SHELLS

DORLING KINDERSLEY
—HANDBOOKS—

SHELLS

S. PETER DANCE

Photography by
MATTHEW WARD

A Dorling Kindersley Book

Reprinted with corrections in 2000

Copyright © 1992
Dorling Kindersley Limited, London
Text copyright ©
1992 S. Peter Dance

A CIP catalogue record for this book is
available from the British Library

ISBN 0-7513-2702-6

Computer page make-up by
The Cooling Brown Partnership,
Great Britain

Text film output by Creative Ace,
Great Britain

Reproduced by
Colourscan, Singapore

Printed and bound by
Kyodo Printing Co., Singapore

see our complete
catalogue at
www.dk.com

CONTENTS

COLLECTING SHELLS

Seashells delight all of us, and have done since ancient times. Their curious shapes, bright colours, and spectacular patterns make them among the most fascinating of nature's creations. The universal appeal of shells is due to their tactile qualities as much as their intrinsic beauty. While some shells are fragile and easily broken, many are solid and pleasant to hold. Such characteristics make shells a satisfying subject to study and to collect.

WHEN WE ADMIRE seashells, we may have no idea how they are formed, and might even be unaware that a shell is the external skeleton of a soft-bodied animal known as a mollusc. This book is for all those who want to know more about the fascinating and exotic world of seashells and those who wish to start or expand a collection.

STARTING A COLLECTION

There are three ways to build up a shell collection: by picking them up from their natural habitats yourself, by exchange with other collectors, and by purchase from dealers. Collecting shells at the seaside is the most enjoyable and instructive alternative, and may also be the cheapest; for the conservation-conscious collector it is the ideal way because it does not interfere with the natural habitat. The shells we find lying on the beach, especially those wrenched from offshore habitats by storms, are often well preserved and very suitable for a collection. With a minimum of effort it is possible to make a large and varied exhibition of such "beached" shells. Other ways to collect shells, such as picking them off rocks or diving to collect

all-purpose stainless steel knife

plastic bags for temporarily storing your shells

beached shells may be pristine

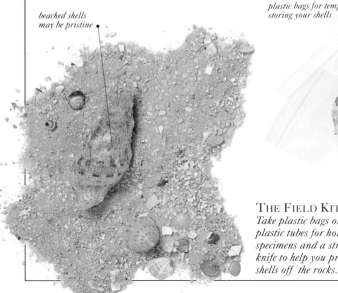

THE FIELD KIT
Take plastic bags or plastic tubes for holding specimens and a strong knife to help you prise shells off the rocks.

plastic film tube for storing small shells

them from the depths of the ocean, ultimately involve removing the animals within, by means some may consider objectionable. However, these alternative methods bring you into closer contact with the living occupants of shells and their real-world habitats.

OUT IN THE FIELD

Some basic equipment is essential if you are to examine the world of shells effectively, and to remove from it a few– but not too many– of its occupants. First, take care of yourself: wear protective clothing, and a hat, to prevent sunburn. Canvas-soled shoes or rubber boots will guard against cuts from coral and rough rock. In addition to the equipment shown here, useful all-purpose collecting items may include a plastic bucket or two (to hold equipment and specimens) and a small rake (to drag through sand). Use white plastic labels to record information about specimens.

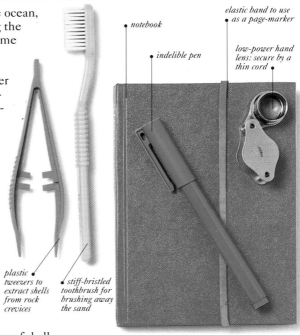

notebook

indelible pen

elastic band to use as a page-marker

low-power hand lens: secure by a thin cord

plastic tweezers to extract shells from rock crevices

stiff-bristled toothbrush for brushing away the sand

MAKING NOTES
You will need a pen and notebook to record relevant information on the spot. Make notes about the appearance of the living animals, the nature of the habitat, and the state of the tides.

times of low and high tides

height of the tides in metres

SAFETY
Consult a local tide table for the tide times.

STUDYING LIVE SPECIMENS

Before you collect any live specimens, always make sure you are not disobeying local conservation regulations. In some places you may need a permit for this. It is fascinating and instructive to watch live molluscs move around in a container of seawater. Like the measled cowrie shown above, many are lively and very beautiful.

Collecting underwater will of course require special equipment. In shallow water, a mask and snorkel will suffice but if you are deep-sea diving you will need special breathing apparatus.

CLEANING SEASHELLS

If you have collected live specimens, you must speedily kill the animals and extract them from their shells; this can be an unpleasant and often smelly business. Unless the specimens are delicate and highly polished, place them in a strainer and immerse them for about five minutes in water brought slowly to the boil. Extract the still-warm animals,

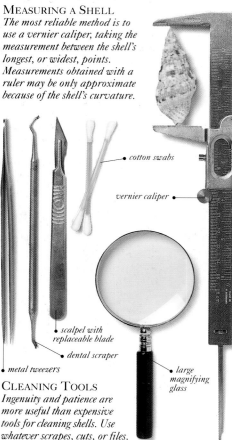

round plastic containers

rectangular, lidded, plastic container

glass tube with dry specimens

glass tube with specimens in alcohol to preserve the soft-bodied animals

foam base

SHELL STORAGE
For convenience, store shells in clear plastic containers with removable lids.

MEASURING A SHELL
The most reliable method is to use a vernier caliper, taking the measurement between the shell's longest, or widest, points. Measurements obtained with a ruler may be only approximate because of the shell's curvature.

cotton swabs

vernier caliper

scalpel with replaceable blade

dental scraper

metal tweezers

large magnifying glass

CLEANING TOOLS
Ingenuity and patience are more useful than expensive tools for cleaning shells. Use whatever scrapes, cuts, or files.

using forceps, a knife, scalpel, metal toothpick, and needles. Remove bivalves when their valves gape, and sever the attachment muscles.

Another way to extract live animals is to put specimens, in plastic bags, in a freezer. Take out the shells one or two days later and, after thawing, remove the animals with forceps, knife, and other tools. Flush out any animal remains and wipe the shells all over with tissues and cotton swabs. Let the shells dry out completely before storing them. Plug their apertures with tissue to absorb obnoxious fluids.

Loosen any coral growths and algae from shells by immersing them in concentrated or diluted bleach. Wash all shells thoroughly afterwards, then remove encrustations with needles, a small drill, and stiff brushes.

IDENTIFYING SEASHELLS

Do not expect to identify all of your shells down to species, or even to genus, straight away. Identifying shells is seldom easy and takes time; identified or not, however, you need to record all the information relevant to each shell. A shell that lacks this information – of which its name is the least important element– loses its scientific importance (but none of its appeal). You should first measure a shell, study its form, its surface contours, its colour, and its pattern; expect to find considerable variation in some of its features.

DISPLAYING SEASHELLS

Most collectors keep their shells in shallow drawers in a steel cabinet, which is both economical and convenient; for larger collections it is the only practical arrangement. The colours of shells tend to fade when exposed to light, so storing them in the dark also preserves their appearance. If the collection is organized systematically into families, adopting a sequence like the one used in this book, it should be possible to find a particular species quickly whenever you need to.

LABELLING SHELLS

SPECIES.......... *Cypraea helvola*........

AUTHOR ......*Linnaeus*...............

LOCALITY........*Sri Lanka*..................

....

Make the labels to accompany your specimens from good quality paper which will fold flat if necessary (folded, stiff paper or card may crush delicate shells). The information included on it may be simple or detailed, hand-written or partially printed. Use permanent black ink and, of course, write legibly. You may cross-refer specimens in your collection to relevant information in a notebook, such as where you found the shell, using easily understood symbols.

attractive display of cowries and other shells in small, round containers

space-saving rectangular boxes

place labels underneath shells

two specimens of a species display an apertural view and a dorsal view

CONTAINERS
Shells come in all shapes and sizes – and so do containers for them, as seen in this cabinet drawer.

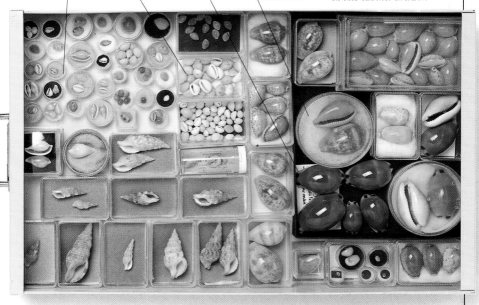

SPECIALIZING
Cone shells from a specialist collection all display a strong family likeness, but they also reveal endless variations among species, which are fascinating to the collector.

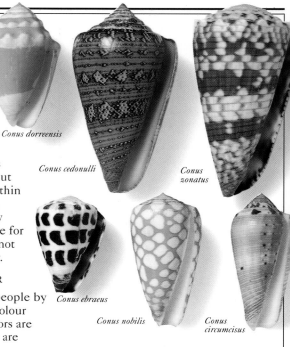

Conus dorreensis

Conus cedonulli

Conus zonatus

Conus ebraeus

Conus nobilis

Conus circumcisus

Label the front of each drawer with the names of the families in it. Use small, shallow boxes to divide shell types within a drawer. You may lay out specimens in their boxes on a thin layer of coloured foam rubber, beneath which you can display their labels. Always leave space for your collection to expand; try not to cram too much into a drawer.

THE SPECIALIST COLLECTOR

Shells give pleasure to many people by the great variety of form and colour they display. But some collectors are specialists by nature, and they are happy to concentrate their attention on a limited range within a larger subject. Seashells provide inexhaustible opportunities for specialization and some collectors have become authorities on certain groups, such as cowries, cones, mitres, and olives. Less space is needed for specialist specimens, which may be an advantage, and you can have fun meeting, corresponding, and exchanging shells with other specialists.

THE SHELL SELECTION

This book includes both collectors' favourites and unfamiliar species from all around the world. The shells chosen show the extraordinary diversity of the second largest group in the animal kingdom, varying from the obscure sea butterfly to the impressively large trumpet shell and giant clam. Although only a fraction of the many thousands of known species is included, it represents a majority of the shell groups likely to be encountered by any collector.

PRESERVING THE OPERCULUM

Collectors often overlook or discard the horny or calcareous operculum attached to the gastropod's muscular foot. But most serious collectors realize that this "trapdoor" is worth preserving as an integral part of the shell. Remove the operculum carefully from the animal's foot, glue it on to cotton wool, and insert it, correctly orientated, into the aperture of the shell.

operculum's inner side glued to a pad of cotton wool

HOW THIS BOOK WORKS

THE BOOK IS ARRANGED according to the five main classes of shell: Gastropods, Bivalves, Tusk Shells, Chitons, and Cephalopods. These classes are sub-divided into different groups. Each separate group has a short introduction describing its general characteristics. The entries that follow give detailed information, in words and pictures, about selected species found in that group. This annotated example shows how a typical entry is organized.

SHELL NOMENCLATURE

The popular name for a species varies from place to place and from language to language, but its scientific name is universal. It is, however, subject to modification because of advances in scientific knowledge. The scientific name consists of the shell's generic, or genus, name, followed by the specific, or species, name. The name of the person who first described the shell, and proposed its name, may be added.

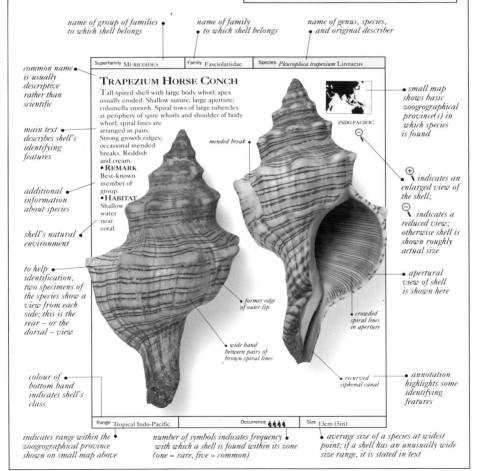

name of group of families to which shell belongs

name of family to which shell belongs

name of genus, species, and original describer

common name is usually descriptive rather than scientific

Superfamily MURICOIDEA   Family Fasciolariidae   Species *Pleuroploca trapezium* Linnaeus

TRAPEZIUM HORSE CONCH

Tall-spired shell with large body whorl; apex usually eroded. Shallow suture; large aperture; columella smooth. Spiral rows of large tubercles at periphery of spire whorls and shoulder of body whorl; spiral lines are arranged in pairs. Strong growth ridges; occasional mended breaks. Reddish and cream.
• REMARK Best-known member of group.
• HABITAT Shallow water near coral.

main text describes shell's identifying features

additional information about species

shell's natural environment

mended break

INDO-PACIFIC

small map shows basic zoogeographical province(s) in which species is found

⊕ *indicates an enlarged view of the shell;*

⊖ *indicates a reduced view; otherwise shell is shown roughly actual size*

to help identification, two specimens of the species show a view from each side; this is the rear – or the dorsal – view

former edge of outer lip

crowded spiral lines in aperture

apertural view of shell is shown here

wide band between pairs of brown spiral lines

colour of bottom band indicates shell's class

recurved siphonal canal

annotation highlights some identifying features

Range Tropical Indo-Pacific   Occurrence 🐚🐚🐚🐚   Size 13cm (5in)

indicates range within the zoogeographical province shown on small map above

number of symbols indicates frequency with which a shell is found within its zone (one = rare, five = common)

average size of a species at widest point; if a shell has an unusually wide size range, it is stated in text

REGIONS OF THE WORLD

SINCE ALL SPECIES are adapted to a variety of different living conditions, the distribution of molluscs follows a pattern. To help with identification, all the shells in this book are accompanied by miniature maps highlighting where the species occur. These small maps each represent one of the regions, or zoogeographical provinces, shown in context on this world map.

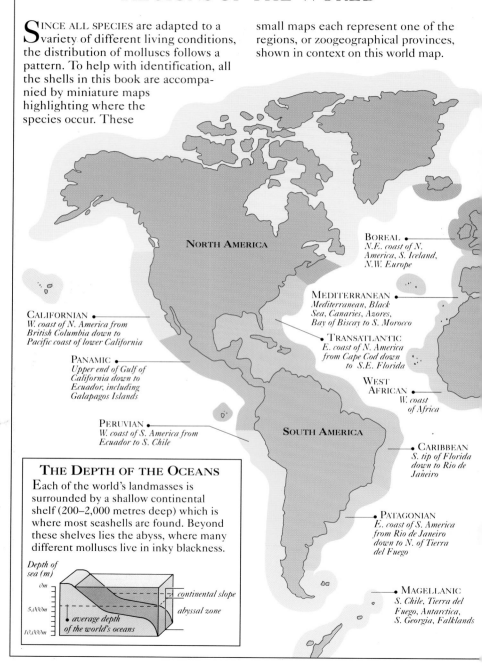

NORTH AMERICA

SOUTH AMERICA

BOREAL •
N.E. coast of N. America, S. Iceland, N.W. Europe

MEDITERRANEAN •
Mediterranean, Black Sea, Canaries, Azores, Bay of Biscay to S. Morocco

CALIFORNIAN •
W. coast of N. America from British Columbia down to Pacific coast of lower California

TRANSATLANTIC •
E. coast of N. America from Cape Cod down to S.E. Florida

PANAMIC •
Upper end of Gulf of California down to Ecuador, including Galapagos Islands

WEST AFRICAN •
W. coast of Africa

PERUVIAN •
W. coast of S. America from Ecuador to S. Chile

CARIBBEAN •
S. tip of Florida down to Rio de Janeiro

PATAGONIAN •
E. coast of S. America from Rio de Janeiro down to N. of Tierra del Fuego

MAGELLANIC •
S. Chile, Tierra del Fuego, Antarctica, S. Georgia, Falklands

THE DEPTH OF THE OCEANS

Each of the world's landmasses is surrounded by a shallow continental shelf (200–2,000 metres deep) which is where most seashells are found. Beyond these shelves lies the abyss, where many different molluscs live in inky blackness.

Depth of sea (m)

0m

5,000m

10,000m

continental slope

abyssal zone

average depth of the world's oceans

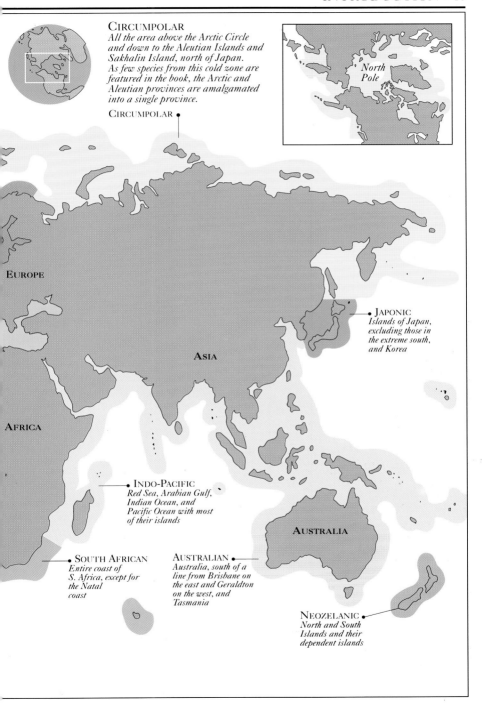

CIRCUMPOLAR
*All the area above the Arctic Circle
and down to the Aleutian Islands and
Sakhalin Island, north of Japan.
As few species from this cold zone are
featured in the book, the Arctic and
Aleutian provinces are amalgamated
into a single province.*

CIRCUMPOLAR

*North
Pole*

EUROPE

ASIA

JAPONIC
*Islands of Japan,
excluding those in
the extreme south,
and Korea*

AFRICA

INDO-PACIFIC
*Red Sea, Arabian Gulf,
Indian Ocean, and
Pacific Ocean with most
of their islands*

AUSTRALIA

SOUTH AFRICAN
*Entire coast of
S. Africa, except for
the Natal
coast*

AUSTRALIAN
*Australia, south of a
line from Brisbane on
the east and Geraldton
on the west, and
Tasmania*

NEOZELANIC
*North and South
Islands and their
dependent islands*

SHELL HABITATS

L IKE OTHER ANIMALS, molluscs have adapted to a range of widely varying living conditions. From rocks merely splashed by the sea, down to the oozy floor of the deepest abyss, there are several well-defined types of habitat, each of which has its own characteristic molluscan fauna. The tides influence the character and distribution of molluscs that live at the sea's edge. So, too, does the nature of the surface on, and in, which they live. Even more important are the beneficial effects of sunshine on the available food supply.

Molluscs find living conditions most congenial in the tropics, and this is where the greatest variety and the most spectacular shells are found. A coral reef is home to colourful cones, cowries, and volutes, as well as giant clams, while in mangroves, oysters cling to roots, nerites crawl on leaves, and ceriths trail through squelchy mud. Temperate regions offer a variety of opportunities to shell collectors too. A sandy shore shelters many different bivalves, as well as burrowing gastropods such as moon snails. In estuaries, mud mixes with sand to provide a more food-rich environment, which is sometimes astonishingly productive for cockles. A rocky shore is a good hunting ground for gastropods that can cling fast.

ADAPTING TO THEIR ENVIRONMENT

Molluscs have developed many ways of surviving in different situations. Some burrow into coral and grow with it, while others – coral shells – attach themselves to its root-like bases. Thinner-shelled, burrowing species abound in coral sand. Bivalves that frequent mangroves seem moulded to the roots to which they cling; other, narrow-shelled bivalves move effortlessly in firm sand. The streamlined razor shells burrow even faster than a man can dig. Limpets are the obvious success story of rocky places; their dome-shaped shells are admirably adapted to withstand buffeting by the waves.

HABITAT CONSERVATION

It is important that habitat is disturbed as little as possible. Under almost every stone or coral block is a community of living animals and plants which may perish if their little world is overturned and not returned to its original position. Every time a piece of coral is removed from a reef, a part of the reef dies. Constant scouring of a particular shore by shell collectors and others may gradually ruin the shore as a natural habitat. Always treat habitats and their lowly, defenceless occupants with respect.

THE LIVE MOLLUSC

C ollectors may spend a lifetime picking up seashells without ever seeing the animal, since most molluscs are secretive and nocturnal by preference. In warm and tropical waters the beauty of molluscan animals can be breathtaking, frequently eclipsing the shells they inhabit. This is vividly illustrated by the animal of Roosevelt's margin shell, shown here. Even in cool and temperate waters, the molluscan animals may be surprisingly attractive.

ROCKY SHORE

A rocky shore may consist of rounded boulders and stones, flat pavements, sharp-edged rocks, or cliffs. Clinging molluscs, such as winkles, dog whelks, and limpets, all live in rock pools, as shown below.

CORAL REEF

In tropical regions, where the sun warms the water, corals flourish unchecked and attract many molluscs with colourful shells. They range in size from tiny to much larger, such as this Caribbean trumpet shell.

SANDY SHORE

Many shells found on sandy shores are empty, since the living molluscs spend most of their time buried in the sand. Sandy shores support many burrowing bivalves, such as these cockles.

THE LIVING MOLLUSC

EVERY ONE OF the millions of empty shells washed up on the world's beaches has a life story. Hatched from an egg, a tiny larva which may have spent days or months swimming around, settles on the sea floor. As it feeds and grows, it secretes a hard covering around itself. When it grows bigger it becomes recognizable for what it is: a mollusc, a soft-bodied, legless animal with a hard, protective shell. It continues growing and eventually reaches maturity. The gastropod animal may develop tentacles, eyes, a proboscis, and a broad, fleshy foot. The bivalve animal may develop a narrow, fleshy foot, gills, and siphons, as well as sensory tentacles.

WHAT IS A SHELL?

Calcium carbonate is the basic material of which most shells are made. Another ingredient is conchiolin, a protein substance also found in the operculum of gastropods. Secreted in layers to give added strength, these ingredients sometimes produce a mother-of-pearl effect. The hard shell enlarges from its outside edge, which is thin and brittle until superseded by later growth. The animal secretes tubercles, scales, spines, and ribs at the growing edge. The shell's colour patterns develop because growth is rhythmic and continuous.

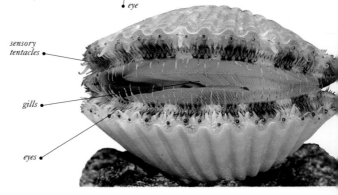

extensible proboscis

position of operculum

muscular foot

eye

A LIVING GASTROPOD
The animal of this Caribbean music volute has a broad foot, an extensible proboscis, and pointed tentacles with eyes at the base. Its colour pattern differs from that of its shell.

sensory tentacles

gills

eyes

A LIVING BIVALVE
A calico scallop from Florida opens to display its fringe of sensory tentacles and its multitude of tiny blue eyes. Notice the gills, which are visible inside the shell.

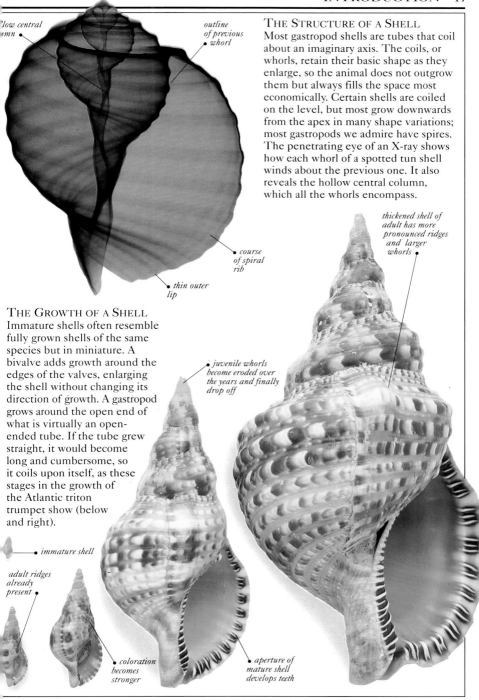

low central
column

outline
of previous
whorl

THE STRUCTURE OF A SHELL

Most gastropod shells are tubes that coil about an imaginary axis. The coils, or whorls, retain their basic shape as they enlarge, so the animal does not outgrow them but always fills the space most economically. Certain shells are coiled on the level, but most grow downwards from the apex in many shape variations; most gastropods we admire have spires. The penetrating eye of an X-ray shows how each whorl of a spotted tun shell winds about the previous one. It also reveals the hollow central column, which all the whorls encompass.

*course
of spiral
rib*

*thin outer
lip*

*thickened shell of
adult has more
pronounced ridges
and larger
whorls*

THE GROWTH OF A SHELL

Immature shells often resemble fully grown shells of the same species but in miniature. A bivalve adds growth around the edges of the valves, enlarging the shell without changing its direction of growth. A gastropod grows around the open end of what is virtually an open-ended tube. If the tube grew straight, it would become long and cumbersome, so it coils upon itself, as these stages in the growth of the Atlantic triton trumpet show (below and right).

*juvenile whorls
become eroded over
the years and finally
drop off*

immature shell

*adult ridges
already
present*

*coloration
becomes
stronger*

*aperture of
mature shell
develops teeth*

THE PARTS OF A SHELL

NEARLY ALL MEMBERS of the five main classes of Mollusca have a shelly covering. Most seashells belong in one of two main classes: gastropods or bivalves. Gastropods have one-piece shells that are usually coiled. Bivalves have two-piece shells, normally hinged along one side. To identify the different shell species, you must first familiarize yourself with the various parts of a shell. The multifeatured, hypothetical shells illustrated below show all the features you are likely to come across in the gastropod and bivalve entries of this book.

GASTROPOD SHELL

Many gastropod shells have a small notch or canal at the rear (upper) end of the aperture and a siphonal canal at the front (lower) end. There may be folds on the columella, and folds or teeth on the outer lip. The illustration brings together all common surface features.

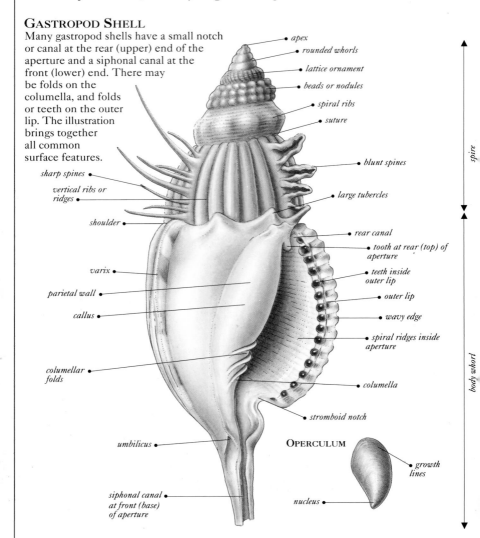

apex

rounded whorls

lattice ornament

beads or nodules

spiral ribs

suture

blunt spines

large tubercles

rear canal

tooth at rear (top) of aperture

teeth inside outer lip

outer lip

wavy edge

spiral ridges inside aperture

columella

stromboid notch

sharp spines

vertical ribs or ridges

shoulder

varix

parietal wall

callus

columellar folds

umbilicus

siphonal canal at front (base) of aperture

spire

body whorl

OPERCULUM

growth lines

nucleus

BIVALVE SHELL

This illustration of a hypothetical bivalve shows the commonly occurring surface and internal features. A bivalve has a left and a right valve, joined by a ligament which is usually visible externally when the valves are closed. With the umbones uppermost and the external ligament placed between them and you, the right valve is on your right and the left on your left.

HINGE VIEW OF A BIVALVE

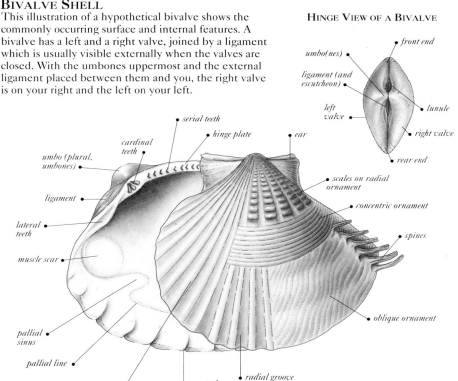

- front end
- umbo(nes)
- ligament (and escutcheon)
- left valve
- lunule
- right valve
- rear end

- serial teeth
- cardinal teeth
- hinge plate
- ear
- umbo (plural, umbones)
- scales on radial ornament
- ligament
- concentric ornament
- lateral teeth
- spines
- muscle scar
- oblique ornament
- pallial sinus
- pallial line
- radial rib
- serrated edge
- radial groove

SHELLS OF THE MINOR CLASSES

The three minor classes have far fewer species and show much less variety in shell shape than the gastropods and bivalves. Tusk shells are monotonously similar, and the few cephalopods are much the same shape and size. The valves of chitons may be decorated.

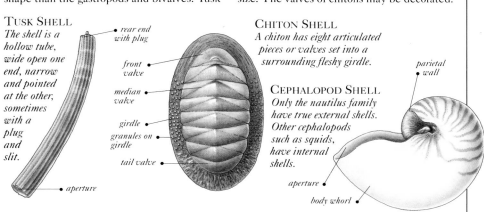

TUSK SHELL
The shell is a hollow tube, wide open one end, narrow and pointed at the other, sometimes with a plug and slit.

- rear end with plug
- front valve
- median valve
- girdle
- granules on girdle
- tail valve
- aperture

CHITON SHELL
A chiton has eight articulated pieces or valves set into a surrounding fleshy girdle.

- parietal wall

CEPHALOPOD SHELL
Only the nautilus family have true external shells. Other cephalopods such as squids, have internal shells.

- aperture
- body whorl

SHELL IDENTIFICATION KEY

THE KEY on the following pages is designed to help you identify your shells. The first stage in the process of identification is to establish which of the five main classes of shell you are dealing with (see Stage 1, right).

Stage 2 sub-divides the major shell classes into groups according to basic shape. Decide which shape applies to your specimen and then move on to Stage 3, which breaks down the shape categories featured in Stage 2 into sub-shapes. Establish which sub-shape your shell most closely resembles and you will find next to it a list of all the genera to which your shell could belong, with their page numbers indicated – provided, of course, that your shell is one of the 500 species included in this book.

STAGE 1

Shells are divided into five main classes. About 80 per cent of living molluscs belong to the gastropods class, whose features are described on page 18. Bivalves comprise the second largest class (see page 19), and the far less numerous tusk shells, chitons, and cephalopods the minor classes (see page 19).

The Five Main Classes of Shell

 GASTROPODS

 BIVALVES

 TUSK SHELLS

 CHITONS

 CEPHALOPODS

STAGE 2: GASTROPODS

The shape category is based on the shell's form and outline and mostly ignores any extraneous decoration or ornament, such as nodules or spines. When trying to identify a shell, it is important to look at it from the same angle as that from which we have described it – gastropods are usually viewed from the apertural side. Some gastropods are cap-shaped or ear-shaped. Shells shaped like an upturned spinning top are much more common, as are corkscrew-shaped shells. A majority of shell groups may be loosely described as being shaped like a pear, a spindle, a barrel, or a club. Decide which shape your gastropod most closely resembles, then turn to the key on pages 22–27.

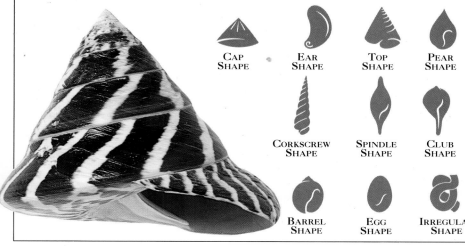

CAP SHAPE   EAR SHAPE   TOP SHAPE   PEAR SHAPE

CORKSCREW SHAPE   SPINDLE SHAPE   CLUB SHAPE

BARREL SHAPE   EGG SHAPE   IRREGULAR SHAPE

STAGE 2: BIVALVES

Bivalves are less varied in shape than gastropods. Discus- and fan-shaped shells are less common than triangular shells, such as tellins. The largest shape category of all – boat-shaped – comprises arks and other low, broad bivalves, while certain groups, such as mussels, are paddle-shaped. Several bivalves have an irregular form, while two or three are roughly heart-shaped. For identification purposes, you should always view bivalves with the hinge uppermost. It is also important to recognize the left and right valves of a bivalve (see page 19). Decide which of the shape categories below matches your bivalve and turn to the key on pages 26–29.

| DISCUS SHAPE | FAN SHAPE | TRIANGULAR SHAPE | BOAT SHAPE | PADDLE SHAPE | IRREGULAR SHAPE | HEART SHAPE |

STAGE 2: TUSK SHELLS

All tusk-shaped shells are members of the tusk shell class. Apart from being different lengths and having different curvatures, they vary only in minor characteristics which do not influence their shape. It is not usually easy to identify species of tusk shell.

TUSK SHAPE

STAGE 2: CHITONS

Although at first glance a large collection of chitons displays a variety of shapes, most chitons fit into a single category. Narrow or broad, long or short, their shells usually resemble jointed shields.

SHIELD SHAPE

STAGE 2: CEPHALOPODS

Only about half a dozen different cephalopod species have external shells, and these are members of the nautilus family. Placed here, in the same category, is the small internal shell of the common spirula, which is a true shell, and the so-called shell of an argonaut, although it is merely a temporary egg case.

HELMET SHAPE

STAGE 3

This final stage in the identification of shells will guide you quickly to a particular entry in the book. Once you decide which of the main shapes your gastropod resembles, whether it is like a cap, or a spindle, for example, you will see that

GASTROPODS

CAP SHAPE

 *Patella* **33**, *Nacella* **34**, *Patelloida* **34**, *Helcion* **34**

 *Diodora* **32**

 *Fissurella* **32**

EAR SHAPE

 *Haliotis* **30**

 *Crepidula* **54**, *Concholepas* **112**

Nerita **46**

TOP SHAPE

Architectonica **52**

Perotrochus **31**, *Entemnotrochus* **31**

Maurea **35**, *Calliostoma* **35**, *Monodonta* **3**, *Tectus* **37**, *Umbonium*, *Trochu*

PEAR SHAPE

Cantharidus **35**, *Tectarius* **47**, *Turbo* **39-41**, *Modulus* **50**, *Trigonostoma* **181**

Phasianella **45**, *Cominella* **131**, *Phos* **132**, *Nassarius* **143-6**, *Hinia* **143**, *Ilyanassa* **146**, *Nassaria* **132**

Neritina **46**, *Littorina* **47**, *Planaxis* **52**, *Struthiolaria* **56**, *Cuma* **114**, *Trophon* **122**, *Buccinum* **127-8**, *Northia* **131**

CORKSCREW SHAPE

Rhinoclavis **51**, *Cerithium* **51**, *Cerithidea* **51**

Bankivia **36**, *Bullia* **142**

Pyramidella **200**

each category has been further divided into sub-shapes. Work out which sub-shape your shell most closely resembles and turn to the pages listed against each of the genera (or in some cases only one genus) to find the relevant species entry.

Emarginula **32**

Capulus **54**

Carinaria **75**

Purpura **112**

Neverita **77,**
Sinum **78**

Stomatia **37**

Oxystele **36,**
Janthina **53**

Bolma **42-3,**
Guildfordia **42,**
Astraea **43,**
Angaria **44,**
Xenophora **55,**
Stellaria **55**

Telescopium **50**

Charonia **92,** *Tutufa* **100-1,**
Bursa **102-3,** *Crossata*
103, *Phyllonotus* **107,**
Hexaplex **110,**
Ocenebra **111,**
Trochia **111,**
Nucella **111,**
Rapana **113,**
Thais **113-14,**
Phyllocoma **117,**
Coralliophila **118**

Nassa **115,**
Acanthina **117,**
Fasciolaria **148**

Gyrineum **93,** *Cabestana* **93,**
Ranella **94,** *Mayena* **94,**
Argobuccinum **95,** *Fusitriton* **95,**
Cymatium **96-8,** *Gelagna* **96**
Distorsio **99,** *Bufonaria* **104,**
Vitularia **115,** *Burnupena* **131,**
Buccinulum **132,** *Pisania* **133,**
Solenosteira **134,**
Cantharus **134,**
Colubraria **136**

Turritella **48,**
Epitonium **53**

Terebra **195-9,**
Hastula **199**

STAGE 3

GASTROPODS

SPINDLE SHAPE

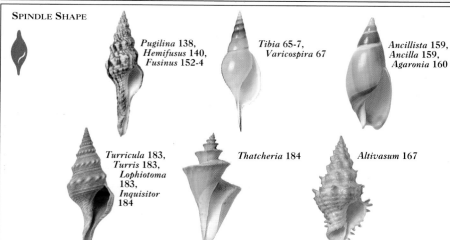

Pugilina 138,
Hemifusus 140,
Fusinus 152-4

Tibia 65-7,
Varicospira 67

Ancillista 159,
Ancilla 159,
Agaronia 160

Turricula 183,
Turris 183,
Lophiotoma
183,
Inquisitor
184

Thatcheria 184

Altivasum 167

CLUB SHAPE

Volema
138,
Vasum
165-6,
Turbinella
169

Para-
metaria
124,
Cryptospira
180,
Conus 185-94

Siratus 105
Bolinus 109,
Rapa 119

Murex 109

Homalocantha
107,
Tudivasum 168,
Tudicla 168

Melongena 137,
Voluta 172-3,
Cymbiolacca 173,
Scaphella 176

BARREL SHAPE

Tonna 87-90,
Volutharpa 128,
Harpa 170-1

Cassis 79-81,
Cypraecassis 82,
Galeodea 82,
Phalium 83,
Morum 84,
Malea 91

Macron 133,
Opeatostoma 150

Mazatlania
124,
Strombina
124,
Pyrene
125,
Columbella
126,

Terebellum 67,
Metula 130,
Mitra 161-2,
Pterygia 162,
Scabricola 163,
Neocancilla 163,
Cancilla 163,
Vexillum 164

Fulgoraria 174,
Alcithoe 174,
Lyria 175

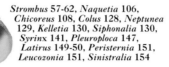

Strombus 57-62, *Naquetia* 106,
Chicoreus 108, *Colus* 128, *Neptunea*
129, *Kelletia* 130, *Siphonalia* 130,
Syrinx 141, *Pleuroploca* 147,
Latirus 149-50, *Peristernia* 151,
Leucozonia 151, *Sinistralia* 154

Columbarium 123,
Afer 168

Haustellum 105

Ficus 85-6

Busycon 139

Eunaticina 78,
Drupa 116,
Latiaxis 120,
Cancellaria
181-2

Lunatia 76,
Natica 76-7,
Mammilla 77,
Euspira 78

Babylonia 135,
Demoulia 146,
Bullina 200, *Acteon*
201, *Pupa* 201,
Micromelo 202,
Aplustrum 202,
Atys 202, *Bulla* 203,
Hydatina 203

STAGE 3

GASTROPODS

EGG SHAPE

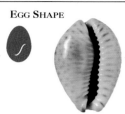 *Cypraea 68-73, Cyphoma 74*

 *Volva 74, Ovula 75*

 *Oliva 155- Olivella 1! Olivancil- laria 158*

IRREGULAR SHAPE

 Vermicularia 49

 *Serpulorbis 49*

 *Pteropurpura 10 Typhisala 121, Typhisopsis 121 Typhina 121*

BIVALVES

DISCUS SHAPE

  *Dosinia 241*

 Lucina 225

 Glycyme 213

FAN SHAPE

 Pinctada 216, Crenatula 217, Pecten 218, Chlamys 219, Aequipecten 220, Amusium 220, Lyropecten 221, Cryptopecten 221

 Lyrocard- ium 229

Spondylus 222

TRIANGULAR SHAPE

  Astarte 226, Donax 237

 Nucula 210

 Tellina 234-5, Phylloda 23

Afrivoluta 178,
Persicula 178-9,
Bullata 179,
Marginella 179-80

Volutoconus 175,
Harpulina 175,
Livonia 176,
Cymbium 177,
Cymbiolista 177

Aporrhais 56,
Lambis 63-4

Cavolinia
204

Diacria 204

Codakia 225

Divaricella
225

Neotrigonia
224

Cerastoderma
228,
Fragum 229,
*Acantho-
cardia* 229,
*Plagio-
cardium* 230

Tridacna
231

Eucrassatella 226,
Chione 243

Spisula 232,
Mactrellona
232,
Mactra
232,
Hecuba
237

Tellidora
236

STAGE 3

BIVALVES

BOAT SHAPE

Megacardita 227, *Asaphis* 238, *Paphia* 242

Callista 241

Trapezium 239

Semele 239, *Pitar* 240, *Gafrarium* 240, *Circe* 240, *Lioconcha* 242, *Chamelea* 242

PADDLE SHAPE

Pinna 215

Lima 224

Mytilus 214, *Choromytilus* 214

IRREGULAR SHAPE

Malleus 217

Trisidos 212

Pteria 216

HEART SHAPE

Corculum 230

Glossus 244

Solemya 210, *Ensis* 233,
Siliqua 233

Arca 211,
Anadara 211,
Barbatia 212

Hiatula 238, *Sanguinolaria* 238,
Panopea 243, *Mya* 244, *Pholas* 245,
Cyrtopleura 245, *Thracia* 246,
Lyonsia 246, *Laternula* 247

Atrina 215

Laevicardium 228

Anomia 223

Lopha 223

Tusk Shells

Tusk Shape

Pictodentalium
205, *Dentalium*
205, *Fissident-*
alium 206,
Antalis 206

Chitons

Shield Shape

Chiton 207-8,
Ischnochiton 208,
Tonicia 208,
Chaetopleura
209, *Acantho-*
pleura 209

Cephalopods

Helmet Shape

Nautilus 248,
Argonauta 249,
Spirula 249

GASTROPODS

ABALONES

THESE FLATTENED SHELLS have few whorls; the large body whorl is perforated with small holes that are used for respiration. The iridescent lining has a central muscle impression. The animal clings firmly to rocks and coral. Worldwide in distribution, the large species are from temperate waters.

Superfamily PLEUROTOMARIOIDEA	Family Haliotidae	Species *Haliotis rufescens* Swainson

RED ABALONE

This shell is very thick. Its large, oval body whorl is ornamented with irregular spiral ridges, fine spiral riblets, and occasional coarse growth ridges; normally has three or four open holes; later ones usually have elevated sides. Pink to brick-red outside; iridescent inside.
• **HABITAT** Rocks offshore.

early whorls erode revealing layer below

CALIFORNIAN

part of muscle impression tucks under rim of shell

Range California	Occurrence 🌢🌢🌢🌢	Size 25cm (10in)

Superfamily PLEUROTOMARIOIDEA	Family Haliotidae	Species *Haliotis asinina* Linnaeus

DONKEY'S-EAR ABALONE

A thin, elliptical shell with apex close to the margin; six or seven open holes, each with slightly raised edge. Body whorl is sparsely ornamented with spiral ridges and some growth lines. Outside creamy, with green and brown blotches, triangles and streaks.
• **HABITAT** Rocks offshore.

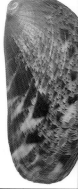

INDO-PACIFIC

groove runs parallel with row of holes

Range W. Pacific	Occurrence 🌢🌢🌢🌢	Size 7.5cm (3in)

SLIT SHELLS

FRAGILE AND TOP-SHAPED, only a few species of slit shell survive in the deeper parts of our oceans. These rarely seen living fossils represent a family which flourished millions of years ago. The main feature of a slit shell is the open-ended slit (for the discharge of waste) in the body whorl.

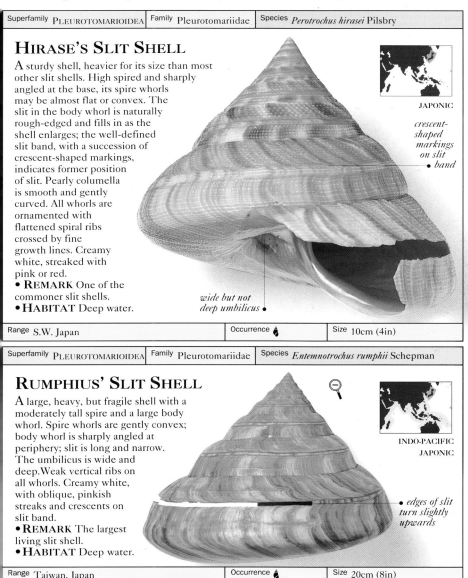

| Superfamily PLEUROTOMARIOIDEA | Family Pleurotomariidae | Species *Perotrochus hirasei* Pilsbry |

HIRASE'S SLIT SHELL

A sturdy shell, heavier for its size than most other slit shells. High spired and sharply angled at the base, its spire whorls may be almost flat or convex. The slit in the body whorl is naturally rough-edged and fills in as the shell enlarges; the well-defined slit band, with a succession of crescent-shaped markings, indicates former position of slit. Pearly columella is smooth and gently curved. All whorls are ornamented with flattened spiral ribs crossed by fine growth lines. Creamy white, streaked with pink or red.
• **REMARK** One of the commoner slit shells.
• **HABITAT** Deep water.

JAPONIC

crescent-shaped markings on slit band

wide but not deep umbilicus

| Range S.W. Japan | Occurrence | Size 10cm (4in) |

| Superfamily PLEUROTOMARIOIDEA | Family Pleurotomariidae | Species *Entemnotrochus rumphii* Schepman |

RUMPHIUS' SLIT SHELL

A large, heavy, but fragile shell with a moderately tall spire and a large body whorl. Spire whorls are gently convex; body whorl is sharply angled at periphery; slit is long and narrow. The umbilicus is wide and deep. Weak vertical ribs on all whorls. Creamy white, with oblique, pinkish streaks and crescents on slit band.
• **REMARK** The largest living slit shell.
• **HABITAT** Deep water.

INDO-PACIFIC
JAPONIC

edges of slit turn slightly upwards

| Range Taiwan, Japan | Occurrence | Size 20cm (8in) |

KEYHOLE LIMPETS

T HIS LARGE FAMILY of cap-shaped shells gets its name from the characteristic apical hole or slit on the anterior margin. Ribbed outside, the shells are porcelain-like inside and have horseshoe-shaped muscle scar. They have no operculum. The animals adhere to rocks, where they browse on algae.

Superfamily FISSURELLOIDEA	Family Fissurellidae	Species *Fissurella barbadensis* Gmelin

BARBADOS KEYHOLE LIMPET

A thick, elevated shell with a central, almost circular orifice. Strong radiating ribs, irregularly spaced, extend from the apex and are crossed by weaker spiral ribs. Outside creamy white to brownish, and sometimes can be varied with purple-brown blotches. The inside of the shell is greenish, with concentric white bands; border white.
• HABITAT Intertidal rocks.

sharp-edged ribs

CARIBBEAN

green edge of orifice, bordered by red line

Range Caribbean	Occurrence 🐚🐚🐚🐚🐚	Size 2.5cm (1in)

Superfamily FISSURELLOIDEA	Family Fissurellidae	Species *Emarginula crassa* Sowerby

THICK EMARGINULA

This moderately elevated, thick, oval shell has 40 to 50 radiating ribs intersected by much weaker spiral ribs. A short vertical slit is extended to the apex by a flat-bottomed groove. Inside of shell is smooth, wrinkled at the margin. Outside yellowish white; inside porcellaneous white.
• HABITAT Rocky coasts offshore.

apex close to rear end of shell

BOREAL

groove appears as a smooth ridge inside

Range N.W. Europe, Virgin Is.	Occurrence 🐚🐚	Size 2.5cm (1in)

Superfamily FISSURELLOIDEA	Family Fissurellidae	Species *Diodora listeri* Orbigny

LISTER'S KEYHOLE LIMPET

A solid, oval, elevated shell with strong, radiating ribs alternating with weaker ones. Where these are crossed by concentric ribs, nodes are formed. Inside the shell, radiating ribs appear as grooves; margin wrinkled. White, cream, or grey outside; glossy interior.
• HABITAT Intertidal rocks.

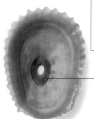

CARIBBEAN

black rim to inside edge of orifice

Range S. Florida, W. Indies	Occurrence 🐚🐚🐚🐚🐚	Size 4cm (1½in)

TRUE LIMPETS

T HE ELEVATED or flattened shells belonging to this large group occur along seashores worldwide. Smooth or radially ribbed outside, they are smooth inside, and have a horseshoe-shaped muscle impression. The animals stick tightly to rocks, their shell shape helping them withstand battering by the waves.

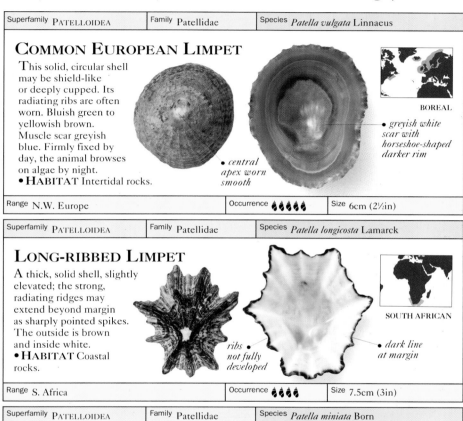

Superfamily PATELLOIDEA	Family Patellidae	Species *Patella vulgata* Linnaeus

COMMON EUROPEAN LIMPET

This solid, circular shell may be shield-like or deeply cupped. Its radiating ribs are often worn. Bluish green to yellowish brown. Muscle scar greyish blue. Firmly fixed by day, the animal browses on algae by night.
• **HABITAT** Intertidal rocks.

BOREAL

• *greyish white scar with horseshoe-shaped darker rim*

• *central apex worn smooth*

Range N.W. Europe	Occurrence 🐚🐚🐚🐚🐚	Size 6cm (2½in)

Superfamily PATELLOIDEA	Family Patellidae	Species *Patella longicosta* Lamarck

LONG-RIBBED LIMPET

A thick, solid shell, slightly elevated; the strong, radiating ridges may extend beyond margin as sharply pointed spikes. The outside is brown and inside white.
• **HABITAT** Coastal rocks.

SOUTH AFRICAN

ribs not fully developed

• *dark line at margin*

Range S. Africa	Occurrence 🐚🐚🐚🐚	Size 7.5cm (3in)

Superfamily PATELLOIDEA	Family Patellidae	Species *Patella miniata* Born

CINNABAR LIMPET

Moderately thick, flattened shell. Radiating ribs, regularly spaced. Outside brownish pink, mottled with pale brown. Inside smooth and shiny; muscle scar whitish. Shell often encrusted.
• **REMARK** Sunlight may alter the shell's colour.
• **HABITAT** Intertidal rocks.

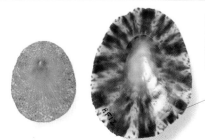

SOUTH AFRICAN

• *radial ribs form sharp points at margin*

Range S. Africa	Occurrence 🐚🐚🐚🐚	Size 6cm (2½in)

Superfamily PATELLOIDEA	Family Patellidae	Species *Helcion pellucidus* Linnaeus

BLUE-RAYED LIMPET

A thin, translucent, smooth shell, rounded or oval across the base; apex nearer the front end, directed forwards. Horn coloured with pale blue radial lines that are brilliant under water. Muscle scar is charcoal-grey colour.
• **REMARK** Specimens found on stalks of weed lack blue lines.
• **HABITAT** Oarweeds offshore.

blue lines radiate from apex

BOREAL

dark, opaque muscle scar

Range E. Atlantic	Occurrence ♦♦♦♦	Size 2cm (¾in)

Superfamily PATELLOIDEA	Family Patellidae	Species *Nacella deaurata* Gmelin

GOLDEN LIMPET

Moderately thin but strong, deeply excavated shell, also known as the Patagonian Copper Limpet. Apex is nearer front end. Broad and narrow radiating ribs crossed by concentric growth lines. The inside is glossy; the outside is dull brown.
• **HABITAT** Seaweeds offshore.

undulations on margin

PATAGONIAN MAGELLANIC

pearly glaze overlays reddish brown colour

Range Patagonia, Falkland Is.	Occurrence ♦♦♦♦	Size 5cm (2in)

Superfamily PATELLOIDEA	Family Lottiidae	Species *Patelloida saccharina* Linnaeus

PACIFIC SUGAR LIMPET

Small but sturdy shell with low apex situated in front of central point. Seven or eight strong radiating ridges, with lesser ridges between; these are crossed by irregular, concentric growth lines. The shell is dull grey and white on the outside; opaque white on the inside, sometimes tinged with violet. Yellowish muscle scar often spotted with darker brown; margin dark brown.
• **HABITAT** Intertidal rocks.

INDO-PACIFIC

yellowish brown muscle scar

strong ridges project at margin

Range Tropical Pacific	Occurrence ♦♦♦♦♦	Size 3cm (1¼in)

TOP SHELLS

EARLY CONCHOLOGISTS compared; these sturdy shells, of which there are hundreds of species worldwide, to the old-fashioned spinning top, hence their common name. Colourful outside, the inside is lined with mother-of-pearl. Many have an open umbilicus. The corneous operculum has many whorls.

Superfamily TROCHOIDEA	Family Trochidae	Species *Calliostoma zizyphinum* Linnaeus

EUROPEAN PAINTED TOP

A strongly built shell with straight sides and base. Body whorl is sharply keeled and encircled by a thick band which is repeated at the suture up to a sharply pointed apex. A few low ridges on the base. No umbilicus. The columella bulges slightly. Yellowish or reddish, with smooth, shiny surface.
• **HABITAT** Rocky shores.

straight sides

MEDITERRANEAN
BOREAL

patterned spiral bands

Range Mediterranean, W. Europe	Occurrence 🐚🐚🐚🐚	Size 2.5cm (1in)

Superfamily TROCHOIDEA	Family Trochidae	Species *Cantharidus opalus* Martyn

OPAL JEWEL TOP

Thin but strong shell, taller than it is broad. The suture is very shallow; growth lines are oblique and only faintly marked. Columella is slightly curved; there is no umbilicus. Purplish green body whorl has zigzag reddish streaks; spire whorls are greener and more faintly marked than body whorl.
• **HABITAT** Weeds offshore.

early whorls straight sided

NEOZELANIC

iridescent inside

Range New Zealand	Occurrence 🐚🐚🐚	Size 4cm (1½in)

Superfamily TROCHOIDEA	Family Trochidae	Species *Maurea tigris* Martyn

TIGER MAUREA

Thin but strongly built shell with a large body whorl and steeply sloping spire, ending with a sharply pointed apex. Sides are flat except for a bulge at the base. Weakly developed spiral ridges are shown to be slightly beaded under magnification. No umbilicus; large aperture. Cream, with zigzag brown stripes down almost the entire length of shell.
• **HABITAT** Intertidal rocks.

slight bulge above suture of first spire whorl

NEOZELANIC

sharp angle at base of columella

pattern visible through aperture

Range New Zealand	Occurrence 🐚🐚	Size 5.5cm (2¼in)

Superfamily TROCHOIDEA	Family Trochidae	Species *Monodonta turbinata* Born

CHEQUERED TOP

A solid, thick, heavy shell with well-rounded whorls and a deep but narrow suture. Broad, flattened spiral ribs encircle lower whorls; rib on body whorl below the suture is pinched in, forming angle with succeeding rib. Oblique growth lines are conspicuous on lower whorls. Edge of aperture thin. Columella has prominent blunt tooth. Umbilicus concealed. Greyish, yellowish, or off-white, with spiral rows of purple, red, or black dashes; aperture and columella white.
• **REMARK** Often covered with algae.
• **HABITAT** Intertidal rocks.

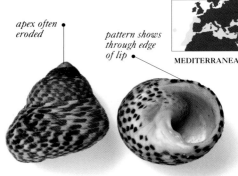

apex often eroded

pattern shows through edge of lip

MEDITERRANEAN

Range Mediterranean	Occurrence 🐚🐚🐚🐚	Size 3cm (1¼in)

Superfamily TROCHOIDEA	Family Trochidae	Species *Oxystele sinensis* Gmelin

ROSY-BASE TOP

A thick, short-spired, and somewhat flattened shell with well-rounded whorls and almost non-existent suture. The columella slopes acutely to meet lower part of lip. Thick, blackish periostracum conceals most of smooth, bluish surface; aperture and columella white.
• **HABITAT** Rock pools.

SOUTH AFRICAN

black rim to inside edge of aperture

Range S. Africa	Occurrence 🐚🐚🐚🐚	Size 3.5cm (1¼in)

Superfamily TROCHOIDEA	Family Trochidae	Species *Bankivia fasciata* Menke

BANDED BANKIVIA

A small, elongate shell with a sharply pointed apex and straight-sided or slightly rounded whorls. Shallow suture is well defined. Thin apertural lip often damaged; columella is twisted. Parietal wall has only a thin callus covering. Glossy surface exhibits many colour patterns. Ground colour is white, yellow, or pink; patterns, mostly brown in colour, include bands, vertical streaks, and zigzags.
• **REMARK** The narrowly elongate spire is unique among top shells.
• **HABITAT** Weeds inshore.

translucent thread covers suture

AUSTRALIAN

coloured zigzag pattern

Range Australia	Occurrence 🐚🐚🐚🐚🐚	Size 2cm (¾in)

Superfamily TROCHOIDEA	Family Trochidae	Species *Umbonium vestiarium* Linnaeus

COMMON BUTTON TOP

Flattened, glossy and smooth, the whorls of this small shell culminate in an acutely shouldered body whorl with a relatively small aperture. Suture is very shallow. Large, greyish callus plug smothers the umbilicus, giving shell an ungainly appearance seen from below. Brown, pink, white, or yellow ground colour, superimposed with bands patterned with streaks, spots, or blotches.
• **HABITAT** Sandy beaches.

pale rim to callus plug

INDO-PACIFIC

shell has flattened button-like appearance

Range Tropical Indo-Pacific	Occurrence 🐚🐚🐚🐚🐚	Size 1.2cm (½in)

Superfamily TROCHOIDEA	Family Trochidae	Species *Stomatia phymotis* Helbling

SWOLLEN-MOUTH SHELL

Immediately recognizable shell that produces a conventionally coiled spire as a juvenile, then seemingly forgets to continue coiling and develops a large, elongated body whorl dwarfing the spire. Looks like a tiny abalone. Greyish white, mottled with brown.
• **REMARK** Apex often eroded.
• **HABITAT** Offshore rocks.

INDO-PACIFIC
JAPONIC

lightly iridescent shell interior

large knobs on periphery of body whorl

Range Indo-W. Pacific, Japan	Occurrence 🐚🐚🐚	Size 3cm (1¼in)

Superfamily TROCHOIDEA	Family Trochidae	Species *Tectus conus* Gmelin

CONE-SHAPED TOP

A solid, robust shell with a tall, pointed spire and a blunt apex. The base is rounded; the whorls are almost straight sided, and are separated by a shallow suture. Coarse spiral ridges on all whorls are strongest at the periphery of the body whorl; oblique growth lines are rather faint. The umbilicus is large and deep, its sides smooth; the columella is smooth and thickened. White or pinkish ground colour, with red or grey streaks on the whorls, and dashes and spots on the base; the aperture is pinkish white or greyish colour.
• **REMARK** The outer lip of the aperture is very sharp.
• **HABITAT** Near coral reefs.

INDO-PACIFIC

columella thickens at base

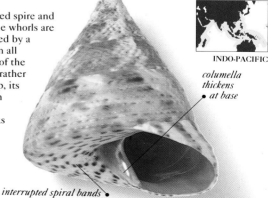

interrupted spiral bands

Range Pacific	Occurrence 🐚🐚🐚🐚	Size 6cm (2½in)

Superfamily TROCHOIDEA	Family Trochidae	Species *Trochus niloticus* Linnaeus

COMMERCIAL TROCHUS

This, the largest and heaviest of the top shells, is almost an equilateral triangle in profile. In mature examples most whorls are smooth except for fine oblique striae; earlier whorls in medium-sized examples, and all whorls of juvenile examples, are ornamented with tubular nodules which are someimes fluted at the shallow suture. The columella has a ridge-like tooth. Pinkish white, with broad, deep red oblique stripes.
• **REMARK** Once used to provide the material for buttons, and still fished commercially in small quantities for decorative purposes.
• **HABITAT** Near coral reefs.

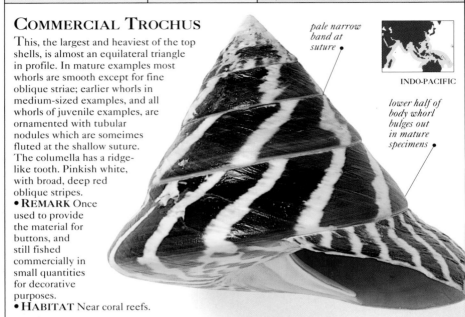

pale narrow band at suture

INDO-PACIFIC

lower half of body whorl bulges out in mature specimens

Range Tropical Indo-Pacific	Occurrence 🐚🐚🐚🐚	Size 11cm (4½in)

Superfamily TROCHOIDEA	Family Trochidae	Species *Trochus maculatus* Linnaeus

MOTTLED TOP

This thick, solid shell is taller than it is wide. The base is almost flat, the body whorl sharply angled. The suture is about equal in depth to the grooves between the beaded spiral ribs. The irregular, vertical growth ridges are not continued on to the base. The pearly umbilicus is edged with four or five blunt nodules (representing the columella). Shell is creamy in colour, mottled with red; base is patterned with red dashes.
• **REMARK** A very variable species in both colour and overall shape.
• **HABITAT** Coral reefs.

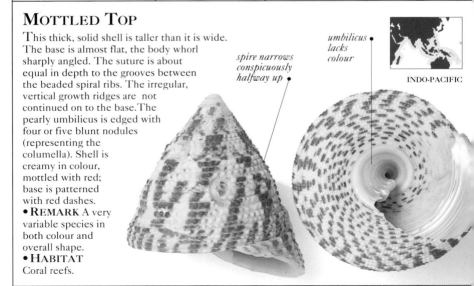

spire narrows conspicuously halfway up

umbilicus lacks colour

INDO-PACIFIC

Range Tropical Indo-Pacific	Occurrence 🐚🐚🐚🐚	Size 5cm (2in)

TURBAN SHELLS

T HE MEMBERS OF THIS large group differ from top shells in several respects, notably by possessing a thick, calcareous operculum which can often be bumpy, or ornamented with curved ridges. The various species may be almost spherical or top-shaped, smooth or strongly ornamented; some have spines or flutings. Few turban shells have an umbilicus. The aperture is pearly. Most species occur in warm waters, especially around coral reefs.

Superfamily TROCHOIDEA	Family Turbinidae	Species *Turbo marmoratus* Linnaeus

GREAT GREEN TURBAN

The biggest turban shell, its spire is small in relation to its widely expanded body whorl. Spire whorls smooth; body whorl develops two or three keels which tend to separate into warty lumps; lowermost keel skirts around umbilical region. Suture shallow; columella smooth. Dull green with brown blotches.
• **REMARK** Still being fished commercially to provide mother-of-pearl for making decorative buttons, beads, and jewellery.
• **HABITAT** Near coral reefs.

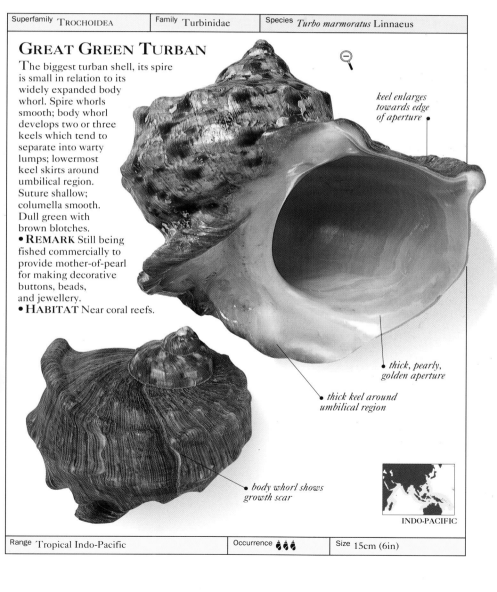

keel enlarges towards edge of aperture

thick, pearly, golden aperture

thick keel around umbilical region

body whorl shows growth scar

INDO-PACIFIC

Range Tropical Indo-Pacific	Occurrence 🐾🐾🐾	Size 15cm (6in)

Superfamily TROCHOIDEA	Family Turbinidae	Species *Turbo petholatus* Linnaeus

TAPESTRY TURBAN

This thick, heavy shell is glossy and completely smooth except for occasional, shallow striae. The spire is high, the apex blunt, and the suture is shallow. All whorls are convex but the body whorl is often concave below the suture. The well-rounded aperture has a sharp edge to its outer lip. There is no umbilicus. Except for the lip, which is usually yellow or greenish yellow, the colour and pattern vary considerably. Often dark brown in colour with darker bands, blotched and striped with white, but may be greenish yellow without a pattern.
• **REMARK** The outside of the operculum is bluish green at the centre and is sometimes known as a "cat's eye".
• **HABITAT** Shallow reefs.

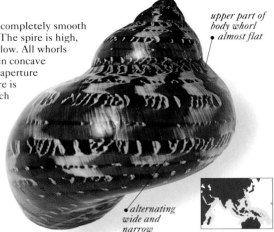

upper part of body whorl almost flat

alternating wide and narrow spiral bands

INDO-PACIFIC

Range Tropical Indo-Pacific	Occurrence 🐚🐚🐚	Size 6cm (2½in)

Superfamily TROCHOIDEA	Family Turbinidae	Species *Turbo argyrostomus* Linnaeus

SILVER MOUTH TURBAN

A moderately large, thick, and heavy shell, higher than it is wide, with its spire less than half the total height. The spire whorls are well rounded but the body whorl is sometimes square-sided in appearance. The suture is well impressed; a small umbilicus may be present. All whorls have strong spiral ribs which may be either flat-topped or have strong, fluted scales. These ribs are well developed towards the edge of the aperture, which has corrugations corresponding to the ribs. Colour whitish or cream, blotched with brown or green. Outer edge of aperture greenish; inside and columella silvery.
• **REMARK** Outside of operculum is white and green, covered with pustules.
• **HABITAT** Intertidal near coral reefs.

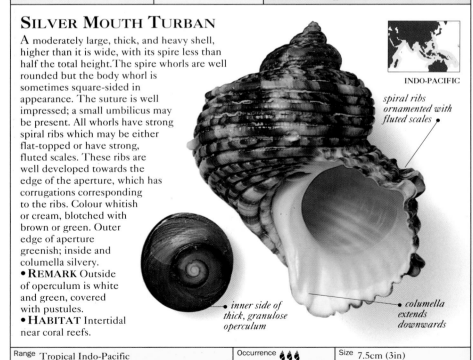

INDO-PACIFIC

spiral ribs ornamented with fluted scales

inner side of thick, granulose operculum

columella extends downwards

Range Tropical Indo-Pacific	Occurrence 🐚🐚🐚	Size 7.5cm (3in)

Superfamily TROCHOIDEA	Family Turbinidae	Species *Turbo sarmaticus* Linnaeus

SOUTH AFRICAN TURBAN

DORSAL VIEW

A large, thick, and heavy shell with a low spire of few whorls, a large body whorl, and a widely expanded aperture. The very thick columella is continuous with the lower edge of the aperture. The three or four spiral rows of broad, evenly spaced tubercles are often eroded. The pristine shell is covered with a thick, red periostracum; a large black patch extends from the upper aperture.

• **REMARK** Collectors appreciate this shell's attractive appearance when rubbed down to reveal the nacreous inner layer.

• **HABITAT** Offshore rocks.

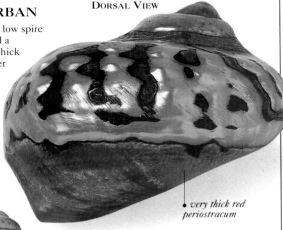

• *very thick red periostracum*

APERTURAL VIEW

• *prominent pustules cover thick, white operculum*

periostracum remains in grooves of polished specimen •

• *reddish brown inside margin of outer lip*

TOP VIEW

• *polishing reveals glossy mother-of-pearl layer underneath*

SOUTH AFRICAN

Range S. Africa	Occurrence ♦♦♦♦	Size 7.5cm (3in)

STAR SHELLS

A DISTINCTIVE FEATURE of these attractive shells is the thick and often brightly coloured operculum. A few species have peripheral spines, others a fringe resembling saw-teeth Most shells lack an umbilicus. Most c the species are subtidal rock dweller but some are from deep water.

Superfamily TROCHOIDEA	Family Turbinidae	Species *Guildfordia triumphans* Philippi

TRIUMPHANT STAR TURBAN

A moderately thick but light shell, top shaped but flattened so that it appears almost disc-like in cross section. Eight or nine pointed spines project from the body whorl, some of their ends usually broken off. Suture is very shallow and umbilicus covered by shelly deposit. Spire whorls display prominent rows of beads; similar beads surround umbilical area of base. Spire whorls pinkish, with darker band of brownish pink; base creamy white, with brownish pink band surrounding umbilical area. Operculum white.
• **REMARK** The commonest of three or four similar species.
• **HABITAT** Deep water.

narrow spines project at right angles to whorl

angles on top edge of whorl

longest spine

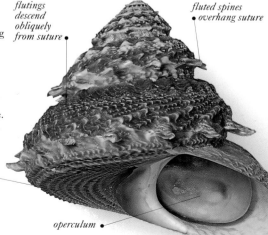

JAPONIC
INDO-PACIFIC

Range Japan, Philippines	Occurrence 🐚🐚🐚	Size 5cm (2in)

Superfamily Turbinidae	Family Turbinidae	Species *Bolma aureola* Hedley

BRIDLED BOLMA

A solid, robustly constructed shell with spine whorls more steeply sloping than body whorl. Short, fluted spines encircle whorls. On the body whorl each spine is seen as the most extravagant of a series of flutings coming down from suture. Edge of aperture is thin. Reddish orange, with columella and inside of aperture white. Operculum white, tinged with orange.
• **REMARK** Rare in good condition.
• **HABITAT** Deep water.

flutings descend obliquely from suture

fluted spines overhang suture

concentric strong beaded ribs on base of shell

operculum

AUSTRALIAN

Range N.E. Australia	Occurrence 🐚🐚	Size 7.5cm (3in)

Superfamily Trochoidea	Family Turbinidae	Species *Bolma girgyllus* Reeve

Girgyllus Star Shell

This light but robust shell has rounded whorls encircled by rows of beaded riblets, those on the base becoming progressively stronger. Each whorl is separated by a narrow but well-defined suture. Above and below the periphery of each whorl is a row of foliated spines which make the whorls appear angled. Colour mostly yellow or green, with brown streaks at suture and also on the spines.
• **REMARK** Orange edge to white columella.
• **HABITAT** Deep water.

INDO-PACIFIC

hollow peripheral spines in two rows expand at their ends

spines on upper row longer than on lower row

Range Philippines, Taiwan	Occurrence 🐚🐚	Size 5cm (2in)

Superfamily Trochoidea	Family Turbinidae	Species *Astraea heliotropium* Martyn

Sunburst Star Turban

A large, robust shell with a moderately tall spire and a wide, deep umbilicus. The spire whorls are well rounded while the body whorl is angled at the base. Large, fluted scales form prominent saw-tooth ornament on the body whorl, which hides suture. Spiral rows of tubercles cover all whorls and extend over scales; border of umbilicus is smooth. Fresh shells dull white, with yellowish umbilicus and pearly aperture. Operculum thick.
• **REMARK** An impressive species discovered during one of Captain Cook's famous sea voyages.
• **HABITAT** Deep water.

hollow fluted scales at periphery

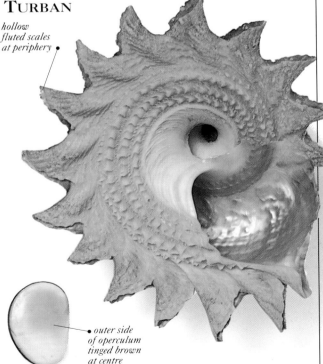

NEOZELANIC

outer side of operculum tinged brown at centre

Range New Zealand	Occurrence 🐚🐚🐚	Size 9cm (3½in)

DOLPHIN SHELLS

MEMBERS OF THIS small group have thick, heavily ornamented, and colourful shells with a wide, deep umbilicus. The pearly, round aperture is sealed with a thin corneous operculum. Some species develop long, curved spines. Inhabitants of coral reefs, they abound in the Philippines.

Superfamily TROCHOIDEA	Family Turbinidae	Species *Angaria sphaerula* Kiener

KIENER'S DELPHINULA

A solid and highly variable shell with a large body whorl and flat-topped spire. Umbilicus wide and deep; suture of upper whorls scarcely perceptible. A row of flattened, curved spines encircles the later whorls. Lower half of the body whorl has spiral rows of stunted spines. Spiral bands of olive-green and red.
• **REMARK** Complete specimens rarely found during 19th century.
• **HABITAT** Coral reefs.

hollow spines

INDO-PACIFIC

umbilicus circled by incurved spines

edge of outer lip not pearly

coarse spiral ribs on upper half of body whorl

Range Philippines	Occurrence 🐚🐚	Size 6cm (2¼in)

Superfamily TROCHOIDEA	Family Turbinidae	Species *Angaria vicdani* Kosuge

VICTOR DAN'S DELPHINULA

APERTURAL VIEW

This solid shell has a large body whorl and a short spire. Base of body whorl flattened. Spines at periphery of whorls are thin, flattened, and straight on early spire whorls; longer, more tubular, and more curved towards aperture. The wide, deep umbilicus is encircled by a double row of short spines. Upper side of later whorls has coarse spiral ribs; the base of the body whorl has strong spiral ribs. Pinkish orange, with green highlights; basal ribs whitish.
• **REMARK** Named after a keen Filipino shell collector.
• **HABITAT** Deep water.

INDO-PACIFIC

TOP VIEW
The arrangement of the spines becomes clearly evident when seen from the top

deep red around umbilicus

subsidiary spines

spines open along one side

Range Philippines	Occurrence 🐚🐚	Size 7cm (2¾in)

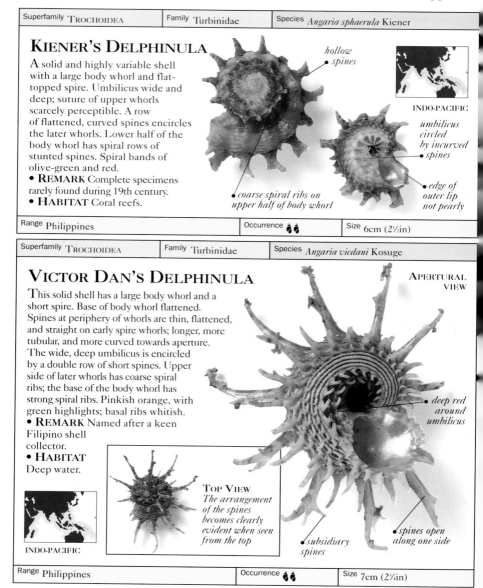

PHEASANT SHELLS

T HE SPECIES in this group of glossy, mostly egg-shaped shells have no umbilicus. The whorls are smooth and swollen, displaying attractive colours and variable patterns; the pear-shaped aperture is sealed with a chalky white operculum. They are widely distributed in temperate and warm waters.

Superfamily TROCHOIDEA	Family Phasianellidae	Species *Phasianella variegata* Lamarck

VARIEGATED PHEASANT

This small shell is smooth and moderately glossy; it has a high spire with a rounded apex, convex whorls, and shallow suture. Aperture pear-shaped; columella smooth and gently curved. Brownish, reddish, or creamy, with brown spots and brown and white dashes.
• **REMARK** Varies in colour and pattern.
• **HABITAT** Shallow water among weeds.

INDO-PACIFIC

• *colour pattern shows through edge of outer lip*

Range Indo-West Pacific	Occurrence 🐚🐚🐚	Size 2cm (¾in)

Superfamily TROCHOIDEA	Family Phasianellidae	Species *Phasianella australis* Gmelin

PAINTED LADY

A moderately thick, very shiny shell, almost twice as high as broad, with a pointed apex, convex whorls, and a well-defined suture. Body whorl slightly taller than spire; aperture pear-shaped, its lower edge projecting well below base of columella; upper end of outer lip bends inwards slightly. Inside of aperture is dull, not pearly. Commonest colour form is blotchy pink with spiral bands of reddish blotches, chevron-like markings, and vertical streaks. Examples displaying vertical brown streaks crossed by whitish spiral lines occur frequently; and the shell may also be covered with spiral rows of rectangular brownish blotches.
• **REMARK** The largest pheasant shell, the patterns are infinitely varied and include some of great beauty.
• **HABITAT** Shallow water.

• *apical whorls have no pattern*

AUSTRALIAN

• *spiral white lines*

• *short vertical streaks just below suture*

• *upper edge of outer lip slightly thickened*

base of columella •

Range S. Australia, Tasmania	Occurrence 🐚🐚🐚🐚	Size 7.5cm (3in)

NERITES

THESE THICK, SHORT-SPIRED shells have a thickened outer lip which is often toothed; the columella may be toothed or furrowed. The calcareous operculum may be granulated. Some species vary greatly in colour. There i no umbilicus. Nerites abound on rock shores and among mangroves.

Superfamily NERITOIDEA	Family Neritidae	Species *Nerita peloronta* Linnaeus

BLEEDING TOOTH

This shell, large among nerites, is thick and short-spired. Its surface may have slightly raised spiral ridges. The dark red operculum is granulated on its inner side. Yellow, reddish, or creamy, with darker streaks or zigzags.
• **REMARK** The teeth give rise to the common name.
• **HABITAT** Rocks inshore.

CARIBBEAN

orange-stained, squarish teeth

zigzag markings on a lighter background

Range W. Indies, W. Florida, Bermuda	Occurrence 🐚🐚🐚🐚🐚	Size 3cm (1¼in)

Superfamily NERITOIDEA	Family Neritidae	Species *Nerita polita* Linnaeus

POLISHED NERITE

Almost flat-topped, thick, and heavy shell with a flattened body whorl. The suture is very shallow. The broad parietal shield is smooth except for irregular, sometimes square-edged, teeth. Parietal shield and aperture creamy, often with orange margin. The rest of the shell is pink or whitish, mottled with white, black, or red.
• **HABITAT** Rocks inshore.

INDO-PACIFIC

spire almost immersed in body whorl

teeth are square edged

Range Tropical Indo-Pacific	Occurrence 🐚🐚🐚🐚🐚	Size 3cm (1¼in)

Superfamily NERITOIDEA	Family Neritidae	Species *Neritina communis* Quoy & Gaimard

ZIGZAG NERITE

A thin but robust shell with a moderately raised spire and conspicuously swollen body whorl. Surface almost perfectly smooth and shiny, the only ornament being indistinct vertical striae. The apex is pointed or rounded; the suture is very shallow. Fine parietal teeth. Red, pink, black, yellow, usually arranged in both zigzags and bands.
• **HABITAT** Mangrove swamps.

body whorl swells out towards aperture

INDO-PACIFIC

very striking colour patterns

Range S.W. Pacific	Occurrence 🐚🐚🐚🐚🐚	Size 2cm (¾in)

WINKLES

THESE SOLIDLY BUILT shells are found in both warm and cool waters, often swarming on rocks and harbour walls. Some can be strikingly marked, and vary considerably in colour. The suture is usually shallow and an umbilicus is never present. There is a thin, corneous operculum.

Superfamily LITTORINOIDEA	Family Littorinidae	Species *Littorina littorea* Linnaeus

COMMON WINKLE

This thick, short-spired shell has a fine suture, moderately swollen whorls, and a pointed apex. Superficially smooth, the shell has weak ridges and faintly marked vertical growth lines. Most are dark brown or grey, usually with spiral bands, but an occasional orange or reddish example occurs.
• **REMARK** Reversed specimens are known but are very rare.
• **HABITAT** Intertidal rocks.

BOREAL

sharp edge to outer lip

fine spiral ridges and grooves

Range W. Europe, N.W. United States	Occurrence 🐚🐚🐚🐚🐚	Size 3cm (1¼in)

Superfamily LITTORINOIDEA	Family Littorinidae	Species *Littorina scabra* Linnaeus

MANGROVE WINKLE

This thin but strong shell is usually high-spired and has rounded, spirally ribbed whorls and a well-defined suture. The straight columella forms a sharp angle with the base of the outer lip. Yellowish or whitish background, variegated with dark and light brown streaks.
• **REMARK** Also known as rough winkle.
• **HABITAT** Mangroves.

pointed high spire

INDO-PACIFIC

columella forms angle with lip

Range Indo-Pacific, S. Africa	Occurrence 🐚🐚🐚🐚🐚	Size 3cm (1¼in)

Superfamily LITTORINOIDEA	Family Littorinidae	Species *Tectarius coronatus* Valenciennes

CROWNED PRICKLY WINKLE

The suture of this straight-sided shell is scarcely perceptible among the spiral rows of nodules, which enlarge towards the periphery of body whorl. Spire creamy to pinkish orange; base white, with brown flecks on outer lip.
• **REMARK** A particularly rugged species of winkle.
• **HABITAT** Intertidal rocks.

dark brown band below suture

INDO-PACIFIC

nodules align vertically and horizontally

Range Philippines	Occurrence 🐚🐚🐚	Size 3cm (1¼in)

SCREW SHELLS

MORE STRIKING for their slender proportions than for their colour, these shells differ from other families mainly in the character of their spiral ornament. The suture is distinct b[...] there is no umbilicus and the outer l[...] is seldom complete. Species are foun[...] in sandy places all over the world.

Superfamily CERITHIOIDEA	Family Turritellidae	Species *Turritella communis* Risso

EUROPEAN SCREW SHELL

Thin and light, this shell has rounded whorls, a well-impressed suture, and sharply pointed apex. Coarse spiral ridges are crossed by fine vertical lines and occasionally by more distinct, uneven growth ridges. Always reddish or yellowish brown, except for columella which is whitish.
• **HABITAT** Sand in both shallow and deep water.

sharper spiral ridges in middle of whorls

BOREAL
MEDITERRANEAN

• *uneven edge to aperture*

Range W. Europe, Mediterranean	Occurrence 🐚🐚🐚🐚🐚	Size 6cm (2¹/₂in)

Superfamily CERITHIOIDEA	Family Turritellidae	Species *Turritella terebra* Linnaeus

TOWER SCREW SHELL

A tall, elegant shell with 30 or more regularly descending, rounded whorls. The outer lip of the rounded aperture is thin, but it is usually complete; the columella is also rounded.

INDO-PACIFIC

turreted, very tall spire

whorls widest just above the suture

perfectly round aperture, with thin, sharp lip

Up to six strong spiral ribs, with lesser ribs in-between, crossed by fine vertical lines. The concave base has spiral grooves. The colour often varies from light to dark brown, but the shell is without markings or patterns. Some specimens may develop swollen whorls, a deeper suture, and much weaker ribs.
• **REMARK** The largest screw shell, it derives its specific name from its resemblance to the auger shells of the genus *Terebrida*.
• **HABITAT** Sandy mud.

• *white-edged columella*

Range Tropical Indo-Pacific	Occurrence 🐚🐚🐚🐚	Size 14cm (5¹/₂in)

WORM SHELLS

A LL WORM SHELLS, as their name suggests, are irregularly coiled and resemble worm tubes. In their earlier growth stages, some are almost indistinguishable from screw shells and their anatomy shows they are related. Others grow more haphazardly and are generally coiled upon themselves.

Superfamily CERITHIOIDEA	Family Turritellidae	Species *Vermicularia spirata* Philippi

WEST INDIAN WORM SHELL

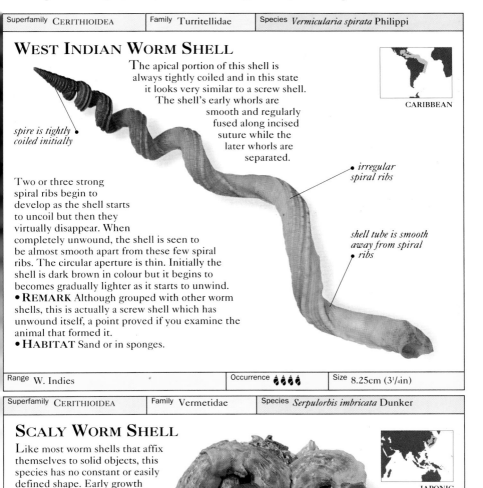

The apical portion of this shell is always tightly coiled and in this state it looks very similar to a screw shell. The shell's early whorls are smooth and regularly fused along incised suture while the later whorls are separated.

spire is tightly coiled initially

irregular spiral ribs

shell tube is smooth away from spiral ribs

Two or three strong spiral ribs begin to develop as the shell starts to uncoil but then they virtually disappear. When completely unwound, the shell is seen to be almost smooth apart from these few spiral ribs. The circular aperture is thin. Initially the shell is dark brown in colour but it begins to becomes gradually lighter as it starts to unwind.
• **REMARK** Although grouped with other worm shells, this is actually a screw shell which has unwound itself, a point proved if you examine the animal that formed it.
• **HABITAT** Sand or in sponges.

Range W. Indies	Occurrence ♦♦♦♦	Size 8.25cm (3¼in)

Superfamily CERITHIOIDEA	Family Vermetidae	Species *Serpulorbis imbricata* Dunker

SCALY WORM SHELL

Like most worm shells that affix themselves to solid objects, this species has no constant or easily defined shape. Early growth stage is completely hidden by later growth. Irregular ridges run whole length of shell.
• **REMARK** Two specimens may be joined together, as here.
• **HABITAT** Rocks.

CARIBBEAN

JAPONIC

thin edge to circular aperture

Range Japan	Occurrence ♦♦♦♦	Size 6cm (2½in)

MODULUS SHELLS

T HE FEW SPECIES of this warmth-loving, shallow-water group look superficially like small turban shells. Solid and spherical, they all have a wide aperture and a small, blunt tooth at th base of the columella. The spire may b depressed or conical. A tiny umbilicu is sometimes, but not always, visible.

Superfamily CERITHIOIDEA	Family Modulidae	Species *Modulus tectum* Gmelin

COVERED MODULUS

A solid shell with depressed spire, ornamented with oblique vertical folds which appear as lumps at periphery. There are coarse spiral ribs. Smooth columella is prominently toothed at the base. Creamy or pale yellow, blotched with brown; columella may be dark brown.
• HABITAT Weedy sand.

ill-defined suture

INDO-PACIFIC

columellar tooth curves into aperture

Range Tropical Indo-Pacific	Occurrence ♠♠♠	Size 2.5cm (1in)

HORN SNAILS

O NLY A FEW SPECIES of horn snail exist, but in mangrove swamps and mud flats the shells of some may occur in countless thousands. Solid and dull coloured, their many whorls are usually ornamented with spiral ribs and tubercles. The base of the outer lip curves towards the siphonal canal.

Superfamily CERITHIOIDEA	Family Potamididae	Species *Telescopium telescopium* Linnaeus

TELESCOPE SNAIL

The tall, straight-sided spire of this heavy shell gives it the appearance of an elongated top shell. The flat base is separated from the columella by a deep channel. Seen in profile, the edge of the uneven aperture descends in a sweeping curve, with a basal projection. The shallow suture is sometimes difficult to distinguish from the edges of the flat spiral ribs encircling the whorls, one narrow rib and three wider ones per whorl. A light brown, white, or grey band occasionally relieves the shell's uniformly dark brown colour.
• REMARK Despite appearances, it is rare for this shell to have more than a total of 16 whorls.
• HABITAT Mangrove swamps.

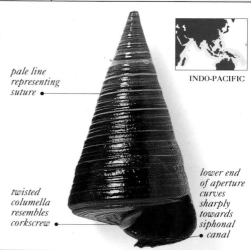

pale line representing suture

INDO-PACIFIC

lower end of aperture curves sharply towards siphonal canal

twisted columella resembles corkscrew

Range Tropical Indo-Pacific	Occurrence ♠♠♠♠	Size 9cm (3½in)

| Superfamily CERITHIOIDEA | Family Potamididae | Species *Cerithidea cingulata* Gmelin |

GIRDLED HORN SHELL

A solid shell with flat-sided whorls and a deep suture. Apex is often eroded. Vertical ribs are prominent on all whorls, but become obsolete on body whorl; ribs are divided into knobs on each whorl by three spiral grooves. Outer lip is thickened and arched. Dark brown, with two or three brown or white lines per whorl.
• **HABITAT** Mangrove swamps.

INDO-PACIFIC

• *body whorl has more pale lines*

| Range Tropical Indo-Pacific | Occurrence 🐚🐚🐚🐚 | Size 4cm (1½in) |

CERITHS

T HE CERITHS are among the most abundant of all the shallow-water gastropods. Generally not colourful, some are attractively banded. Many of the species vary a great deal in size and ornament, which makes them hard to identify. Most are intertidal and prefer sandy places near coral reefs.

| Superfamily CERITHIOIDEA | Family Cerithiidae | Species *Cerithium vulgatum* Bruguière |

EUROPEAN CERITH

This robust shell has a sharply pointed apex, steeply sloping whorls, and a shallow suture. Spiral grooves are strongest mid-whorl; spiral rows of tubercles may develop as short spines. Columella is sinuous, with a thickening at upper end of inner lip. Edge of outer lip wavy, ending in short siphonal canal. Grey or pale brown, with darker brown blotches.
• **HABITAT** Sandy areas.

MEDITERRANEAN

• *very well developed spiral rows of spines*

| Range Mediterranean | Occurrence 🐚🐚🐚🐚 | Size 4.5cm (1¾in) |

| Superfamily CERITHIOIDEA | Family Cerithiidae | Species *Rhinoclavis asper* Linnaeus |

ROUGH CERITH

One of the more slender ceriths, this shell has a sharply pointed apex and a well-impressed suture; the whorls expand evenly throughout its length. Inner lip is clearly separated from body whorl, its upper part thickened. Short siphonal canal is strongly bent away from aperture. Strong vertical ribs, sometimes bearing sharp points, run obliquely the length of shell. White, with spiral brown lines.
• **HABITAT** Sandy areas.

INDO-PACIFIC

• *ribs not aligned vertically on later whorls*

| Range Indo-Pacific | Occurrence 🐚🐚🐚🐚 | Size 5cm (2in) |

PLANAXIS SNAILS

THE FEW SPECIES comprising this group have thick, conical shells. Some are smooth; others are spirally ribbed; the aperture is often ridged and the columella may have a single tooth; the siphonal canal is well defined. There is a thin, corneous operculum. These shells occur on intertidal rocks.

Superfamily CERITHIOIDEA	Family Planaxidae	Species *Planaxis sulcatus* Born

FURROWED PLANAXIS

The body whorl occupies up to two-thirds of this shell's total height; it has broad, flat spiral ribs that are sometimes indistinct. There is a parietal swelling and the columella ends in a notch. Purplish brown and grey in colour, arranged in streaks and spots.
• **REMARK** Surface has opaque periostracum.
• **HABITAT** Intertidal rocks.

body whorl puckered at suture

concave columella

INDO-PACIFIC

Range Tropical Indo-Pacific	Occurrence 🐚🐚🐚🐚🐚	Size 2.5cm (1in)

SUNDIALS

THE FEW MEMBERS of this decorative warm-water group are sometimes known as winding-staircase shells. Corrugations resembling steps line the large, wide, and deep umbilicus of these flat, round shells. Usually their aperture has a damaged edge. The operculum is usually corneous.

Superfamily ARCHITECTONICOIDEA	Family Architectonicidae	Species *Architectonica perspectiva* Linnaeus

CLEAR SUNDIAL

A solid shell with evenly expanding whorls and a deep suture. The spiral and vertical grooves on the whorls produce a lattice pattern. The ridge above and below the suture resembles a string of flattened beads. The outer edge of the base is encircled by two flat-topped ribs. Grey to yellowish brown, with alternating spiral bands of white and dark brown; edge of umbilicus spotted dark brown.
• **REMARK** Ridges inside the umbilicus resemble the steps of a spiral staircase.
• **HABITAT** Sandy areas.

TOP VIEW

suture set below the narrower dark band

INDO-PACIFIC

BOTTOM VIEW

narrow rib separates two broad ribs

Range Tropical Indo-Pacific	Occurrence 🐚🐚🐚🐚🐚	Size 5cm (2in)

WENTLETRAPS

T HE POPULAR NAME for these deli-cate and attractive shells comes from the Dutch word for a winding staircase. The aperture is round and smooth, the umbilicus open or closed. Most species are thin and white. They live in sandy places, sometimes among sea anemones; many are intertidal.

Superfamily EPITONIOIDEA	Family Epitoniidae	Species *Epitonium scalare* Linnaeus

PRECIOUS WENTLETRAP

This lightweight shell has eight or nine well-rounded, loosely coiled whorls connected to each other by thin, varix-like ribs. The separation of the whorls is so complete that there is no suture. The umbilicus is wide and deep. Pale pink or beige, with white ribs and aperture.
• REMARK Rare in the last century, this shell has become much more common during the last three decades.
• HABITAT Subtidal in sand.

weak spiral grooves between ribs

INDO-PACIFIC

delicate rib ornament holds separated whorls together

ten to eleven white ribs on body whorl

Range Tropical Indo-Pacific	Occurrence 🌢🌢🌢	Size 5.7cm (2¹/₄in)

PURPLE SEA SNAILS

T HE HALF-DOZEN species in this group have thin, fragile shells and most of them are purple or violet. The animals spend their lives out at sea, forming mucus-covered "bubble rafts" in which their eggs float on the water surface. When disturbed they emit a violet-coloured fluid.

Superfamily EPITONIOIDEA	Family Janthinidae	Species *Janthina janthina* Linnaeus

COMMON PURPLE SEA SNAIL

A thin, fragile shell of about five whorls, the early ones convex. The suture is well defined. Apertural edge is continuous all round; columella is slightly twisted. Vertical growth striae are crossed by faint spiral grooves. Underlying violet colour overlain with white, except for the apex, suture, and base.
• REMARK Floats upside down.
• HABITAT Free-swimming.

WORLD

base of body whorl angled towards base

Range Worldwide	Occurrence 🌢🌢🌢	Size 4cm (1¹/₂in)

CAP SHELLS

ALTHOUGH RESEMBLING limpets in shape, these shells are less sturdy and their apex, which may be coiled, is often situated towards the rear. Smooth, vertically ribbed, or spirally groove they lack an operculum. The anima attach themselves to solid objects; son are parasitic on other molluscs.

Superfamily CREPIDULOIDEA	Family Capulidae	Species *Capulus ungaricus* Linnaeus

FOOL'S CAP

APERTURAL VIEW   SIDE VIEW

A thin, cap-shaped shell varying considerably in outline and height, usually wider than its height. Recurved apex points backwards and slightly overhangs rear edge. Fine vertical striae and concentric growth ridges. Inside white or pinkish, glossy; outside whitish, dull.
• **HABITAT** Solid objects.

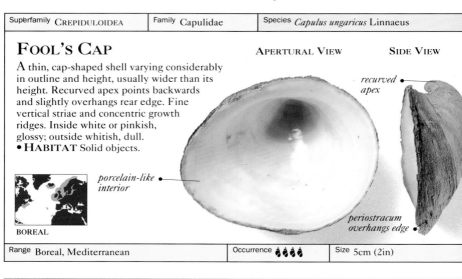

recurved apex

porcelain-like interior

BOREAL

periostracum overhangs edge

Range Boreal, Mediterranean	Occurrence 🌢🌢🌢🌢	Size 5cm (2in)

SLIPPER SHELLS

THESE SHELLS look like limpets when viewed from above but have a broad internal shelf, or cup-shaped structure, which protects the creature's soft organs. Flattened, with apex situated centrally or towards the rear, they may be smooth or variously ornamented. There is no operculum.

Superfamily CREPIDULOIDEA	Family Crepidulidae	Species *Crepidula fornicata* Linnaeus

ATLANTIC SLIPPER

This flattened, oval shell has a gently coiled apex scarely visible at rear end. Aperture is half closed by thin, shell-like partition. Outside surface smooth or wrinkled. Creamy, yellow, or brownish, mottled and streaked with reddish brown. Inside white, with outside colour showing; shelf has reddish brown edge.
• **HABITAT** Attached to each other, and to solid objects, offshore.

sinuously curved edge to shelf

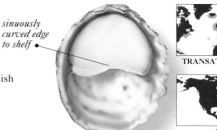

TRANSATLANTIC

BOREAL

Range N.E. U.S.A., N.W. Europe	Occurrence 🌢🌢🌢🌢🌢	Size 4cm (1½in)

CARRIER SHELLS

T HESE DELICATE top-shaped shells have a characteristic tendency, sometimes taken to extremes, to amass shells, stones, and other sea-floor debris to their upper surface. They may or may not have an umbilicus but all have a thin, corneous operculum. Most of the species are from tropical seas.

Superfamily XENOPHOROIDEA	Family Xenophoridae	Species *Xenophora pallidula* Reeve

PALLID CARRIER

A thin, moderately high-spired shell with a small umbilicus sometimes obscured by shelly growth. Upper surface has oblique vertical ribs, covered by shells and debris. White or yellowish white.
• **REMARK** Attached objects include various elongate shells, arranged radially at the periphery.
• **HABITAT** Deep water.

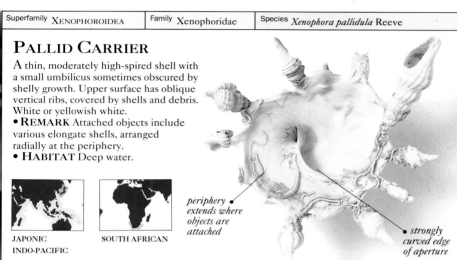

JAPONIC
INDO-PACIFIC

SOUTH AFRICAN

periphery extends where objects are attached

strongly curved edge of aperture

Range Indo-Pacific, S. Africa, Japan	Occurrence 🐚🐚🐚	Size 7.5cm (3in)

Superfamily XENOPHOROIDEA	Family Xenophoridae	Species *Stellaria solaris* Linnaeus

SUNBURST CARRIER

A low-spired shell with long, tubular, blunt-ended, and slightly upturned spines at periphery of all whorls; spines are pressed into succeeding whorls, except on outer body whorl. The upper surface has fine, obliquely sloping riblets; the underside is ornamented with strong, wavy, radiating ribs. Umbilicus is deep, revealing all whorls within it. Creamy, with early spines generally paler.
• **REMARK** Only apical whorls are covered with debris.
• **HABITAT** Offshore sand.

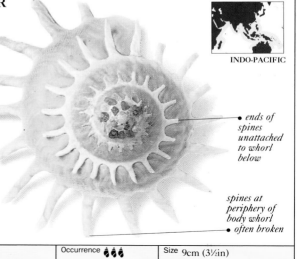

INDO-PACIFIC

ends of spines unattached to whorl below

spines at periphery of body whorl often broken

Range Tropical Indo-Pacific	Occurrence 🐚🐚🐚	Size 9cm (3½in)

OSTRICH FOOT SHELLS

THESE SOLID, medium-sized shells have a prominent suture and no umbilicus. The aperture is large, the siphonal canal short, and the whorls are usually nodulous. The columella and parietal wall are thickly callused. The few species in this group have a thin corneous operculum.

Superfamily STROMBOIDEA	Family Struthiolariidae	Species *Struthiolaria papulosa* Martyn

LARGE OSTRICH FOOT

A thick, heavy shell with a tall spire and well-marked suture. Whorls are sharply angled where a row of prominent tubercles encircles the periphery. Above and below tubercles are several rows of evenly spaced, thin, and flat-topped spiral ridges. Distinguished by strongly curved outer lip and callus on columella. Whitish, with vertical brown stripes.
• **HABITAT** Sand intertidally and offshore.

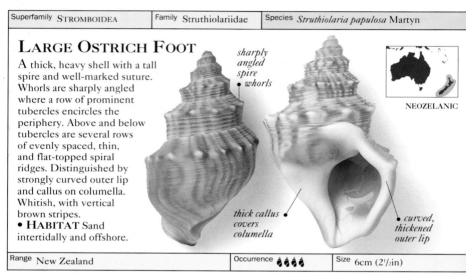

sharply angled spire
• *whorls*

NEOZELANIC

thick callus covers columella •

• *curved, thickened outer lip*

Range New Zealand	Occurrence 🐚🐚🐚🐚	Size 6cm (2¹⁄₂in)

PELICAN'S FOOT SHELLS

WHEN MATURE, the flattened apertural lip of these shells has a "webbed-foot" extension; the immature spiral shells look very different. The shape and the number of finger-like extensions may vary within a species. The few species in this family live in cool and temperate waters.

Superfamily STROMBOIDEA	Family Aporrhaidae	Species *Aporrhais pespelecani* Linnaeus

COMMON PELICAN'S FOOT

The spire has angulated whorls bearing blunt tubercles and fine spiral grooves. The well-marked suture has a spiral rib above. Ribs along the four finger-like extensions to the flattened lip appear as grooves internally. Pale brown, with white aperture.
• **HABITAT** Muddy gravel.

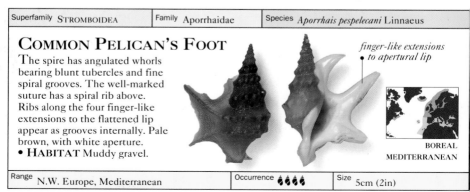

finger-like extensions • *to apertural lip*

BOREAL
MEDITERRANEAN

Range N.W. Europe, Mediterranean	Occurrence 🐚🐚🐚🐚	Size 5cm (2in)

TRUE CONCHS

E ACH OF THE SIX GENERA in this tropical family has its own very distinctive shape (and its own popular name). Despite a variety of differing features, all are closely related.

———— • ————

Strombs have a flaring lip, spider conchs have long, finger-like extensions, while tibias are spindle-shaped with a long siphonal canal. Many conch shells are colourful; most are thick and heavy. A long, curved operculum helps locomotion. A prominent feature, of strombs in particular, is the "stromboid notch" towards the front end of the outer lip, through which the animal protrudes its stalked left eye. They live mostly in shallow water. Many are sand dwellers, some prefer mud or gravel, while others live on the reef.

Superfamily STROMBOIDEA	Family Strombidae	Species *Strombus gigas* Linnaeus

PINK CONCH

A solid, heavy shell with a broad, flaring lip when mature; also known as queen conch. Spire whorls have large tubercles which are often developed into long, blunt spines; these spines may be clearly seen in immature shells. At maturity, the outer lip extends the length of the shell; it tends to be thin and brittle at the edge. Creamy exterior colour is obscured by a brownish periostracum. The aperture is bright pink.
• **REMARK** The animal is edible.
• **HABITAT** Grass or sand.

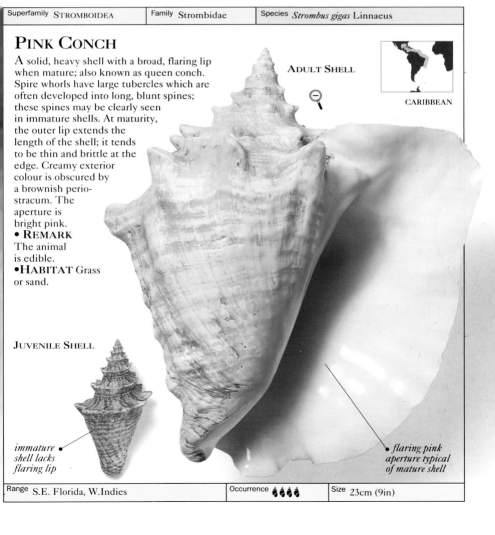

ADULT SHELL

CARIBBEAN

JUVENILE SHELL

immature shell lacks flaring lip

flaring pink aperture typical of mature shell

Range S.E. Florida, W.Indies	Occurrence 🐚🐚🐚🐚	Size 23cm (9in)

Superfamily STROMBOIDEA	Family Strombidae	Species *Strombus sinuatus* Lightfoot

SINUOUS CONCH

A solid, moderately large shell with a high, stepped, knobbed spire and body whorl with a wing-like extension. The lip's thin upper edge has four rounded, fingernail-shaped projections. Creamy, marked with yellowish brown, wavy streaks; aperture purple.
• **REMARK** May have five projections.
• **HABITAT** Coral sand, shallow water.

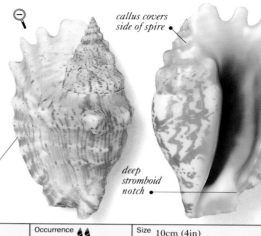

callus covers side of spire

wavy, thickened outer edge of lip

deep stromboid notch

INDO-PACIFIC

Range S.W. Pacific	Occurrence 🐚🐚	Size 10cm (4in)

Superfamily STROMBOIDEA	Family Strombidae	Species *Strombus gallus* Linnaeus

ROOSTER TAIL CONCH

This high-spired, solid shell is lightweight for its size. The flared edge of the aperture projects at an angle to the spire, visually balancing the extended siphonal canal at the opposite end. Spire whorls are encircled with prominent blunt knobs below the narrow, deep suture. Body whorl and flared extension orna-mented with flattened ridges. Deep stromboid notch. Creamy, with brown streak; aperture golden brown.
• **REMARK** Ground colour sometimes violet.
• **HABITAT** Sand offshore.

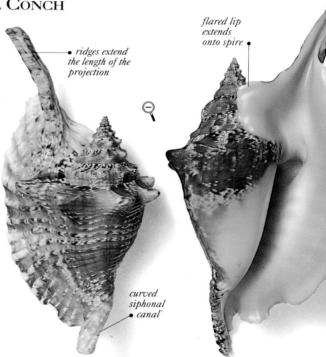

ridges extend the length of the projection

flared lip extends onto spire

curved siphonal canal

CARIBBEAN

Range W. Indies	Occurrence 🐚🐚🐚	Size 13cm (5in)

Superfamily STROMBOIDEA	Family Strombidae	Species *Strombus listeri* T. Gray

LISTER'S CONCH

The body whorl of this thin, lightweight, slender-spired shell is more than half the total height. Early spire whorls are rounded; later ones slope initially, then descend vertically. Suture is shallow. Smooth body whorl is curved; the apertural lip extends outwards, its outer edge parallel with shell axis, and ending with a finger-like projection. Smooth columella is lightly callused. Spire whorls have strong vertical ribs crossed by finer spiral riblets. White, streaked and mottled with brown.
• **REMARK** Once a great rarity, now found more often.
• **HABITAT** Deep water.

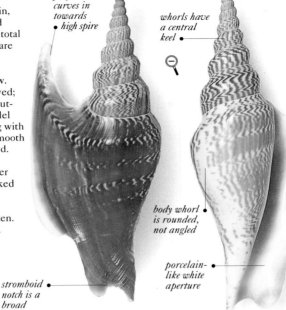

projection curves in towards high spire

whorls have a central keel

body whorl is rounded, not angled

porcelain-like white aperture

stromboid notch is a broad embayment

INDO-PACIFIC

Range Indian Ocean	Occurrence ♦♦♦	Size 13cm (5in)

Superfamily STROMBOIDEA	Family Strombidae	Species *Strombus pugilis* Linnaeus

WEST INDIAN FIGHTING CONCH

A solid, heavy shell with a short, pointed spire and large body whorl. The thickened outer lip ends in a broad stromboid notch. Early whorls are smooth or encircled with blunt knobs. On later whorls, the knobs are more pointed, and are often strongly developed on the penultimate whorl. Apart from the smooth middle of the body whorl, all whorls have spiral riblets and grooves. Pale brown or yellowish orange in colour; both the aperture and the columella are red.

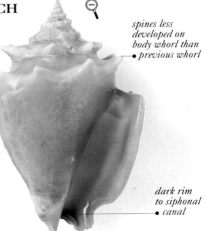

spines less developed on body whorl than previous whorl

dark rim to siphonal canal

• **REMARK** The name is derived from the animal's energetic movements. The operculum is often used by the animal to dig into sand when it is lunging about.
• **HABITAT** Sand inshore.

CARIBBEAN

Range Caribbean	Occurrence ♦♦♦♦♦	Size 7.5cm (3in)

| Superfamily STROMBOIDEA | Family Strombidae | Species *Strombus urceus* Linnaeus |

LITTLE BEAR CONCH

An elongate shell which varies considerably in form and colour. Body whorl more than twice as long as spire. Aperture narrow at top and bottom, its inner edge straight and smoothly rounded; stromboid notch deep or shallow. Spire whorls may be smooth or have vertical ribs or tubercles. Aperture usually strongly ribbed. Spiral grooves around lower part of otherwise smooth body whorl. White, cream or brown, blotched and spotted with shades of brown.
• **HABITAT** Sandy places.

thickened ribs on spire whorls

INDO-PACIFIC

outer lip of aperture parallel with inner lip

black-mouthed Malaysian form

| Range W. Pacific | Occurrence ♦♦♦♦ | Size 5cm (2in) |

| Superfamily STROMBOIDEA | Family Strombidae | Species *Strombus mutabilis* Swainson |

CHANGEABLE CONCH

A solid, squat shell varying in form and colour according to location. Broad body whorl is more than twice the length of spire. Apex is sharply pointed. Vertical ribs on spire whorls may be thick and nodulous. Body whorl may have rounded projections at the shoulder. Outer lip is thickened. Aperture and columella ridged. White or cream, mottled with brown.
• **HABITAT** Sandy places inshore.

INDO-PACIFIC

stromboid notch very shallow

| Range Tropical Indo-Pacific | Occurrence ♦♦♦♦ | Size 3.5cm (1¼in) |

| Superfamily STROMBOIDEA | Family Strombidae | Species *Strombus dentatus* Linnaeus |

SAMAR CONCH

This glossy shell has an inflated body whorl over twice the length of its spire. The suture is shallow. All whorls are smooth, the vertical ribs rounded and fading out about halfway down the body whorl. The aperture is just over half the height of the body whorl and appears to be cut away towards base. Outer lip is thin; stromboid notch is shallow. Columella smooth and glossy. Creamy, blotched brown.
• **REMARK** Lower part of aperture may be purplish brown.
• **HABITAT** Near coral reefs.

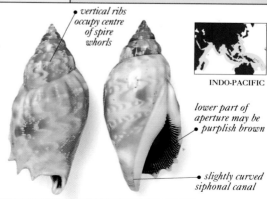

vertical ribs occupy centre of spire whorls

INDO-PACIFIC

lower part of aperture may be purplish brown

slightly curved siphonal canal

| Range Tropical Pacific | Occurrence ♦♦♦ | Size 4cm (1½in) |

Superfamily STROMBOIDEA	Family Strombidae	Species *Strombus latissimus* Linnaeus

BROAD PACIFIC CONCH

A massive, heavy shell with an inflated body whorl. Flared outer lip sweeps up and over the short spire, obliterating its apertural side. Spire whorls are keeled and have small, blunt knobs. The dorsal view reveals a large, rounded knob below shoulder of body whorl and spiral ridges on upper part of outer lip. Thickened inner edge of lip forms a broad ridge. Thick callus on columella. Cream, mottled with brown.
• **REMARK** Stromboid notch may be narrow and deep or wide and shallow.
• **HABITAT** Sand outside coral reefs.

INDO-PACIFIC

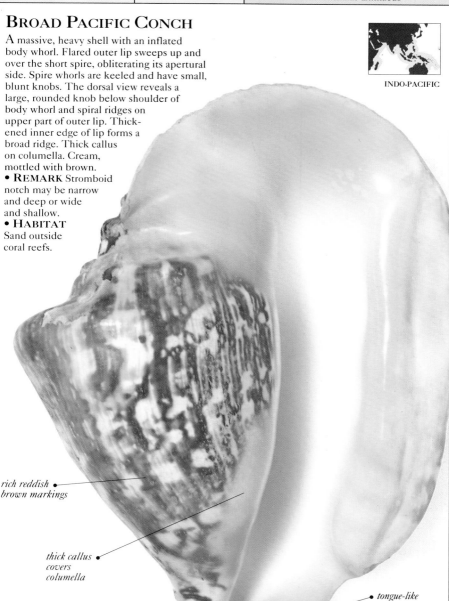

rich reddish brown markings

thick callus covers columella

tongue-like projection separates siphonal canal from stromboid notch

Range W. Pacific	Occurrence 🌢🌢🌢	Size 15cm (6in)

| Superfamily STROMBOIDEA | Family Strombidae | Species *Strombus lentiginosus* Linnaeus |

SILVER CONCH

A solid shell with an inflated body whorl, squarish in outline, and a short, pointed spire. The expanded outer lip is almost as high as the apex and is thickened and reflected. The stromboid notch is deep and the siphonal canal is short and broad. Impressed suture is wavy. Body whorl has five spiral rows of knobs, the uppermost row standing out prominently like bony knuckles. Spiral threads on all whorls. Smooth aperture and columella. A transparent callus covers the parietal wall. Creamy, with orange-brown streaks and blotches; the aperture is pinkish orange.
• **REMARK** A very heavy shell for its size.
• **HABITAT** Shallow water on coral sand.

INDO-PACIFIC

lip has orange-brown bands

stromboid notch has a reflected edge

| Range Tropical Indo-Pacific | Occurrence 🐚🐚🐚🐚 | Size 7.5cm (3in) |

| Superfamily STROMBOIDEA | Family Strombidae | Species *Strombus canarium* Linnaeus |

DOG CONCH

This shell, heavy for its size, has a pear-shaped body whorl and flared outer lip. The short spire has a sharply pointed apex. The rounded spire whorls are smooth or ornamented with spiral grooves and ridges; smooth body whorl is grooved at the base. The outer lip has a thickened edge and a shallow stromboid notch. The straight columella is thickly callused. White, cream, or brown, with darker streaks.
• **REMARK** Varies greatly in size.
• **HABITAT** Sand inshore.

pale band at base of spire whorls

white edge to outer lip

both ground colour and markings are very variable

INDO-PACIFIC

| Range Tropical Indo-Pacific | Occurrence 🐚🐚🐚🐚 | Size 6cm (2½in) |

Superfamily STROMBOIDEA	Family Strombidae	Species *Lambis lambis* Linnaeus

COMMON SPIDER CONCH

A large, solid shell with a spire almost as long as its body whorl. The widely flared aperture has six long, hollow spines, open throughout their length, which mostly curve upwards. The siphonal canal is almost a mirror image of the uppermost spine; the stromboid notch is deep. Blunt knobs decorate the body whorl, the knob nearest the lip being the largest. The rest of the shell has poorly developed spiral ribs. Each spire whorl is concave. A parietal callus covers the shell's apertural side. Creamy white, mottled and streaked with brown.
• **REMARK** Projections longer on shells of females than males.
• **HABITAT** Sand inshore.

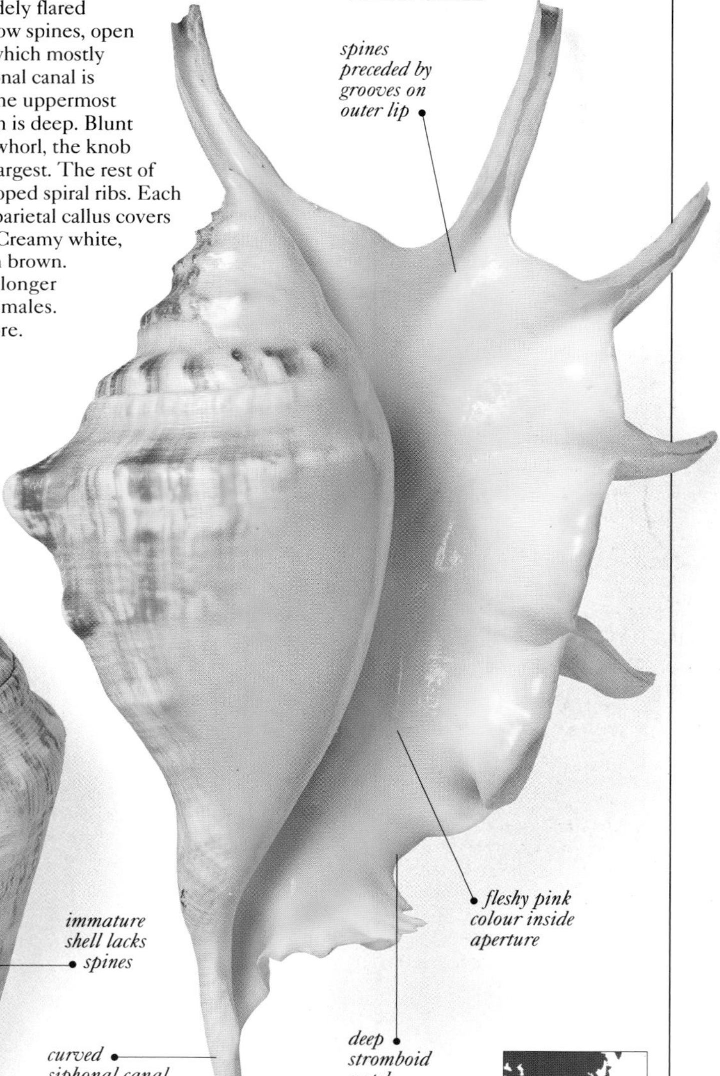

ADULT SHELL

spines preceded by grooves on outer lip

JUVENILE SHELL

immature shell lacks spines

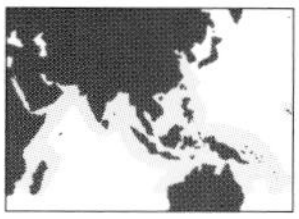

curved siphonal canal

fleshy pink colour inside aperture

deep stromboid notch

INDO-PACIFIC

Range Indo-Pacific	Occurrence	Size 15cm (6in)

Superfamily STROMBOIDEA	Family Strombidae	Species *Lambis violacea* Swainson

VIOLET SPIDER CONCH

An inflated shell with a flared outer lip bearing 15–17 projections. The siphonal canal is long and recurved towards aperture; stromboid notch is wide and deep. Spiral ribs run from top to bottom, bearing irregularly spaced nodules on the later whorls. Aperture delicately ridged. White, flecked and streaked with brown; aperture deep violet colour; orange blotches on the outer lip.
• **HABITAT** Moderately deep water.

upper projections longer and flatter than lower ones

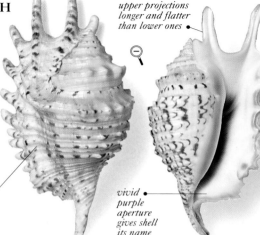

INDO-PACIFIC

ribs are strongest on projections

vivid purple aperture gives shell its name

Range W. Indian Ocean	Occurrence 🐚	Size 9cm (3½in)

Superfamily STROMBOIDEA	Family Strombidae	Species *Lambis chiragra* Linnaeus

CHIRAGRA SPIDER CONCH

A large, thick, and heavy shell with an inflated body whorl and a short spire. The projections are so massively developed around the edge of the aperture that it is difficult to see the spire. The apex is sharply pointed and all the whorls are angulated. The body whorl has irregular and lumpy spiral ribs, the thickest of them ending as curved projections. The five projections from the outer lip (the apparent sixth one at the base of the ridged columella being the siphonal canal) are all open throughout their length. White, mottled and spotted with brown; aperture pink, red, or brownish.
• **REMARK** Shells of female larger, with a more strongly ridged columella.
• **HABITAT** Sand inshore.

canal continuous around extended top of apertural lip

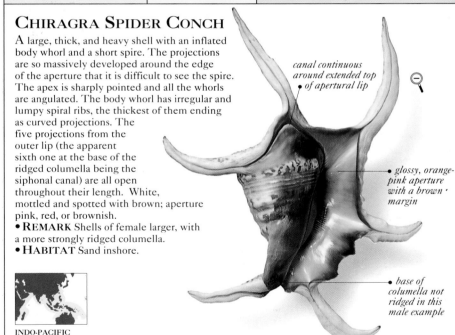

glossy, orange-pink aperture with a brown margin

base of columella not ridged in this male example

INDO-PACIFIC

Range Tropical Indo-Pacific	Occurrence 🐚🐚🐚🐚	Size male 16cm (6¼in)

Superfamily STROMBOIDEA	Family Strombidae	Species *Tibia insulaechorab* Röding

ARABIAN TIBIA

A heavy shell with a straight-sided spire and an inflated body whorl. A thick columellar callus begins at the lower end of the penultimate whorl and eventually joins the siphonal canal. The aperture narrows above and below. Seen from the rear, the outer lip has a well-defined rim extending to the base of the siphonal canal; its lower half has five or six short, blunt points, below which is a shallow stromboid notch. Pale brown colour, with white aperture and columellar callus.
• **REMARK** One form of this species has a dark brown band at the suture.
• **HABITAT** Sandy places offshore.

vertically ribbed, early spire whorls

INDO-PACIFIC

blunt tooth on columella

white lines at suture

Range Indian Ocean, Red Sea	Occurrence 🐚🐚🐚	Size 14cm (5¹/₂in)

Superfamily STROMBOIDEA	Family Strombidae	Species *Tibia fusus* Linnaeus

SHINBONE TIBIA

A slender shell with a narrow, elongate, high spire and long, straight, needle-like siphonal canal. Also known as spindle tibia. Early whorls ornamented with vertical ribs and fine spiral ridges.

INDO-PACIFIC

sculpture more marked on early whorls

projections on outer lip of aperture become longer towards front end

Base of body whorl is spirally grooved while other whorls are smooth. All whorls are distinctly convex, with an impressed suture. The columellar callus, which has a small blunt tooth at its upper end, joins the long siphonal canal, almost equal in length to the rest of the shell. The moderately thickened outer lip forms a canal where it meets the columellar callus; a series of five blunt projections or teeth increase in length from top to bottom. Pale brown in colour, lighter at suture; outer lip and columella creamy white or white. Horny operculum oval, slightly arched, with apical nucleus.
• **REMARK** Highly prized by collectors when the long, slender siphonal canal is undamaged.
• **HABITAT** Deep water.

pointed operculum helps animal's foot to grip sea bed

tip of siphonal canal sometimes gently curved

Range S.W. Pacific	Occurrence 🐚🐚	Size 20cm (8in)

Superfamily STROMBOIDEA	Family Strombidae	Species *Tibia martini* Marrat

MARTIN'S TIBIA

A thin, lightweight, silky shell with a tall spire, pointed apex, and swollen body whorl; the spine-like siphonal canal is slightly curved. Just below the shallow suture is a distinct spiral groove. The outer lip, thickened at the edge, bears six or seven short spines. Pale creamy brown, with white edge to outer lip and lower part of columella; middle spire whorls darker brown.
• **REMARK** Described in 1877, this large species was virtually unobtainable for almost one hundred years.
• **HABITAT** Deep water.

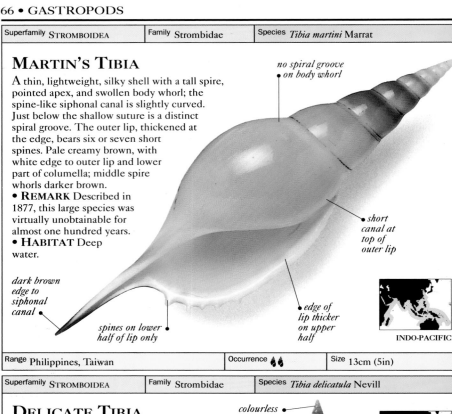

no spiral groove on body whorl

short canal at top of outer lip

dark brown edge to siphonal canal

spines on lower half of lip only

edge of lip thicker on upper half

INDO-PACIFIC

Range Philippines, Taiwan	Occurrence 🐚🐚	Size 13cm (5in)

Superfamily STROMBOIDEA	Family Strombidae	Species *Tibia delicatula* Nevill

DELICATE TIBIA

This sturdy, compact shell is smooth and glossy. Its gently convex spire whorls are separated by a shallow suture and end in a pointed apex. The well-rounded body whorl curves inwards sharply on the lower half to end in a short, slightly curved, and pointed siphonal canal. Outer lip has up to five prominent, blunt spines. Yellowish or pale brown, with faint, darker brown vertical streaks and widely spaced, spiral white lines; inside of outer lip white, outside brown.
• **REMARK** Most of us lack facilities to collect shells like this from the ocean depths but, as with many other deep-water species, one lucky haul of the dredge may bring to the surface enough examples to satisfy the needs of several keen collectors.
• **HABITAT** Deep water.

colourless apical whorls

narrow, transparent band below suture

INDO-PACIFIC

narrow canal at top of aperture

top spine thickest

claw-shaped operculum

aperture purplish brown inside

Range Arabian Sea	Occurrence 🐚🐚	Size 7cm (2¾in)

Superfamily STROMBOIDEA	Family Strombidae	Species *Tibia powisi* Petit

POWIS'S TIBIA

A small, thick, narrowly elongate shell with gently rounded whorls, a deeply incised suture, pointed apex, and short, straight, pointed siphonal canal. Spire longer than body whorl and siphonal canal combined. Apertural side of body whorl compressed. Aperture small; thickened outer lip is reflected and armed with five strong, blunt spines; smooth columella is heavily callused. Later whorls are encircled by rounded ribs between which are indistinct vertical ridges. Pale brown, with white outer lip and columella; dark brown blotches behind the outer lip.
• **HABITAT** Offshore.

• *early whorls perfectly smooth*

INDO-PACIFIC

• *suture darker brown than whorls*

end of siphonal canal brown

• *broad and flattened top spine*

Range S.W. Pacific	Occurrence 🐚🐚	Size 6cm (2½in)

Superfamily STROMBOIDEA	Family Strombidae	Species *Varicospira cancellata* Lamarck

CANCELLATE BEAK SHELL

A thick, elongate shell. The aperture is narrow; the thickened outer lip has a wavy edge; columella continues upwards as part of a curved canal. Smooth ribs have deep spiral grooves between. Brown; aperture purple; outer lip and columella white.
• **REMARK** Unique for its long, narrow, sinuous canal at the top of the aperture.
• **HABITAT** Offshore.

INDO-PACIFIC

• *narrow canal around whorl*

• *puckered surface on lip*

Range Indo-West Pacific	Occurrence 🐚🐚	Size 3cm (1¼in)

Superfamily STROMBOIDEA	Family Strombidae	Species *Terebellum terebellum* Linnaeus

TEREBELLUM CONCH

This slender shell has a very short spire of straight-sided whorls separated by a sharply incised suture. A narrow band encircles whorls above suture. Body whorl longer than spire, tapering, then parallel-sided, ending in a broad siphonal notch. Aperture is narrow; long columella thickly callused; smooth outer lip slightly thickened. Colour and pattern vary, often creamy with spiral rows of pear-shaped, brownish spots.
• **REMARK** No other shell has such a distinct torpedo-like shape.
• **HABITAT** Sand inshore.

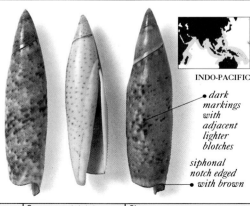

INDO-PACIFIC

• *dark markings with adjacent lighter blotches*

siphonal notch edged with brown

Range Tropical Indo-Pacific	Occurrence 🐚🐚🐚🐚	Size 6cm (2½in)

COWRIES

COWRIES HAVE BEEN universally collected, admired, and treasured for centuries; their beautiful colours, their glossy surface, and simply just holding them are all good reasons for their popularity. There are about two hundred different species and some are abundant, especially in the tropics.

In the first stage of its growth, a cowrie develops a short, pointed spire and a large body whorl; then the body envelops the spire and its growing edge thickens; finally, it forms teeth along each side of the restricted aperture.

The basic shape varies little, but the species differ greatly in size, colour pattern, arrangement of the aperture teeth, and margins. The line seen down the length of the shell is where the animal's mantle flaps meet. Active at night, but hidden by day, these animals browse on algae around coral reefs.

Superfamily CYPRAEOIDEA	Family Cypraeidae	Species *Cypraea helvola* Linnaeus

HONEY COWRIE

A small, solid, elliptical shell with a convex base. Thickened and pitted margins are clearly separated from the sides. Teeth on each side are well developed, those on the columella side reaching about halfway to the margin. Lilac or pale blue, patterned with large brown spots and tiny pale spots; brown spots coalesce towards margins. Base reddish brown; margins lilac at ends.
• **REMARK** Colours soon fade.
• **HABITAT** Coral reefs.

pale line where sides of animal's fleshy mantle meet

INDO-PACIFIC

darker brown colours between teeth of aperture

Range Tropical Indo-Pacific	Occurrence 🐚🐚🐚🐚	Size 2.5cm (1in)

Superfamily CYPRAEOIDEA	Family Cypraeidae	Species *Cypraea caputserpentis* Linnaeus

SNAKE'S HEAD COWRIE

A thick, heavy, rather hump-backed shell with an egg-shaped outline and flattened base. Margins splay out to form a surrounding flange with a strongly ridged edge. Teeth on each side of aperture are short; canals at each end of aperture are scarcely indented. Humped back brown, with small white spots of varying size; deep, chocolate-brown band covers margin, except for creamy white above location of canals at both ends of aperture; teeth and adjacent area of base white.
• **REMARK** Juveniles are bluish.
• **HABITAT** Rocks and coral.

creamy blotches at both ends

INDO-PACIFIC

base sides about equal in width

Range Tropical Indo-Pacific	Occurrence 🐚🐚🐚🐚	Size 3cm (1¼in)

Superfamily CYPRAEOIDEA	Family Cypraeidae	Species *Cypraea ocellata* Linnaeus

OCELLATE COWRIE

A moderately thick, ovate, inflated shell with raised canals at each end. Narrow margin is clearly separated from sides and intermittently pitted; margin on columellar side is thicker and extends slightly on to upper surface. Base fairly rounded; teeth on outer side of aperture longer and thicker. Yellowish brown, sprinkled with rounded white dots and a few larger black dots, ringed by a fine white line. Base creamy.
• **REMARK** Mantle line is bluish.
• **HABITAT** Muddy rocks.

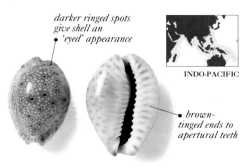

darker ringed spots give shell an 'eyed' appearance

INDO-PACIFIC

brown-tinged ends to apertural teeth

Range Indian Ocean	Occurrence ♦♦♦	Size 2.5cm (1in)

Superfamily CYPRAEOIDEA	Family Cypraeidae	Species *Cypraea lamarckii* Gray

LAMARCK'S COWRIE

This thick, ovate shell has slightly developed margins. Base is convex; teeth strong but short. Coffee coloured, liberally spattered with evenly spaced, round, white dots; many have bluish grey centres. Margins and extremities paler, with dark brown blotches; base white.
• **HABITAT** Muddy rocks inshore.

INDO-PACIFIC

brown lines on canal rim

Range Indian Ocean	Occurrence ♦♦♦	Size 4cm (1½in)

Superfamily CYPRAEOIDEA	Family Cypraeidae	Species *Cypraea moneta* Linnaeus

MONEY COWRIE

This familiar cowrie is one of the most variable of all seashells, and therefore hard to describe comprehensively. It is thick, somewhat flattened, and angular. Margins may be heavily callused, particularly at top, but may be lightly callused and less angular. Aperture is narrow; few strong, short teeth. Ground colour yellowish; three greyish blue bands show through; margins, base, and teeth white, often tinged yellow.
• **REMARK** Once used as a form of currency in tropical areas.
• **HABITAT** Coral reefs.

angular shell widest here

INDO-PACIFIC

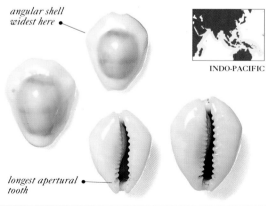

longest apertural tooth

Range Tropical Indo-Pacific	Occurrence ♦♦♦♦♦	Size 2.5cm (1in)

Superfamily CYPRAEOIDEA	Family Cypraeidae	Species *Cypraea aurantium* Gmelin

GOLDEN COWRIE

A large, ovate, heavy shell with a slightly convex base.
Margin is conspicuously developed at top and bottom,
around upper and lower canals. Teeth on outer lip
larger, longer, and farther apart than those on
columellar lip. Deep orange, with greyish white
margin; base white. Strong light turns shell
a warm peach or golden colour.
• **REMARK** Formerly a great rarity, it is
still among the world's most
prized seashells.
• **HABITAT** Outer
side of reefs.

*teeth appear
orange against
creamy white
base*

*groove separates
margin from side
of whorl*

*canal very
narrow*

INDO-PACIFIC

Range S.W. Pacific	Occurrence 🐚	Size 9cm (3¹/₂in)

Superfamily CYPRAEOIDEA	Family Cypraeidae	Species *Cypraea vitellus* Linnaeus

PACIFIC DEER COWRIE

A solid, ovate, or elliptical
shell with a slightly convex
base and somewhat bumpy
margin. Teeth short and
thick. Creamy brown,
with broad bands of
darker brown, overlaid
with porcelain-like spots.
Margin faintly striped;
base and teeth white,
tinged with beige.
• **HABITAT** Under coral slabs.

INDO-PACIFIC

*• teeth on outer
lip thicker
and more
numerous than
those opposite*

Range Tropical Indo-Pacific	Occurrence 🐚🐚🐚🐚	Size 5cm (2in)

Superfamily CYPRAEOIDEA	Family Cypraeidae	Species *Cypraea tigris* Linnaeus

TIGER COWRIE

This large shell is heavy and inflated, its base flat or slightly concave. The margin is an elongate lump each side of upper half of shell. Teeth on outer lip are broad and short; those opposite finer and longer, except for the four lowest ones which are larger and shorter. The colour pattern, seen against a white ground colour, occurs in two layers: the pattern of the under-lying layer is bluish grey, the upper layer reddish to dark brown. Pattern of both layers comprises crowded and often fused spots and blobs, those of the upper layer often surrounded by yellowish orange colour.

• **REMARK** All-black and giant forms are known.

• **HABITAT** Under coral blocks.

margin little developed on this side

hardly any markings on base

indistinct edges to blotches

apex of juvenile shell

a line indicates where mantle edges meet

INDO-PACIFIC

Range Indo-Pacific	Occurrence 🐚🐚🐚	Size 9cm (3¹/₂in)

Superfamily CYPRAEOIDEA	Family Cypraeidae	Species *Cypraea mus* Linnaeus

MOUSE COWRIE

A thick, inflated cowrie with a convex base and squarish outline. Margin is often greatly thickened, making the shell appear misshapen. Teeth are developed on the outer lip; rudimentary on the columellar lip. Fawn with dark-brown smudged spots.
• **REMARK** Don Moore Cowrie (*Cypraea mus donmoorei*) is a bigger, heavier sub-species.
• **HABITAT** Offshore rocks.

CARIBBEAN

• *pale intervals between teeth*

• *darker than usual specimen*

Range N. Colombia, W. Venezuela	Occurrence 👣👣	Size 4cm (1¼in)

Superfamily CYPRAEOIDEA	Family Cypraeidae	Species *Cypraea mauritiana* Linnaeus

HUMPBACK COWRIE

This is a thick, heavy, markedly humped shell; the outer-lip side of the base is flat and the columellar side convex. The margin is more conspicuous at the ends but is not clearly separated from the sides. The aperture is strongly curved, its lower end significantly wider than its upper end. Flattened projections point downwards around the lower end of the aperture. The teeth are well developed, especially on the outer lip. Cream, over-laid with dense brown but leaving rounded, often fused, light-coloured spots visible. Margins, base, and teeth are dark brown; intervals between teeth always paler.
• **REMARK** The teeth of this shell are more numerous on the outer lip than on the opposite, columellar lip.
• **HABITAT** Under rocks.

inside edge of canal pale

rich, dark brown to black thickened margin

INDO-PACIFIC

Range Tropical Indo-Pacific	Occurrence 👣👣👣👣	Size 7.5cm (3in)

Superfamily CYPRAEOIDEA	Family Cypraeidae	Species *Cypraea mappa* Linnaeus

MAP COWRIE

A large, heavy, and rotund
shell with a convex base and
callused margins. Aperture
straight for most of length,
curving in at top. Numerous
small teeth, those on outer
lip more prominent than
those opposite. Whitish or
pale brown, blotched and
streaked with darker brown;
distinctive mantle line,
resembling a river with trib-
utaries, hence the name.
• **HABITAT** Under coral.

*prominent callused
apex of spire*

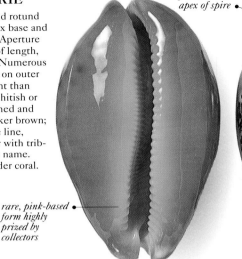

INDO-PACIFIC

*rare, pink-based
form highly
prized by
collectors*

Range Indo-Pacific	Occurrence	Size 7.5cm (3in)

Superfamily CYPRAEOIDEA	Family Cypraeidae	Species *Cypraea argus* Linnaeus

EYED COWRIE

A heavy, broadly cylindrical shell
with slightly convex base. The
margin on the columellar side is
slightly callused; the other margin
is narrow forming a distinct shelf.
Teeth are long and thin, the
longest ones on outer lip situated
just above the aperture's widest
part. Pale brown ground colour has
four, broad, darker brown bands,
which are all overlaid with brown
circle; base light brown, crossed
with two darker bands.
• **REMARK** Apex a flattened coil
of about three whorls.
• **HABITAT** Coral reefs.

INDO-PACIFIC

*two sides of
shell are almost
parallel*

*aperture much
wider at front
than at rear*

Range Indo-Pacific	Occurrence	Size 7.5cm (3in)

SHUTTLE SHELLS

THESE CLOSE RELATIVES of the true cowries mostly have thin, light shells with narrow, generally smooth-edged apertures, which are extended at both ends. They are white, pink, red, o yellow in colour. The animals ar brightly patterned with bands, spots, o blotches. There is no operculum.

Superfamily CYPRAEOIDEA	Family Ovulidae	Species *Cyphoma gibbosum* Linnaeus

FLAMINGO TONGUE

This solid, smooth, elongate shell is one of half a dozen related species. A humped ridge bisects its upper surface but does not continue onto its underside. The shell is smooth either side of the narrow aperture. Glossy and orange, paler underneath.
• **REMARK** Animal marked like a giraffe.
• **HABITAT** Seafans.

CARIBBEAN

aperture widest at front end

Range S.E. Florida to Brazil	Occurrence 🐚🐚🐚	Size 2.5cm (1in)

Superfamily CYPRAEOIDEA	Family Ovulidae	Species *Volva volva* Linnaeus

SHUTTLE VOLVA

This unmistakable shell could easily be compared nowadays to a thin, rolled-up pasta shape which has subsequently swollen out at the middle.

INDO-PACIFIC

ends of canals frequently beaked

thickened outer lip is paler than rest of shell

wide aperture lacks teeth

Its very long front and rear extensions are hollow and open, becoming extremely thin at their ends. Its outer lip is thickened and smooth. It is ornamented with shallow, spiral grooves. Pinkish or pale brown in colour.
• **REMARK** The shell's name reflects its remarkable resemblance to a weaver's shuttle.
• **HABITAT** Coral reefs.

spiral grooves around body whorl

canals gently curved at either end

Range Indo-Pacific	Occurrence 🐚🐚🐚🐚	Size 10cm (4in)

Superfamily CYPRAEOIDEA	Family Ovulidae	Species *Ovula ovum* Linnaeus

COMMON EGG COWRIE

This thick, egg-shaped shell is considerably larger than many true cowries. Shiny and superficially smooth, close examination of an older example would reveal delicate spiral elevations crossed by irregular vertical growth ridges. The thickened outer lip has a puckered inner edge and is unevenly toothed throughout its length; seen from the back, the outer lip is margined and lumpy. The upper canal is extended and strongly twisted, the lower canal extended but straight. All white outside; aperture chocolate-brown.
• **REMARK** Once used throughout the Pacific for personal adornment and for decorating the prows of canoes.
• **HABITAT** Black sponges.

INDO-PACIFIC

inconspicuous low ridge

aperture smoothly curved over its whole length

siphonal canals extend at each end

Range Indo-Pacific	Occurrence 🌢🌢🌢🌢	Size 7.5cm (3in)

HETEROPODS

HETEROPODS SWIM freely in the upper layers of the sea and have fragile, translucent shells. Most species are very small and have disc- or cap-shaped, flattened shells with a minute operculum. The soft parts of the larger species are too large for the shell, causing the animal to swim upside down.

Superfamily HETEROPODA	Family Carinariidae	Species *Carinaria cristata* Linnaeus

GLASSY NAUTILUS

Largest of four species in its genus. The shell is paper-thin, translucent, and flexible (when fresh), shaped like a pointed cap and flattened on two sides, with a small, coiled tip directed towards its rear end. It is encircled by smooth, wavy ribs meeting at a keel that runs the whole length of the sharply angled front edge.
• **REMARK** Name reflects the original belief that the shell was a cephalopod, allied to the group of paper nautiluses.
• **HABITAT** Floats on the surface of the sea.

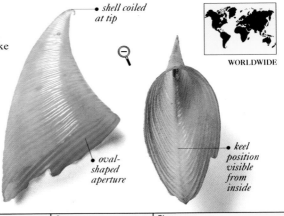

shell coiled at tip

WORLDWIDE

oval-shaped aperture

keel position visible from inside

Range All warm seas	Occurrence 🌢	Size 7.5cm (3in)

MOON SHELLS

MOON SHELLS are globular in shape and have a half-moon aperture. A thick, sometimes rib-like callus largely, or completely, obscures the umbilicus. The operculum may be either corneo or calcareous. Moon shells bore holes i other types of molluscan shell and e the inhabitants. They occur worldwid

Superfamily NATICOIDEA	Family Naticidae	Species *Natica maculata* von Salis

HEBREW MOON

A thick, solid, heavy shell, with a flattened spire of a few whorls and a large body whorl. The whorls are rounded except for a flat shelf below a shallow suture. A wide and deep umbilicus with fine vertical grooves is partly plugged by a rib-like callus. The columella is straight and smooth. Creamy, with reddish brown blotches and spots; aperture violet or brown.
• **REMARK** Varies greatly in size.
• **HABITAT** Sandy places offshore.

MEDITERRANEAN

thin, sharp edge of lip

markings form broken bands

Range Mediterranean	Occurrence 🐚🐚🐚	Size 4cm (1½in)

Superfamily NATICOIDEA	Family Naticidae	Species *Lunatia lewisi* Gould

LEWIS'S MOON

A heavy, large, rotund shell with a distinct shoulder to the body whorl below the suture. The surface of the body whorl is crossed by fine, oblique grooves disappearing into the round, deep umbilicus. At the columellar side of the aperture a small, blunt projection partially obscures the umbilicus. Outer lip is rounded; its slightly wavy outline corresponds with the shoulder. The corneous operculum has a nucleus placed near the lower margin. Brown or greyish brown; dark brown apex; aperture creamy.
• **REMARK** Largest moon shell.
• **HABITAT** Shallow water on sand.

uneven suture

dark brown, inner side to apertural lip

CALIFORNIAN

Range California	Occurrence 🐚🐚🐚🐚	Size 9cm (3½in)

Superfamily NATICOIDEA	Family Naticidae	Species *Neverita albumen* Linnaeus

EGG-WHITE MOON

APERTURAL VIEW

A thick, flattened, glossy shell almost circular in outline. Its apex scarcely rises above succeeding whorls; the body whorl dwarfs the spire whorls. Upper surface smooth except for fine growth lines on the body whorl. Body whorl deep brown; spire whorls and underside of shell white.
• **HABITAT** Sand offshore.

• half-moon-shaped aperture

• irregular curving growth lines

TOP VIEW

INDO-PACIFIC

Range Pacific	Occurrence 🌢🌢🌢	Size 5cm (2in)

Superfamily NATICOIDEA	Family Naticidae	Species *Natica stellata* Hedley

STARRY MOON

violet apex •

A solid shell with a short spire, well-defined suture, and a large body whorl. Its smooth surface has a matt finish. Deep umbilicus is partially hidden by smooth plug. Orange, with two rows of white blotches; aperture is white, tinged with pink.
• **HABITAT** Sand offshore.

• white spots largest at base

INDO-PACIFIC

Range Pacific	Occurrence 🌢🌢	Size 4cm (1½in)

Superfamily NATICOIDEA	Family Naticidae	Species *Mammilla melanostoma* Gmelin

BLACK-MOUTH MOON

gently curved columella •

A sturdy, but not very thick, ovate shell with a very short, pointed spire and almost non-existent, wavy-edged suture. Its very large body whorl has a pear-shaped, thin-edged aperture. A callus projects from the columella over a deep umbilicus. Whitish or grey, with three brownish, spiral bands; columella and umbilical area darker brown.
• **HABITAT** Shallow water.

• thin edge to wide aperture

INDO-PACIFIC

Range Indo-Pacific	Occurrence 🌢🌢🌢🌢	Size 4cm (1½in)

Superfamily NATICOIDEA	Family Naticidae	Species *Euspira poliana* Chiaje

POLI'S NECKLACE SHELL

A small shell with a short spire and very large body whorl. A shallow suture separates four or five rounded spire whorls. Fine, irregular growth lines may be visible. The aperture is a half-moon; the outer lip is thin, the columellar lip thickened and straight. A callus pad on the columellar lip partially obscures a narrow umbilicus. Buff or yellow, with rows of brown chevron-like markings; columella brown.
• **HABITAT** Sand offshore.

spire often less elevated than on this specimen

MEDITERRANEAN
BOREAL

• inside pattern visible

Range Mediterranean, N.W. Europe	Occurrence 🌢🌢🌢🌢	Size 1.2cm (½in)

Superfamily NATICOIDEA	Family Naticidae	Species *Eunaticina papilla* Gmelin

PAPILLA MOON

A solid but light shell with a voluminous, pear-shaped body whorl and a short, conical spire. Apart from the smooth spire, the shell is ornamented with 40–60 regularly spaced, narrow grooves, becoming less regular in the umbilical region; occasional growth lines across the grooves. Shell all white, but covered, when fresh, with a yellowish periostracum. Operculum thin and corneous.
•**HABITAT** Sand inshore.

conical spire has • two or three whorls

INDO-PACIFIC

• columella is curved and thickened here

Range Indo-Pacific	Occurrence 🌢🌢	Size 2.5cm (1in)

Superfamily NATICOIDEA	Family Naticidae	Species *Sinum cymba* Menke

BOAT EAR MOON

This thin, light shell is low-spired, with a voluminous body whorl angled at its base and a shallow suture that becomes deeper as shell grows. Its very wide aperture has a thin outer lip which, by contrast with most moon shells, is not connected to the columella by a thick callus. Fine spiral grooves encircle the whorls. Purple-brown on early whorls, pale brown on body whorl; aperture chocolate-brown.
• **HABITAT** Shallow water.

white band below • shallow suture

PERUVIAN
MAGELLANIC

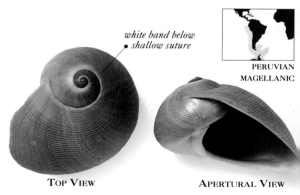

TOP VIEW   APERTURAL VIEW

Range W. S. America, Galapagos	Occurrence 🌢🌢🌢	Size 5cm (2in)

HELMET SHELLS

THERE ARE 80 or more living species of helmet shell. They usually have a short spire and a voluminous body whorl which may be ornamented with knobs, ribs, or varices. The outer lip is thickened, often toothed and, in some larger species, greatly expanded; the columella may also be thickened. Male shells may differ from female shells. The animals are sand dwellers, feeding mostly on sea urchins; they have a small, thin and corneous operculum.

Superfamily TONNOIDEA	Family Cassidae	Species *Cassis fimbriata* Quoy & Gaimard

FRINGED HELMET

A thick, globose shell with short spire and bulbous apex. Its large body whorl is very inflated; umbilicus narrow but deep; its siphonal canal is a narrow channel. Early whorls have wavy vertical ribs and spiral lines; the body whorl has irregular vertical ribs and there are spiral ribs above the siphonal canal. Spire whorls usually have two or three varices, and there may be one on the body whorl. The columellar shield is broad but thin; it is usually smooth but may have spiral folds. The outer lip is normally smooth, but may be toothed. Creamy, with spiral brown lines and vertical brown blotches.
• **REMARK** Examples from northern end of the range usually pink.
• **HABITAT** Sand offshore.

deeply impressed suture

knobs at shoulder are most pronounced

broad columellar shield covers almost all front surface of body whorl

strongly recurved, short siphonal canal

AUSTRALIAN

Range W. Australia	Occurrence ♠♠♠	Size 10cm (4in)

Superfamily TONNOIDEA	Family Cassidae	Species *Cassis flammea* Linnaeus

FLAME HELMET

A low-spired, solid shell of seven whorls with a varix occurring every two-thirds of a whorl in early stages. A parietal shield gives a triangular outline in apertural view; the corners of the shield are rounded. The shell is ornamented with vertical growth lines, a row of large knobs at its shoulder, three or four rows of lesser knobs below; there is no spiral ornament. It has about 20 long, raised, horizontal ridges on the columella. Inner edge of the thickened lip has about ten prominent blunt teeth. White, mottled with brown; darker brown markings arranged in vertical zig-zags. Approximately six brown blotches appear on the outer lip.
• **REMARK** Pattern is visible through the parietal shield.
• **HABITAT** Shallow water on sand.

CARIBBEAN

knobs most prominent at shoulder

strongly recurved siphonal canal

dark blotches on outer lip of aperture

Range W. Indies, S. Florida	Occurrence 🐚🐚🐚🐚	Size 10.8cm (4¹/₂in)

Superfamily TONNOIDEA	Family Cassidae	Species *Cassis nana* Tenison-Woods

DWARF HELMET

A thin, light shell, broad at the shoulder, then narrowing anteriorly. It has five or six whorls with early varices showing, a low spire, and a smooth, swollen nucleus. Its shoulder has two spiral rows of regularly spaced, sharp nodules; below these are two or three rows of weaker nodules. The parietal shield is thin; columella has a row of strong teeth. The outer lip is thickened and bluntly toothed. Pale brown colour, with darker brown blotches; nodules and teeth are both pale.
• **REMARK** The smallest of all the living helmet shells.
• **HABITAT** Sand offshore.

white knobs spaced with almost geometric precision

INDO-PACIFIC

parietal shield is very thin at edge

Range E. Australia	Occurrence 🐚🐚	Size 5.7cm (2¹/₄in)

Superfamily TONNOIDEA	Family Cassidae	Species *Cassis cornuta* Linnaeus

HORNED HELMET

A heavy shell with a large, thick parietal shield, a short spire, and varices at right angles to each other. Its shoulder has a row of large knobs with three spiral, humped ribs below. The surface is covered with rows of small pits. A very thick outer lip has large teeth grouped at middle. The columella has a few strong, wavy folds. Grey or white, with brown bands behind outer lip. Orange on columella and on teeth of outer lip.
• **REMARK**
Males are smaller with knobs like horns.
• **HABITAT**
Coral sand.

parietal shield usually large enough to conceal apertural side of body whorl

INDO-PACIFIC

APERTURAL VIEW

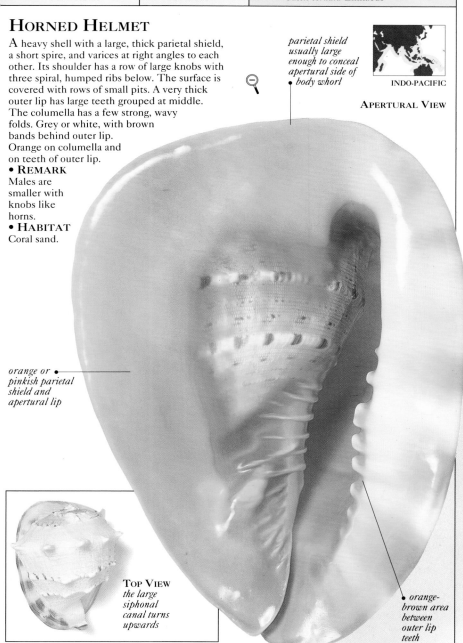

orange or pinkish parietal shield and apertural lip

TOP VIEW
the large siphonal canal turns upwards

orange-brown area between outer lip teeth

Range Indo-Pacific	Occurrence 🐚🐚🐚🐚	Size 22cm (8¾in)

Superfamily TONNOIDEA	Family Cassidae	Species *Cypraecassis rufa* Linnaeus

BULL'S-MOUTH HELMET

A thick, heavy shell with a low
spire, and a large aperture ending
with a small, upturned
siphonal canal. It is
ornamented with three or
four rows of blunt knobs,
decreasing in size towards
the anterior end, with
smaller tubercles and pitted
grooves between the rows.
Above the siphonal canal
distinct, widely spaced
vertical riblets are bisected
by a single, equally distinct
spiral riblet. There are about
22–24 teeth along the outer lip.
Body whorl and spire mottled
with shades of red and brown;
vertical riblets and spiral riblet
whitish. Columellal folds white,
dark brown between.
• **REMARK** Spire lacks varices.
• **HABITAT** Near coral reefs.

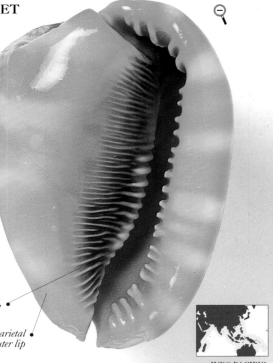

*teeth, sometimes paired,
extend length of lip* •

orange-red parietal •
shield and outer lip

INDO-PACIFIC

Range Tropical Indo-Pacific	Occurrence 🐚🐚🐚🐚	Size 15cm (6in)

Superfamily TONNOIDEA	Family Cassidae	Species *Galeodea echinophora* Linnaeus

SPINY BONNET

A light shell with a tallish
spire. The parietal shield
is thin, the siphonal canal
short and upturned.
Body whorl has five or
six spiral ribs with
blunt knobs. Greyish
brown, with darker
brown between knobs;
aperture whitish.
• **REMARK** Knobs
usually pointed, hence
common name.
• **HABITAT** Sandy
mud offshore.

*dark spots
between
• knobs*

MEDITERRANEAN

*• outer lip
has a few
indistinct
teeth*

*• knobs often
more heavily
developed
than this*

Range Mediterranean	Occurrence 🐚🐚🐚🐚	Size 6cm (2¹/₂in)

Superfamily TONNOIDEA	Family Cassidae	Species *Phalium areola* Linnaeus

CHEQUERED BONNET

A moderately thick shell with an egg-shaped body whorl and a short, pointed spire. It has a single varix on the opposite side of the shell to the thickened outer lip. Body whorl is smooth and shiny except for the finely incised lines below the suture. Parietal shield is thin, and its upper half is transparent. The apex comprises two or three smooth whorls. There are about 20 sharp-edged teeth on outer lip and columellar folds on lower half of the body whorl. Colour pattern on body whorl consists of dark brown blotches that vary in shape but are usually rectangular and appear in five spiral rows. Outer edge of siphonal canal dark brown; outer lip and lower half of parietal shield white.
• **REMARK** The pointed spire has distinctive lattice ornament.
• **HABITAT** Sandy mud.

• conspicuously pointed spire

INDO-PACIFIC

• rectangular brown blotches in spiral rows

• blotches fade out over bottom half of parietal area

Range Tropical Indo-Pacific	Occurrence 🐚🐚🐚	Size 7cm (2³/₄in)

Superfamily TONNOIDEA	Family Cassidae	Species *Phalium saburon* Bruguière

SAND BONNET

This thick, solid, rotund shell has a short spire and shallow suture. The siphonal canal is very short and broad. There is a small, deep umbilicus. Flattened spiral ribs with narrower grooves between them provide characteristic ornament. There are irregular, vertical growth lines all over the shell and fine vertical striae are visible on the spire whorls. The thickened outer lip has small teeth along its length. There is a broad callus on the parietal wall and columella may be thick or thin. Lower part of the columella is wrinkled. Yellowish brown, with broken spiral bands of dark brown; outer lip and columella white.
• **REMARK** Varices sometimes present on body whorl.
• **HABITAT** Sandy mud offshore.

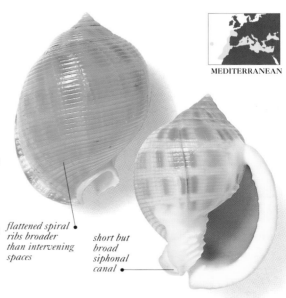

MEDITERRANEAN

flattened spiral ribs broader than intervening spaces

short but broad siphonal canal •

Range Mediterranean	Occurrence 🐚🐚🐚	Size 6cm (2¹/₂in)

Superfamily TONNOIDEA	Family Cassidae	Species *Morum cancellatum* Sowerby

LATTICE MORUM

A thick, sturdy shell with a short spire and elongate body whorl. Suture has a wavy edge. Body whorl has strong, vertical ridges; seen in profile, each ridge has a saw-tooth edge. Topmost ridge is recurved upwards. Outer lip has irregular teeth and warty lumps; columellar callus has warts and folds. Yellowish white, with brown spiral bands.
• **REMARK** All morums are now believed to be related to the harp shells *(see p.170).*
• **HABITAT** Moderate depths.

smooth apical whorls

white interior

clusters of dark brown spots on edge of lip

INDO-PACIFIC

Range China Sea	Occurrence 🐚🐚	Size 4cm (1½in)

Superfamily TONNOIDEA	Family Cassidae	Species *Morum grande* A. Adams

GIANT MORUM

A solid, heavy shell with an elongate body whorl more than twice the length of the spire. Suture is slightly channelled. Spire whorls are strongly shouldered, the body whorl less so. Aperture is long and narrow. Outer lip is greatly thickened; its inner edge bears prominent, evenly spaced teeth. The columellar callus is thin and broad, liberally covered with folds and warts. Strong spiral ribs are crossed by vertical, fluted scales which occasionally form continuous, vertical ridges. Yellowish white, with four spiral brown bands, darker on outer lip; aperture and columellar callus both white.
• **REMARK** Largest species of genus.
• **HABITAT** Deep water.

spire whorls have distinct shoulders

small siphonal canal at front end

edge of columellar callus is thin and sharp

INDO-PACIFIC

Range W. Pacific	Occurrence 🐚🐚	Size 5.7cm (2¼in)

FIG SHELLS

THE FEW SHELLS in this group are thin with a smooth, fig-shaped outline. They have a short spire and a large body whorl with a drawn-out siphonal canal. The whorls have spiral ribs but the aperture and columella are smooth. There is no operculum. All species live offshore on sand.

Superfamily TONNOIDEA	Family Ficidae	Species *Ficus gracilis* Sowerby

GRACEFUL FIG SHELL

Among the most fragile of the larger seashells, this species, like all fig shells, exhibits little variation in form. The elongate, inflated body whorl dwarfs the low, depressed spire. The outer lip is slightly thickened at the top. Seen from above, the spire is a broadly expanded spiral with a well-impressed suture. The columella is straight or slightly curved. Strong, flattened spiral ribs alternate with weaker ones and are crossed by fine vertical striae; apical whorls and aperture are smooth and shiny. Orange-brown ground colour, with vertical streaks and zigzags; aperture orange-brown, paler towards outer lip.
• **REMARK** This is easily the world's largest fig shell.
• **HABITAT** Deep water.

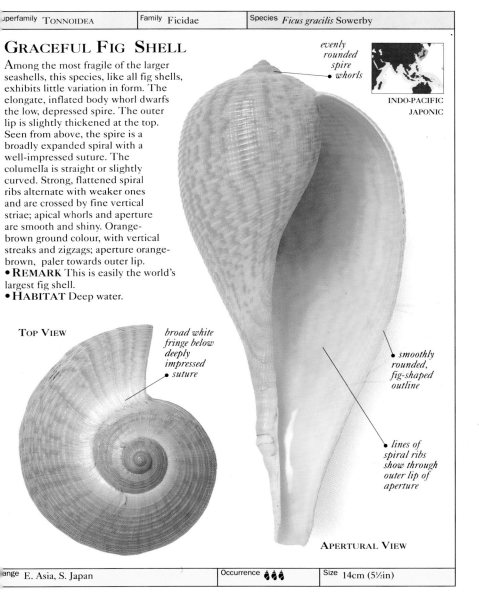

evenly rounded spire whorls

INDO-PACIFIC
JAPONIC

TOP VIEW

broad white fringe below deeply impressed suture

smoothly rounded, fig-shaped outline

lines of spiral ribs show through outer lip of aperture

APERTURAL VIEW

Range E. Asia, S. Japan	Occurrence ♦♦♦	Size 14cm (5½in)

Superfamily TONNOIDEA	Family Ficidae	Species *Ficus ventricosa* Sowerby

SWOLLEN FIG SHELL

A thin, lightweight shell with
a low spire, shallow suture,
and pear-shaped body
whorl. Distinctive, cord-
like spiral ribs. Thin
spiral ridges crossed by
fine vertical ridges pro-
duce a lattice ornament.
Light brown, with paler
spiral ribs spotted darker
brown. Spiral ribs show
through the aperture.
• **REMARK** Swollen body
whorl gives shell its name.
• **HABITAT** Sand offshore.

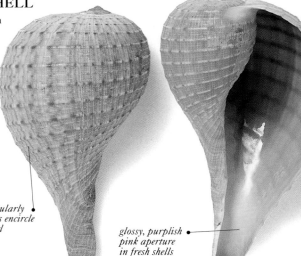

PANAMIC

*strong, regularly
spaced ribs encircle
body whorl*

*glossy, purplish
pink aperture
in fresh shells*

Range W. Mexico to Peru	Occurrence 🌢🌢🌢🌢	Size 9cm (3½in)

Superfamily TONNOIDEA	Family Ficidae	Species *Ficus subintermedia* Orbigny

UNDERLINED FIG SHELL

This thin but sturdy shell has a low spire and
an aperture that runs almost the entire length
of the body whorl. Thin vertical ridges crossed
by fine, intermittently stronger spiral
ridges produce lattice ornament.
Columella and siphonal canal
are sinuously curved. Exterior
pinkish brown, blotched with
shades of brown; four or five
pale spiral bands offset with
darker brown. Aperture
whitish to violet to brown.
• **REMARK** Species has
deep suture.
• **HABITAT** Sandy
mud offshore.

INDO-PACIFIC

*lattice
ornament
over body
whorl and
spire*

*curved
columella
and
siphonal
canal*

Range Indo-Pacific	Occurrence 🌢🌢🌢	Size 10cm (4in)

TUN SHELLS

THE GLOBOSE and often large shells of this small family are thin, with a low or depressed spire, and very inflated body whorl. The siphonal canal is usually deep; some species have a small umbilicus. They are ornamented with spiral ribs, giving a fluted edge to the aperture. In some species, a parietal shield is present. There is no operculum. Most species can be found living in sand, beyond the edge of the coral reef.

Superfamily TONNOIDEA	Family Tonnidae	Species *Tonna cepa* Röding

CHANNELLED TUN

This fairly large, fragile, and globose shell has a moderately high spire and a deeply channelled suture. Widely spaced grooves encircle the shell; the spaces between the grooves appear as smooth, rounded ribs on the spire whorls but are more flattened on the body whorl, where there are about 16 of them. Fine vertical lines cover the shell surface irregularly. The wide aperture has a thin and fluted edge; spiral grooves are clearly visible in the aperture. The umbilicus is small. Exterior light brown, cream, or yellow, with brown, white-edged streaks and patches that are distributed randomly but especially at the shoulder. Aperture brown, whiter at edge; columella white.

• **HABITAT**
Intertidal sand.

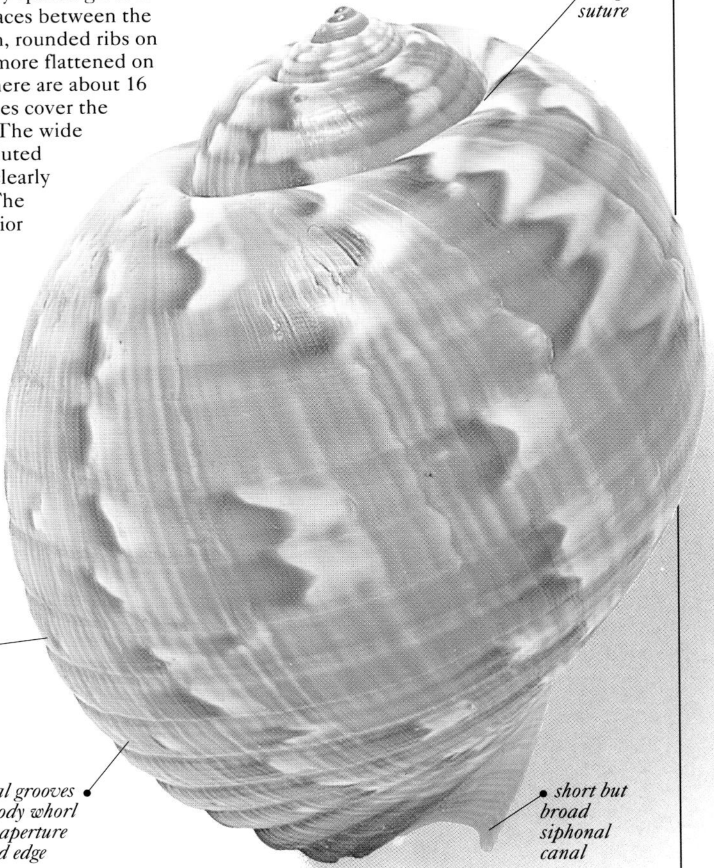

deep suture

widely-spaced grooves

spiral grooves on body whorl give aperture fluted edge

short but broad siphonal canal

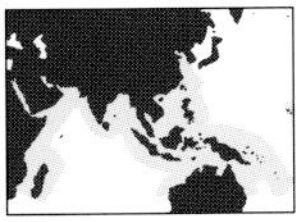

INDO-PACIFIC

Range Indo-Pacific	Occurrence 🐚🐚🐚	Size 10cm (4in)

Superfamily TONNOIDEA	Family Tonnidae	Species *Tonna galea* Linnaeus

GIANT TUN

A lightweight, thin, large shell. Each spire whorl is separated by a deep suture. The umbilicus is very narrow. The body whorl has 15–20 broad, flattened, spiral ribs with lesser ones between them on its upper half. The flutings on the outer lip correspond to the ribs. Chestnut-brown, with paler vertical streaks; apex may be purple; outer lip of aperture white, brown at edge.
• **REMARK** Widely distributed due to long, free-swimming larval stage.
• **HABITAT**
Deep water.

WORLD

short, sunken spire has a purplish apex

deeply channelled suture

columella is strongly twisted

brown blotches correspond to ends of ribs

Range Most seas	Occurrence 🌢🌢🌢	Size 15cm (6in)

Superfamily TONNOIDEA	Family Tonnidae	Species *Tonna allium* Dillwyn

COSTATE TUN

This medium-sized shell has an elevated spire and an ovate body whorl. The suture is deep but not channelled. The twisted columella is covered by a thin callus shield; the umbilicus is narrow and deep. The outer lip is turned outward and backward at the margin. Strong, widely spaced spiral ribs become closer towards the base. Pale brown, tinged violet, ribs darker brown; these colours also seen through aperture; apical whorls purple; outer lip white.
• **REMARK** Spire is relatively tall for a tun shell.
• **HABITAT** Offshore.

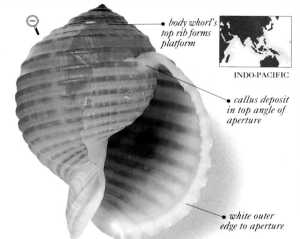

body whorl's top rib forms platform

INDO-PACIFIC

callus deposit in top angle of aperture

white outer edge to aperture

Range W. Pacific	Occurrence 🐾🐾🐾	Size 9cm (3¹/₂in)

Superfamily TONNOIDEA	Family Tonnidae	Species *Tonna perdix* Linnaeus

PACIFIC PARTRIDGE TUN

Large and very fragile, this shell has whorls which slope markedly at shoulders. The spire is fairly high and the body whorl widely expanded. Impressed suture is not channelled. Umbilicus is very small because columella is partly covered by a thin colu-mellar shield which continues over the parietal wall. Outer lip is slightly thickened but not toothed. Broad, flat spiral ribs are separated by shallow grooves. Brown, with cream crescents and dashes between grooves; aperture brownish, outer lip white.
• **REMARK** Colour said to resemble plumage of the common European partridge.
• **HABITAT** Offshore sand.

white outer lip with brown edge

INDO-PACIFIC

white narrow spiral grooves

Range Tropical Indo-Pacific	Occurrence 🐾🐾🐾	Size 13cm (5in)

Superfamily TONNOIDEA	Family Tonnidae	Species *Tonna dolium* Linnaeus

SPOTTED TUN

A large, fragile, globose shell with a low spire and prominently channelled suture. The wavy-edged outer lip ends in a shallow siphonal notch; lower part of columella strongly twisted. Penultimate whorl has two to four spiral ribs; body whorl has from ten to twenty. White, cream, or pale brown, with squarish blotches on ribs; apex brown.
• **REMARK** The greatest number of ribs seems to occur on examples from Taiwan, and the least on those from Malaysia.
• **HABITAT** Offshore.

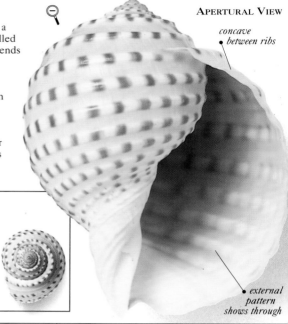

APERTURAL VIEW

concave
• between ribs

• external
pattern
shows through

INDO-PACIFIC
JAPONIC

TOP VIEW
Shows the low, plain rib between patterned ribs, and the plain apical whorls.

Range Indo-Pacific, Japan, New Zealand	Occurrence ♦♦♦	Size 13cm (5in)

Superfamily TONNOIDEA	Family Tonnidae	Species *Tonna sulcosa* Born

BANDED TUN

A thin but sturdy, relatively small, globose shell of about seven whorls, separated by a prominently channelled suture. Reflected outer lip is wavy-edged or bears up to 17 pairs of small teeth; it ends in a shallow, broad siphonal notch. The columella is strongly twisted towards its lower end; there is a thin callus on the parietal wall. Early whorls have thin spiral riblets; there are four to six strong spiral ribs on the penultimate whorl and up to 21 ribs on the body whorl. Creamy white, with three or four dark brown spiral bands on the body whorl; aperture and outer lip white; apex purplish.
• **REMARK** The living shell is covered with an opaque, dark brown periostracum.
• **HABITAT** Offshore.

• single
brown band on
penultimate
whorl

• vertical
growth
lines

INDO-PACIFIC

Range Tropical Indo-Pacific	Occurrence ♦♦	Size 11cm (4½in)

Superfamily TONNOIDEA	Family Tonnidae	Species *Malea ringens* Swainson

GRINNING TUN

This large, thick, globose shell has a short spire and about seven whorls separated by a shallow suture. The reflected outer lip is greatly thickened and ornamented with large, inwardly pointing teeth. The columella is deeply and roundly excavated at its mid-point, with a three-ridged lump below it and a smaller, two-ridged lump above. All whorls are encircled by broad, flat spiral ribs. Yellowish brown; inside of aperture darker brown.
• **REMARK** This shell was named in the 19th century when there was a great tendency to see human attributes in natural objects.
• **HABITAT** Intertidal sand and rocks.

broad parietal callus

PANAMIC

about 18 ribs on body whorl

broad, recurved siphonal notch

wavy edge to outer lip

Range W. Mexico to Peru	Occurrence ♦♦♦♦	Size 15cm (6in)

Superfamily TONNOIDEA	Family Tonnidae	Species *Malea pomum* Linnaeus

PACIFIC GRINNING TUN

A solid, glossy shell with a short spire and about seven whorls, with a globose body whorl and shallow suture. Aperture is narrow; the thickened outer lip bears inwardly pointing, elongated teeth crowded towards the base. Lower half of columella slightly excavated; below it is an irregular twisted fold; above are four to five small folds; siphonal notch is broad and slightly recurved. Creamy brown, blotched with pale brown and white; lip and columella white.
• **REMARK** The umbilicus is usually covered by the well-developed callus.
• **HABITAT** Offshore.

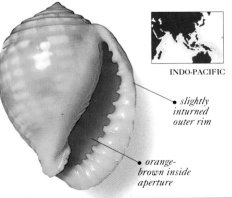

INDO-PACIFIC

slightly inturned outer rim

orange-brown inside aperture

Range Tropical Indo-Pacific	Occurrence ♦♦♦	Size 6cm (2¹/₂in)

TRITONS

LARGE OR MODERATE in size, tritons have thick, often extravagantly ornamented shells. Some tritons are tall, with a large body whorl. Most of the species have columellar folds, prominent varices, and teeth or folds on the outer lip. Many tritons are covered in a hairy periostracum; all have a thick corneous operculum. Some tritons have a long, free-swimming larval period and are consequently widely distributed in warm, mainly tropical seas. The animals are carnivorous, usually feeding on other molluscs and sea urchins.

Superfamily TONNOIDEA	Family Ranellidae	Species *Charonia tritonis* Linnaeus

TRUMPET TRITON

The tall, pointed spire, which invariably lacks the apical whorls, is less than half the height of the shell. The broad body whorl usually has two prominent varices (as does each spire whorl). The smooth, broad, and flattened spiral ribs on the body whorl have deep grooves and an occasional thin, extra rib between. Suture is well impressed and the rib below each whorl is wavy and puckered. Siphonal canal is broad and short. Thin folds along the columellar wall. Creamy, with dark brown blotches and crescents. Aperture orange-brown, with white channels between teeth on outer lip. Columellar teeth white, dark brown between.
• **REMARK** Used as a trumpet.
• **HABITAT** Coral reefs.

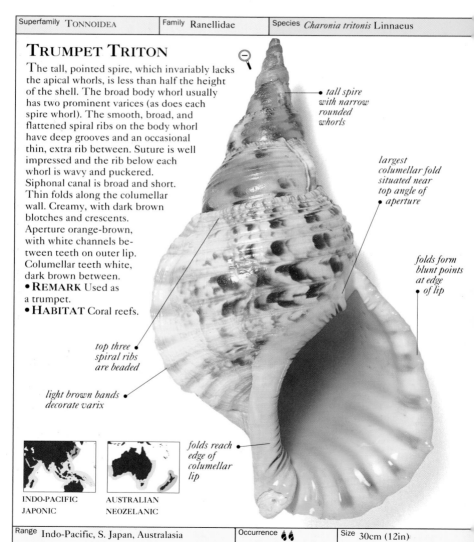

tall spire with narrow rounded whorls

largest columellar fold situated near top angle of aperture

folds form blunt points at edge of lip

top three spiral ribs are beaded

light brown bands decorate varix

folds reach edge of columellar lip

INDO-PACIFIC
JAPONIC

AUSTRALIAN
NEOZELANIC

Range Indo-Pacific, S. Japan, Australasia	Occurrence 🐚🐚	Size 30cm (12in)

Superfamily TONNOIDEA	Family Ranellidae	Species *Gyrineum pusillum* Broderip

PURPLE GYRE TRITON

A small, arrowhead-shaped shell with an impressed suture. Each whorl has a fin-like varix on both sides. Rows of spiral ridges are bisected by vertical ridges. Thick outer lip has seven or eight small, rounded, teeth-like projections (denticles); columella has three or four scattered ones. Siphonal canal short. Banded white and brown, with intersections of ridges white; apertural lips purple.
• **HABITAT** Coral debris.

INDO-PACIFIC

white denticles on outer lip

brown bands on conspicuous varix

small aperture has purple margin

Range Tropical Indo-Pacific	Occurrence	Size 2.5cm (1in)

Superfamily TONNOIDEA	Family Ranellidae	Species *Gyrineum perca* Perry

MAPLE LEAF TRITON

outline of shell reminiscent of maple leaf

A thick, compressed, and slightly distorted shell with a tall spire and moderately long siphonal canal. The fin-like varices on each side of the whorls are drawn out into points, each point being the termination of a prominent rib. Spiral ribs crossing stronger vertical ribs produce vertical rows of nodules. Spiral riblets occur between spiral ribs. The aperture is almost circular. White, with brown spiral bands and blotches; aperture white.
• **HABITAT** Deep water.

INDO-PACIFIC

nodules vary in number

ribs weaker on apertural side of varix

Range Tropical Indo-Pacific	Occurrence	Size 2.5cm (1in)

Superfamily TONNOIDEA	Family Ranellidae	Species *Cabestana cutacea* Linnaeus

MEDITERRANEAN BARK TRITON

This is a thick shell with a turreted spire, and a large body whorl. The suture is deep, the umbilicus narrow, and the siphonal canal short. A thickened outer lip constricts the aperture; the columella is smooth. About eight spiral ridges cross four or five vertical swellings on the body whorl, which also has a varix. Light or dark brown, with a white aperture.
• **REMARK** Thin operculum.
• **HABITAT** Offshore.

MEDITERRANEAN
BOREAL

canal at top of aperture

aperture has greatly thickened outer lip

operculum

Range Mediterranean, E. Atlantic	Occurrence	Size 7.5cm (3in)

Superfamily TONNOIDEA	Family Ranellidae	Species *Ranella olearia* Linnaeus

WANDERING TRITON

This shell varies considerably in size, thickness, and colour pattern, but is fairly constant in shape. It is thick and robust with a tall spire, large body whorl, well-impressed suture, and long, slightly twisted siphonal canal. Each whorl has a varix on either side. The aperture is almost round with a small canal at the top; the reflected outer lip bears about 17 teeth. The columella is smooth; small teeth on columellar side of siphonal canal. Parietal shield is thinly spread. Strong vertical ribs crossed by weak spiral ribs. Creamy, blotched brown; aperture and outer lip white. Yellowish brown periostracum when fresh.
• **REMARK** Name derives from worldwide distribution.
• **HABITAT** Deep water.

prominent nodules at intersections of vertical ribs and spiral riblets

varices make oblique series down sides

operculum

WORLDWIDE

example of shell's usual colour pattern

Range Most warm seas	Occurrence ♦♦♦	Size 14cm (5¹/₂in)

Superfamily TONNOIDEA	Family Ranellidae	Species *Mayena australasia* Perry

SOUTHERN TRITON

A thick, ovate shell with a tall spire and a well-rounded body whorl. The suture is uneven. The siphonal canal is short and broad. Thickened outer lip has seven to ten short, rounded teeth. Thin parietal callus has a tubercle at the upper end. Columella almost smooth, with a few folds at base. Pale to dark brown, varices striped brown and white; aperture, outer lip, and columella white.
• **HABITAT** Rocks offshore.

spiral row of tubercles at shoulder of whorls

operculum

AUSTRALIAN

greatly thickened outer lip

Range S. Australia	Occurrence ♦♦♦♦	Size 9cm (3¹/₂in)

Superfamily TONNOIDEA	Family Ranellidae	Species *Argobuccinum pustulosum* Lightfoot

ARGUS TRITON

A solid, dumpy shell with a moderately tall spire and large, rounded body whorl; the apex and often the entire spire are eroded. The shallow suture is uneven. Outer lip is thickened and provided with low, blunt teeth set well back; siphonal canal short and broad. Columella smooth and straight; tubercle at top of aperture. Spire whorls angled at periphery, less angled on body whorl. Oblique vertical ribs are crossed by low spiral ribs with tubercles at intersections. Pale brown, with darker brown spiral bands; aperture white.
• **REMARK** Often covered by periostracum.
• **HABITAT** Offshore.

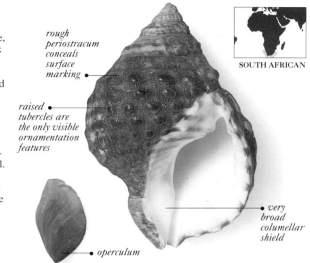

rough periostracum conceals surface marking

raised tubercles are the only visible ornamentation features

SOUTH AFRICAN

very broad columellar shield

operculum

Range S. Africa	Occurrence 🐚🐚🐚	Size 7.5cm (3in)

Superfamily TONNOIDEA	Family Ranellidae	Species *Fusitriton oregonense* Redfield

OREGON TRITON

A thin, lightweight, elongate shell with a tall spire and lengthened, slightly recurved siphonal canal. All the whorls are well rounded and separated by a deeply impressed suture. Aperture is elongate with a tubercle at the top and a slightly thickened outer lip; the columella is sinuously curved and smooth. Strong vertical ribs are crossed by smaller spiral ribs with fine spiral lines between them. Whitish, tinged with yellow; aperture and siphonal canal glossy.
• **REMARK** External markings visible in aperture.
• **HABITAT** Offshore.

varices on early whorls

rounded operculum thick and corneous

bristly periostracum persists even on worn shell

CALIFORNIAN

Range W. United States	Occurrence 🐚🐚🐚🐚	Size 11cm (4½in)

Superfamily TONNOIDEA	Family Ranellidae	Species *Gelagna succincta* Linnaeus

LESSER GIRDLED TRITON

This elegant shell has a low spire, well-rounded whorls, and a deep suture; the body whorl has a long, straight siphonal canal. The elongate aperture has a prominent canal at the top. Central part of the columella is incurved, and the outer lip is thickened and has smooth, rounded teeth along its entire length. Evenly spaced, broad, flat, spiral ribs appear on all but apical whorls. Pale brown, with dark brown ribs; apertural teeth brown, white between.
• **REMARK** No varices develop on this species of shell.
• **HABITAT** Under rocks offshore.

well impressed suture

INDO-PACIFIC

• prominent growth flaw

• inconspicuous folds at base of columella

Range Tropical Indo-Pacific	Occurrence 🐚🐚	Size 5cm (2in)

Superfamily TONNOIDEA	Family Ranellidae	Species *Cymatium femorale* Linnaeus

ANGULAR TRITON

This distinctive, large, thick shell has prominent varices. Its elevated spire is short compared to the very tall body whorl. The siphonal canal is slightly recurved. Body whorl is dominated by the upward-pointing, wing-like varices which give it a triangular outline in apertural view. Strong, broad, spiral ribs, each with a few well-developed nodules. The outer lip, virtually a final varix, is thickened, its strongly inturned edge is wavy. Reddish brown, except for white aperture and extremities of varices.
• **REMARK** When found off Brazilian coast, it is often known as *Cymatium raderi*.
• **HABITAT** Shallow water.

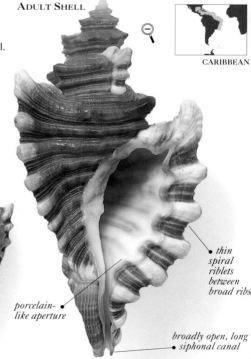

ADULT SHELL

CARIBBEAN

JUVENILE SHELL

young shells are • generally more brightly coloured than adults

porcelain-like aperture

• thin spiral riblets between broad ribs

broadly open, long • siphonal canal

Range S.E. Florida to Brazil	Occurrence 🐚🐚🐚	Size 13cm (5in)

Superfamily TONNOIDEA	Family Ranellidae	Species *Cymatium parthenopeum* von Salis

NEAPOLITAN TRITON

A solid shell with a moderately tall spire, rounded whorls, and a deep suture. There is usually a varix on the body whorl, and sometimes others on the spire whorls. The well-rounded spiral ribs are crossed by vertical ridges. The thickened outer lip is ornamented with six teeth. Pale brown colour, with dark brown blotches on the outer lip, columella, and on the varices.
• **REMARK** Example shown here unusually tall.
• **HABITAT** Stones offshore.

whorl excavated above suture

dark brown spots on varix

WORLD

extremely bristly periostracum

dark brown area between white folds of columella

Range Most warm seas	Occurrence ♦♦♦	Size 10cm (4in)

Superfamily TONNOIDEA	Family Ranellidae	Species *Cymatium pileare* Linnaeus

COMMON HAIRY TRITON

This thick, sturdy shell has a tall spire and an elongate body whorl measuring at least half the height of the shell. The short siphonal canal is slightly curved. There are usually two varices per whorl. The suture is very shallow. The inner lip has folds along its entire length; outer lip has groups of small teeth, evenly distributed. Strong vertical ribs are crossed by strong spiral ribs on all whorls. White, with broad, dark brown bands; aperture reddish.
• **REMARK** Fresh examples are often found to have a sparsely hairy periostracum.
• **HABITAT** Shallow water coral.

slightly bent spire

operculum

WORLD

body whorl may be no broader than penultimate whorl

Range Most warm seas	Occurrence ♦♦♦♦	Size 7.5cm (3in)

Superfamily TONNOIDEA	Family Ranellidae	Species *Cymatium flaveolum* Röding

BROAD-BANDED TRITON

This sturdy, elongate shell has a spire which is shorter than the body whorl, and a long, narrow aperture. There are many folds on the columella and strong teeth on the inside of the outer lip. The regular varices are broadly spaced; the whorls have spiral rows of distinctly rounded beads. The shell is a cream colour, with reddish-brown and yellowish spiral bands, and orange staining between the teeth.
• **REMARK** One of several species closely resembling each other.
• **HABITAT** Coral reefs.

INDO-PACIFIC

• *orange staining between teeth*

• *short siphonal canal slightly twisted*

Range Solomon Is. to Mauritius	Occurrence ♦♦	Size 5cm (2in)

Superfamily TONNOIDEA	Family Ranellidae	Species *Cymatium hepaticum* Röding

BLACK-STRIPED TRITON

The spire is narrower and more straight sided than the rounded body whorl. Varices are regular and broadly spaced. Spiral rows of rounded beads cover all whorls. The columella has strong folds and there are stronger, rounded teeth on the inside of the outer lip. Dark reddish brown, with thin, black spiral bands; the varices have white bands.
• **REMARK** Colour and pattern distinguish this species from its close relatives.
• **HABITAT** Under coral.

INDO-PACIFIC

• *black bands between rows of beads*

• *orange-brown spaces between teeth*

siphonal canal open throughout •

Range Tropical Indo-Pacific	Occurrence ♦♦♦	Size 6cm (2½in)

Superfamily TONNOIDEA	Family Ranellidae	Species *Cymatium rubeculum* Linnaeus

ROBIN REDBREAST TRITON

The irregular growth of its spire whorls give this shell a slightly distorted look. Varices are thick and regular. There are spiral rows of coarse, sometimes fused beads on all whorls. The aperture is broad and the siphonal canal short. Bright red to orange, with an occasional pale spiral band and white varices.
• **REMARK** Exposure to sunlight produces some of the paler colour forms of this species.
• **HABITAT** Coral reefs.

• *apex missing from mature shell*

INDO-PACIFIC

• *white spaces between teeth*

strong folds on columella •

• *spiral ridges inside aperture*

Range Tropical Indo-Pacific	Occurrence ♦♦♦♦	Size 4.5cm (1¾in)

DISTORSIOS

F EW GASTROPOD SHELLS have more bizarre shapes than those in this small group. The aperture is constricted by strongly developed teeth and folds; the body whorl is curiously distorted. Some species have a densely hairy periostracum when fresh. There is a thin, corneous operculum.

Superfamily TONNOIDEA	Family Ranellidae	Species *Distorsio clathrata* Lamarck

ATLANTIC DISTORSIO

Early spire whorls of this shell are almost straight sided; body whorl well rounded and slightly distorted. Large teeth and folds constrict aperture, which ends in a moder-ately long siphonal canal. Lattice ornament covers the shell. Yellowish white, with orange-brown parietal wall and outer lip.
• **REMARK** Shrimp fishermen often find good examples of this species .
• **HABITAT** Offshore.

TRANSATLANTIC
CARIBBEAN

prominent central tooth

inside of aperture white

Range N. Carolina to Brazil	Occurrence 🐚🐚🐚	Size 7.5cm (3in)

Superfamily TONNOIDEA	Family Ranellidae	Species *Distorsio anus* Linnaeus

COMMON DISTORSIO

The apex of this grossly deformed shell is usually broken off. Spiral rows of smooth tubercles and nodules cover all whorls. Apertural side almost covered by broad, glossy shield with sharp edges; underlying tubercles and teeth show through. Cream, with brown spiral bands.
• **REMARK** Largest and most grotesque member of the group.
• **HABITAT** Coral.

edge of former shield

INDO-PACIFIC

wavy edge to shield

short, recurved siphonal canal

Range Tropical Indo-Pacific	Occurrence 🐚🐚	Size 7.5cm (3in)

Superfamily TONNOIDEA	Family Ranellidae	Species *Distorsio constricta* Broderip

CONSTRICTED DISTORSIO

Early whorls are regular; later ones grossly distorted. Lattice ornament, regular at first, becoming irregular later. Aperture is surrounded by a translucent glossy shield. Early whorls white; later whorls brownish.
• **REMARK** Orderly progression of early whorls contrasts with chaotic later ones.
• **HABITAT** Offshore.

PANAMIC

brown inside to siphonal canal

Range Gulf of California to Ecuador	Occurrence 🐚🐚	Size 4cm (1½in)

FROG SHELLS

T HESE SHELLS are distinguished from tritons by a gutter-like canal or a slit-sided tube, which cuts through the edge of the aperture at its rear end. Some are of moderate size, others very large. They assume many shapes; some are squat and coarsely ornamented with thick ribs, knobs, and warty lump giving them the name frog shell Others are tall and lightly ornamented A few species are laterally compressed some have spines, most have varice The operculum is corneous. Most liv on sand and coral rubble.

Superfamily TONNOIDEA	Family Bursidae	Species *Tutufa bubo* Linnaeus

GIANT FROG SHELL

The shell has an inflated body whorl with a moderately tall spire. There are two varices per whorl and six to eight stout, bluntly pointed knobs between each varix. The body whorl also has spiral ribs with lesser riblets, ornamented with nodules, between them. The widely expanded aperture has a short, broad siphonal canal. At the upper edge of the aperture, the canal is short, deep, and open. The outer lip of the shell is not conspicuously thickened and lacks any teeth; the columella has many small folds along its entire length. Creamy in colour, with brown spots and lines all over; aperture white.
• **REMARK** Second largest frog shell.
• **HABITAT** Coral sand offshore.

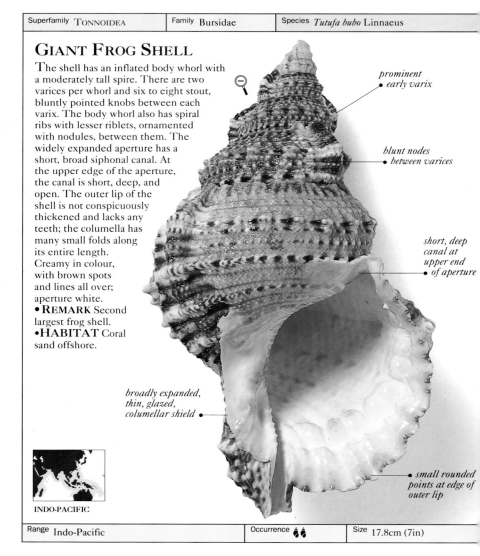

prominent early varix

blunt nodes between varices

short, deep canal at upper end of aperture

broadly expanded, thin, glazed, columellar shield

small rounded points at edge of outer lip

INDO-PACIFIC

Range Indo-Pacific	Occurrence 🐚🐚	Size 17.8cm (7in)

Superfamily TONNOIDEA	Family Bursidae	Species *Tutufa rubeta* Linnaeus

RUDDY FROG SHELL

A large, heavy shell with an ovate body
whorl and an uneven, shallow suture. The
surface is covered by coarse spiral ribs and
a row of bluntly pointed knobs at the
periphery of later whorls. The lower half
of the body whorl has about five
strong spiral ribs; the prominent
varices are widely separated. Strong
teeth lie along the outer lip of
the shell. Creamy, blotched with
brown; inside aperture bright
orange, outer lip bright red,
teeth tipped white.
• HABITAT Under
rocks inshore.

*strong varix is
partially hidden*

*white
channel
and folds
behind teeth*

*white denticles
on outerlip*

INDO-PACIFIC

Range Tropical Indo-Pacific	Occurrence 🐚🐚🐚🐚	Size 10cm (4in)

Superfamily TONNOIDEA	Family Bursidae	Species *Tutufa oyamai* Habe

OYAMA'S FROG SHELL

A solid but not very heavy shell with an
inflated body whorl and a tall spire with
a deep, uneven suture. The spiral ribs are
strongest around the periphery of whorls
where they override prominent, bluntly
pointed tubercles. There may be three
or four additional spiral ribs below
peripheral ones on body whorl. The
broad, thin outer lip is wrinkled and
bluntly toothed within. The parietal
shield is thin and wide; the columella
has slender folds. White in colour, with
brown spiral lines.
• REMARK Edges of aperture
may be pinkish orange.
• HABITAT Offshore.

*flat-topped, blunt-
ended tubercles*

*extremely
narrow
siphonal
canal*

INDO-PACIFIC

Range N. Indian Ocean, W. Pacific	Occurrence 🐚🐚	Size 7.5cm (3in)

Superfamily TONNOIDEA	Family Bursidae	Species *Bursa granularis* Röding

GRANULATE FROG SHELL

varix has prominent angles

A high-spired, slightly compressed shell whose body whorl has a small aperture. The apical whorls are smooth and pointed. Later whorls have two varices which are aligned with other varices. The suture is slightly impressed. The short siphonal canal is narrow and straight. Up to 16 spiral rows of nodules. Apertural lip has small, blunt teeth; columella has folds. Brown, with darker spiral bands; aperture white or yellowish.
• HABITAT Pools and under coral.

INDO-PACIFIC

CARIBBEAN

Range Indo-Pacific, W. Indies	Occurrence ♦♦♦♦	Size 5cm (2in)

Superfamily TONNOIDEA	Family Bursidae	Species *Bursa lamarckii* Deshayes

LAMARCK'S FROG SHELL

A thick, heavy, squat shell with a spire less than half the total height; the suture is shallow. The large aperture is nearly circular; the siphonal canal is short and narrow. Each whorl has two varices; the tube-like former canals are upturned and open on one side. Lumps give shell a warty appearance. Grey or yellowish, with purple-brown blotches; outer lip and columella purple-brown.
• HABITAT Coral reefs.

INDO-PACIFIC

canal is an almost totally enclosed tube

edge of aperture forms into sharp points

thin, horny operculum

Range S.W. Pacific	Occurrence ♦♦	Size 5cm (2in)

Superfamily TONNOIDEA	Family Bursidae	Species *Bursa cruentata* Sowerby

BLOOD-STAIN FROG SHELL

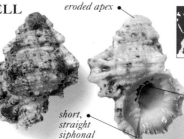

eroded apex

This small, low-spired shell has a large body whorl and almost circular aperture. Suture is deeply impressed. Each whorl has two varices, the last making the body whorl appear wider. Spiral rows of nodules and lumps cover the shell. Inner lip is toothed; columella has strong folds. Whitish, with brown marks; apertural lips brown.
• HABITAT Coral reefs.

INDO-PACIFIC

short, straight siphonal canal

dark brown staining between folds

Range Indo-Pacific	Occurrence ♦♦	Size 4cm (1½in)

Superfamily TONNOIDEA	Family Bursidae	Species *Bursa scrobilator* Linnaeus

PITTED FROG SHELL

A solid, tall shell with a spire less than half the total height, a large body whorl, and an ovate aperture. The well-impressed suture is wavy. The upper half of each whorl is sloping or forms an almost horizontal ramp; There is one varix per whorl. The outer lip has a wavy edge and is irregularly toothed, the teeth being paired; columella has irregularly spaced folds. Spiral ribs are often roundly nodulous; the varices are deeply pitted. Yellow, blotched and lined with brown. Outer lip orange.
• **REMARK** The only frog shell in the Mediterranean.
• **HABITAT** Offshore.

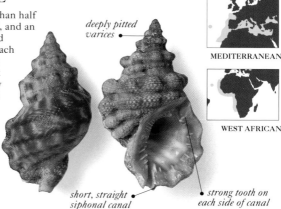

deeply pitted varices

MEDITERRANEAN

WEST AFRICAN

short, straight siphonal canal

strong tooth on each side of canal

Range Mediterranean, W. Africa	Occurrence 🐚🐚	Size 6cm (2½in)

Superfamily TONNOIDEA	Family Bursidae	Species *Crossata californica* Hinds

CALIFORNIA FROG SHELL

This solid, robust shell has a tall, pointed spire, an inflated body whorl, and a large, rounded aperture. Each whorl has two opposing varices, the last with four or five pointed knobs. Knobs are repeated as a spiral series around the whorls. There are coarse spiral ridges. The shallow suture is wavy. The outer lip has a fluted edge and usually blunt teeth; the columellar lip is thin. The columella has slight folds. The short siphonal canal is straight and narrow; upper canal is about the same width. Yellowish brown in colour, with thin brown lines across knobs; the aperture is white, the lip is brown.
• **HABITAT** Offshore rocks.

two knobs between each pair of varices

outer lip of this shell not fully developed

knobs point upwards

CALIFORNIAN

lower row of knobs on body whorl point downwards

thin, corneous operculum

Range California	Occurrence 🐚🐚🐚	Size 10cm (4in)

Superfamily TONNOIDEA	Family Bursidae	Species *Bufonaria echinata* Link

SPINY FROG SHELL

A solid, heavy, compressed shell characterized by long spines protruding from the sides. The body whorl is large, the spire less than half the total shell height. The elongate aperture ends in a long, broad, slightly recurved siphonal canal. The longest spines coincide with former positions of rear canal on the two vertically aligned series of varices; these spines point up on spire whorls, down on body whorl. Each spire whorl has a spiral row of pointed tubercles; body whorl has one or more extra rows. Shell is adorned with spiral riblets; irregularly indented outer lip. Creamy, with brown markings.
• **REMARK** The only frog shell with long spines.
• **HABITAT** Offshore.

INDO-PACIFIC

small tubercle at top of aperture

new spine forming at position of canal

brown dashes on indentations

Range Indian Ocean	Occurrence	Size 5cm (2in)

Superfamily TONNOIDEA	Family Bursidae	Species *Bufonaria rana* Linnaeus

COMMON FROG SHELL

A solid, compressed shell with a large body whorl and short spire which is about one third of total height. Elongate aperture; slightly recurved siphonal canal may be longer or shorter than that illustrated, but is usually same breadth as the rear canal. Opposing series of varices on each side resemble fins; those on the body whorl form sharp points where they coincide with former positions of rear canal and the three spiral rows of pointed tubercles. Outer lip has sharp teeth; lower half of columella has a series of folds. Colour creamy or white, blotched with brown.
• **REMARK** Colour usually darker than shell shown.
• **HABITAT** Rocky shores.

suture well impressed

INDO-PACIFIC
JAPONIC

broad rear canal

spiral riblets continue on varices

lower edge of outer lip serrated

Range W. Pacific, Japan	Occurrence	Size 7.5cm (3in)

MUREXES

S OME MUREXES are colourful, but their charm lies more in their ornamentation. Murexes may be thick and heavy, or sometimes delicate and fragile. The siphonal canal may be short and broad, or long and tubular. The brown, corneous operculum is usually pointed at one end. Murexes can be found in all seas, but are particularly abundant in tropical waters, on or close to coral reefs, where they prey on other invertebrates.

Superfamily MURICOIDEA	Family Muricidae	Species *Haustellum haustellum* Linnaeus

SNIPE'S BILL MUREX

A solid, low-spired shell with a large body whorl and an extremely long, straight siphonal canal. Vertical ribs are prominent on the later whorls, where some develop into varices, three per whorl. The suture may be slightly channelled. Flared aperture, with its outer lip lightly toothed. Smooth varices have points which are crossed by strong spiral riblets. The siphonal canal is almost spineless. Creamy or pinkish, with brown blotches and dashes, barred on varices; apertural lips orange or pink.
• **REMARK** Largest common species in its genus.
• **HABITAT** Intertidal sand flats.

three vertical ribs between varices

bend in siphonal canal

rudimentary spine

INDO-PACIFIC

Range Indo-Pacific	Occurrence ♦♦♦♦	Size 13cm (5in)

Superfamily MURICOIDEA	Family Muricidae	Species *Siratus motacilla* Gmelin

WAGTAIL MUREX

This thick shell has a short spire, a large, inflated body whorl, and a long, straight siphonal canal. The body whorl has three varices, between which are strong vertical knobs. Spiral ribs decorate whorls. Shallow suture; ovate aperture, its outer lip with a wavy edge and a few teeth. The columella has folds. Creamy, suffused with pink, blotched brown.
• **REMARK** Siphonal canal may be bent.
• **HABITAT** Offshore.

CARIBBEAN

brown bands on varix

position of former siphonal canal

single spine on siphonal canal

Range W. Indies	Occurrence ♦♦♦	Size 7cm (2¾in)

Superfamily MURICOIDEA	Family Muricidae	Species *Siratus laciniatus* Sowerby

LACINIATE MUREX

A high-spired shell with a large body whorl. Each whorl has three scaly varices. The rest of the shell has spiral ribs crossed by fluted scales. The siphonal canal is short and broad. Outer lip has small teeth; columella is smooth. Orange or pale brown, with darker varices; apex pink or dark brown; columella violet.
• **HABITAT** Coral and sand.

INDO-PACIFIC

regular rows of frilled scales

narrow channel of siphonal canal

Range Tropical Pacific	Occurrence 🌢🌢	Size 5cm (2in)

Superfamily MURICOIDEA	Family Muricidae	Species *Naquetia trigonula* Lamarck

TRIANGULAR MUREX

This thick, elongate shell has a spire one third of its total length. Body whorl has three low varices, the last being strongest. The suture is deeply impressed between early whorls. Last varix has a flange-like development to outer lip and siphonal canal. Teeth on outer lip; columella smooth. Spiral ribs strongest on lower half of body whorl. Yellowish, with spiral brown bands and dashes.
• **REMARK** The species varies considerably in colour.
• **HABITAT** Near coral reefs.

INDO-PACIFIC

apical whorls lean to one side

flange-like extension

Range Tropical Indo-Pacific	Occurrence 🌢🌢	Size 5cm (2in)

Superfamily MURICOIDEA	Family Muricidae	Species *Pteropurpura trialata* Sowerby

THREE-WINGED MUREX

A lightweight and triangle-shaped shell. The spire is short and pointed, the body whorl large. The siphonal canal is long, broad, and slightly curved. All whorls have three varices, each varix bearing a thin, frilled wing; there are low, rounded tubercles between varices. The outer lip has a frilled or straight edge; the columella is smooth and straight. Yellowish white, with spiral brown bands; columella and aperture white.
• **REMARK** The shell's operculum is shaped like a fan.
• **HABITAT** Intertidal rocks.

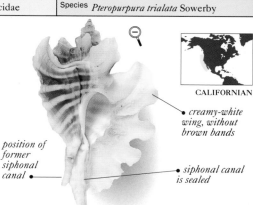

CALIFORNIAN

creamy-white wing, without brown bands

position of former siphonal canal

siphonal canal is sealed

Range California	Occurrence 🌢🌢🌢🌢	Size 6cm (2½in)

Superfamily MURICOIDEA	Family Muricidae	Species *Phyllonotus pomum* Gmelin

APPLE MUREX

This thick, heavy shell with a short spire and round body whorl is notoriously variable, and many forms have been named. The suture is slightly impressed and very uneven. Each whorl has three, evenly spaced, thick varices with one or two short vertical ribs between them. Low spiral ribs are prominent where they cross varices and vertical ribs; pointed scales develop on later varices. The aperture is large and rounded; pointed scales give the outer lip a saw-tooth edge. The columella has a few tubercles but is otherwise smooth. Yellowish to dark brown in colour, marked with whitish or brown blotches and lines; aperture white, orange, or yellow.

• **REMARK** The animal bores holes into oyster shells and eats the occupants.

• **HABITAT** Rocks and sand inshore.

apex smooth and shiny

early varices lack pointed scales

characteristic dark brown blotch

position of former siphonal canal

short, broad siphonal canal

thin, corneous operculum

CARIBBEAN

Range S.E. United States, Caribbean	Occurrence 🐚🐚🐚🐚	Size 7.5cm (3in)

Superfamily MURICOIDEA	Family Muricidae	Species *Homalocantha zamboi* Burch & Burch

ZAMBO'S MUREX

A short-spired, solid shell, character-ized by its extensions. The long, curved siphonal canal is almost closed. There are about five varices per whorl; the last four varices and the siphonal canal have long, hollow projections which are broadened and flattened at their tips. The surface of the shell is smooth, as are the outer lip and columella. White, with purple tinge on spire; aperture pink.

• **REMARK** Deformed appearance of shell is normal.

• **HABITAT** Coral reefs.

tip of projection splays out

siphonal canal delicately flushed pink

all projections flattened

INDO-PACIFIC

Range Philippines, Solomon Is.	Occurrence 🐚🐚🐚	Size 5cm (2in)

Superfamily MURICOIDEA	Family Muricidae	Species *Chicoreus palmarosae* Lamarck

ROSE BRANCH MUREX

A solid, tall-spired shell whose coarse sculpturing makes it very attractive. It has a large, ovate body whorl, a long, broad siphonal canal, and a well-impressed suture. Each whorl has three varices curving down the length of the shell; later varices bear tubular, open-sided projections with fronds at their tips. Blunt teeth inside edge of outer lip. Fine spiral ridges cover shell, with a few knobs between varices. Yellowish, with brown ridges; fronds sometimes violet or pink.
• **REMARK** In Sri Lanka, unscrupulous dealers enhance these shells' appearance by dipping them in a pink or violet dye.
• **HABITAT** Offshore.

fine ridges develop into fronds

Sri Lankan version has more fronds

white aperture

occasional broader brown ridges

projections tend to meet

INDO-PACIFIC

Range Sri Lanka, Philippines	Occurrence ♦♦♦	Size 10cm (4in)

Superfamily MURICOIDEA	Family Muricidae	Species *Chicoreus ramosus* Linnaeus

BRANCHED MUREX

A very large, heavy shell with a low spire and inflated body whorl, angled at the shoulder. Each whorl has three varices, between which there may be one or two, knobbly vertical ribs. Both varices and siphonal canal have short, frilled spines. Fine spiral ridges cover all whorls. The outer lip has a saw-tooth edge and, towards its lower end, a prominent tooth. The columella is smooth. White, with brown ridges and blotches; the columella is pink.
• **REMARK** One of the biggest and heaviest of the murex shells, it is widely used for ornamental purposes.
• **HABITAT** Coral reefs.

longest spine

INDO-PACIFIC

hollow, open spines curve upwards

strong tooth on outer lip of aperture

siphonal canal open

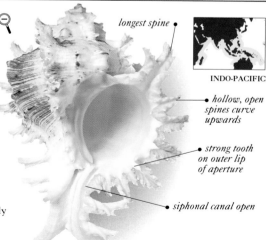

Range Indo-Pacific	Occurrence ♦♦♦♦	Size 20cm (8in)

Superfamily MURICOIDEA	Family Muricidae	Species *Bolinus brandaris* Linnaeus

PURPLE-DYE MUREX

A club-shaped shell with a short spire, inflated body whorl, and a long, straight siphonal canal. Body whorl has six or seven varices with two rows of short spines. Yellowish or buff; aperture reddish brown.
• **REMARK** The Romans took a juice from this shell's animal which stained cloth purple.
• **HABITAT** Sand offshore.

spines point away from each other

MEDITERRANEAN

swelling at top of columella

operculum

corrugated edge to thin outer lip

Range Mediterranean, N.W. Africa	Occurrence ♦♦♦♦♦	Size 7cm (2¾in)

Superfamily MURICOIDEA	Family Muricidae	Species *Murex troscheli* Lischke

TROSCHEL'S MUREX

This large, spine-covered murex has a striking appearance. It is club shaped, with acutely pointed apex, rounded whorls, deeply impressed suture, and very long, straight siphonal canal. The body whorl has three varices bearing alternately long and short spines; longest spines point upwards at shoulder. Spines continue down length of siphonal canal and protrude at right angles to it. Outer lip is corrugated; columella smooth. Thin spiral ribs cross weak vertical ribs. White or pinkish, with reddish-brown spiral lines; aperture white.
• **REMARK** The spines may provide some protection against predatory fish.
• **HABITAT** Sand offshore.

slightly curved spines on upper whorls

spiral lines show through aperture

sharp, thin edge of columellar wall

straight spines on siphonal canal

spiral bands continue on siphonal canal

end of siphonal canal slightly bent

INDO-PACIFIC

Range E. Indian Ocean, Pacific, Japan	Occurrence ♦♦♦	Size 15cm (6in)

Superfamily MURICOIDEA	Family Muricidae	Species *Hexaplex trunculus* Linnaeus

TRUNK MUREX

A thick, robust shell with a large body whorl and pointed spire. The numerous thick varices are flattened against shell wall, each bearing rounded knobs and often a stout spine. Coarse spiral ribs occur on lower half of body whorl. The deep umbilicus is surrounded by tubes which were formerly part of siphonal canal. The columella is smooth. Yellowish white, with brown spiral bands which sometimes coalesce; columella white.
• **REMARK** Like the purple-dye murex *(see p.109)*, the animal of this shell provided the Romans with a juice that stained cloth purple.
• **HABITAT** Rocks and sand offshore.

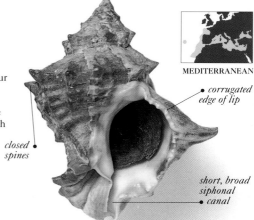

MEDITERRANEAN

corrugated edge of lip

closed spines

short, broad siphonal canal

Range Mediterranean	Occurrence 🐚🐚🐚🐚🐚	Size 6cm (2½in)

Superfamily MURICOIDEA	Family Muricidae	Species *Hexaplex radix* Gmelin

RADISH MUREX

A massive, very heavy shell with a small pointed spire, a very inflated body whorl, and a deep umbilicus. Shallow suture is difficult to see; siphonal canal is moderately long and broad. Body whorl has six to eleven varices, thickly covered with spines, giving shell a prickly appearance. Where spines are intersected by spiral ribs they develop frilled ends which may be slightly recurved. The columella is smooth; edge of outer lip jagged. White, with purplish black spines, darkest on their inside faces, and thin, connecting spiral bands; spire mostly white.
• **REMARK** This species is one of the most spiny and one of the heaviest murex shells.
• **HABITAT** Intertidal rocks.

spines point upwards

PANAMIC

swollen lump at top of columella

thick, corneous operculum

siphonal canal is open

Range Panama to Ecuador	Occurrence 🐚🐚🐚🐚	Size 11cm (4½in)

ROCK SHELLS

T HE SHELLS INCLUDED in this group belong to several genera and display many different shapes and surface features, but most are shades of brown and yellow. They are sturdily built and have a corneous operculum. All are carnivorous, and some infest oyster beds. They abound in warm seas.

Superfamily MURICOIDEA	Family Muricidae	Species *Ocenebra erinacea* Linnaeus

STING WINKLE

A sturdy, variable, high-spired shell with pointed apex, large body whorl, and longish, broad siphonal canal. Body whorl has up to nine varices and thick, widely spaced ribs. Columella smooth. Shell covered in fluted scales. Yellowish; aperture white.
• **REMARK** A damaging parasite of oysters.
• **HABITAT** Oyster beds.

ribs and varices intersect

operculum

BOREAL MEDITERRANEAN

very crowded scales

siphonal canal closed

Range S.W. Europe, Mediterranean	Occurrence 👤👤	Size 3cm (1¼in)

Superfamily MURICOIDEA	Family Muricidae	Species *Trochia cingulata* Linnaeus

CORDED ROCK SHELL

A small, solid, high-spired shell with a flattened apex and smooth columella. The body whorl is encircled by three, broad spiral ribs; fine spiral riblets between. Dark brown to grey or white; aperture brownish orange.
• **REMARK** A variable shell, it may have up to six spiral ribs, or none at all.
• **HABITAT** On rocks at low tide.

curled edges to ribs

SOUTH AFRICAN

widely open siphonal canal

Range S. Africa	Occurrence 👤👤👤👤	Size 4cm (1½in)

Superfamily MURICOIDEA	Family Muricidae	Species *Nucella lapillus* Linnaeus

DOG WINKLE

Solid shell often with a tall, pointed spire and large body whorl, but showing great variation in shape even in one locality. Smooth or rough spiral ribs are crossed by fine vertical lines. White, yellow, purple, or brown; plain or broadly banded.
• **REMARK** A rare form ornamented with wavy frills occurs in sheltered waters.
• **HABITAT** Rocks inshore.

regular, sharp-edged frills

BOREAL

well-impressed suture

Range N.E. United States, W. Europe	Occurrence 👤👤👤👤👤	Size 5cm (2in)

CAP SHELLS

MOST OF THESE thick, brown shells have well-developed tubercles and are often encrusted with coral. The aperture may be smooth or rigid internally. The columella often lacks prominent folds. Many species occur on intertidal rocks in warm water, feeding on invertebrates.

Superfamily MURICOIDEA	Family Muricidae	Species *Purpura patula* Linnaeus

WIDE-MOUTHED PURPURA

A thick shell with an insignificant spire, very large body whorl, wide, elongated aperture, and spiral rows of large tubercles or knobs. Shallow siphonal canal. Brown, with darker tubercles; smooth salmon-pink columella.
• **REMARK** Central American Indians still use a juice obtained from this shell to dye cloth purple.
• **HABITAT** Rocks inshore.

tubercles worn down on older example

purplish black edge to aperture

fine grooves between rows of tubercles

slight kink in columella

edge of aperture weakly toothed

CARIBBEAN

Range S. Florida, Caribbean	Occurrence ♦♦♦♦♦	Size 9cm (3½in)

Superfamily MURICOIDEA	Family Muricidae	Species *Concholepas concholepas* Bruguière

HARE'S EAR SHELL

A very thick, flattened shell in which early spire whorls are smothered by the greatly expanded and reflected body whorl. As with abalones, the spire seldom shows above columellar rim of aperture when shell is fully grown. Strong spiral ribs are crossed by thinner vertical ribs, which become scaly or frilled at later stages of growth. Columella thick and smooth; siphonal canal very shallow. Dull brown or greyish white; aperture whitish; columella pink-edged.
• **REMARK** Animal attaches itself to rocks by the suction of its large foot.
• **HABITAT** Rocks inshore.

PERUVIAN

deep spiral grooves

vertical ribs frilled at midway stage of growth

two large teeth on outer lip

Range Peru, Chile	Occurrence ♦♦♦♦♦	Size 6cm (2½in)

Superfamily MURICOIDEA	Family Muricidae	Species *Rapana venosa* Valenciennes

VEINED RAPA WHELK

A heavy, short-spired shell with a large, inflated body whorl and a deep umbilicus. Aperture is large and ovate; columella broad and smooth; edge of outer lip has small, elongate teeth. Older examples have a flaring outer lip. Smooth spiral ribs develop regular, blunt knobs at shoulder and periphery of body whorl. Fine spiral ridges crossed by low vertical riblets. Greyish or reddish brown, with dark brown dashes on spiral ribs. Aperture and columella deep orange.

• **REMARK** A native of Japanese and Chinese waters, this impressive shell was found in the Black Sea in the 1940s, where it soon destroyed many oyster beds.

• **HABITAT** Oyster beds.

vertical sides to spire whorls

broad rear canal

sharp angle at shoulder

thick, scaly ribs around umbilicus

paired teeth on outer lip

JAPONIC
INDO-PACIFIC

MEDITERRANEAN

columellar lip projects over umbilicus

short, broad siphonal canal

Range Japan, China, Black Sea, Mediterranean	Occurrence 🐚🐚🐚🐚🐚	Size 10cm (4in)

Superfamily MURICOIDEA	Family Muricidae	Species *Thais tuberosa* Röding

HUMPED ROCK SHELL

A thick, heavy shell with moderately tall spire and large body whorl. Impressed suture is difficult to see when spire is eroded. Body whorl is ornamented with two rows of large, blunt nodules and a lesser row towards base. Smooth columella. Yellowish white, with purple-brown spiral bands; aperture creamy, with regularly spaced, orange spiral lines.

• **REMARK** One of several Indo-Pacific species, it varies in size and ornamentation.

• **HABITAT** Near coral reefs.

INDO-PACIFIC

purple-brown patches on lip

Range Pacific	Occurrence 🐚🐚🐚🐚	Size 5cm (2in)

Superfamily MURICOIDEA	Family Muricidae	Species *Thais haemastoma* Linnaeus

RED-MOUTHED ROCK SHELL

A thick, heavy shell with a short, conical spire, large body whorl and expanded aperture. Suture is shallow. The body whorl usually has up to four spiral rows of blunt knobs and the whole shell is covered with fine spiral grooves. The columella is smooth and straight. Greyish to reddish brown in colour; aperture red, orange, or brownish.
• **REMARK** The popular name is not always appropriate.
• **HABITAT** Rocks inshore.

ADULT SHELL

prominent shoulder

JUVENILE SHELL

WEST AFRICAN
SOUTH AFRICAN

MEDITERRANEAN

Range Mediterranean to S. Africa	Occurrence 🐚🐚🐚🐚🐚	Size 7.5cm (3in)

Superfamily MURICOIDEA	Family Muricidae	Species *Thais rugosa* Born

ROUGH ROCK SHELL

A biconic shell with a pagoda-like spire and a large body whorl. Wide aperture, straight columella, and an umbilicus which is often sealed. The body whorl may have four spiral rows of short, fluted spines, the topmost ones curving upwards. Pale or dark brown; the aperture is cream or white.
• **REMARK** The fluted spines are sometimes much reduced.
• **HABITAT** Muddy rocks inshore.

sharply keeled early whorls

INDO-PACIFIC

longest spine

short siphonal notch

operculum

Range India to S.E. Asia	Occurrence 🐚🐚🐚🐚	Size 2.5cm (1in)

Superfamily MURICOIDEA	Family Muricidae	Species *Cuma lacera* Born

KEELED ROCK SHELL

This species has a short spire and a large, inflated body whorl with a wide aperture. The sharp keel on each spire whorl has protuberances which, on the body whorl, become large, pointed knobs. Smooth, straight columella; outer lip is corrugated. Yellowish brown; aperture whitish.
• **REMARK** Collected along Bombay coast for food.
• **HABITAT** Muddy rocks inshore.

secondary row of knobs

INDO-PACIFIC

spine at edge of outer lip

spiral grooves

narrow siphonal notch

Range Indian Ocean, S.E. Asia	Occurrence 🐚🐚🐚🐚🐚	Size 5cm (2in)

Superfamily MURICOIDEA	Family Muricidae	Species *Vitularia salebrosa* King & Broderip

RUGGED SEA-CALF

One of the most conspicuous features of this high-spired shell is the large, elongate aperture and its very thick outer lip. The body whorl is twice the total height of the spire. The sharply keeled early whorls give way to knobbed shoulders on later whorls. The impressed suture is slightly wavy. Fresh examples of the shell may show a series of thin, sharp varices, which are often worn away from older examples. Pale to dark brown in colour, with four or five darker brown spiral bands, which are at their broadest towards the base of the body whorl.

• **REMARK** This is the larger of the only two species in the whole genus.

• **HABITAT** Offshore.

• *blunt teeth along inside of lip*

• *whitish aperture*

• *thin, brittle layers at edge of lip*

PANAMIC

Range Gulf of California to Panama, Galapagos	Occurrence 🐚🐚🐚	Size 7.5cm (3in)

Superfamily MURICOIDEA	Family Muricidae	Species *Nassa francolina* Bruguière

FRANCOLIN JOPAS

This smooth and shiny shell has a capacious body whorl and a small spire. The early whorls have vertical ribs. The columella is smooth, and the outer lip is sharp edged. Pale or dark reddish brown in colour, with greyish white areas variegated with thin vertical streaks and patches; the aperture and columella are either yellowish or orange.

• **REMARK** The shell's scientific name was given to it in 1789 by the French naturalist, Bruguière, and is derived from an old Italian word for partridge.

• **HABITAT** Coral and stones.

concave upper side of body whorl

INDO-PACIFIC

• *tubercle at top of aperture*

• *short, deep siphonal notch*

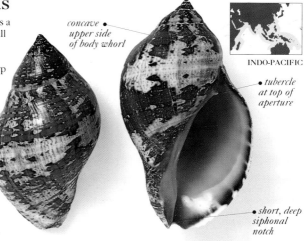

Range Indian Ocean	Occurrence 🐚🐚🐚	Size 6cm (2½in)

DRUPES

T HE SPECIES IN THIS small group have thick shells, a large body whorl and are covered in nodules. The outer lip is prominently toothed on the inside edge; the aperture may further constricted by columellar fold Drupes inhabit Indo-Pacific co reefs, feeding on small invertebrates.

Superfamily MURICOIDEA	Family Muricidae	Species *Drupa morum* Röding

PURPLE PACIFIC DRUPE

The large body whorl of this thick shell obscures the spire. There are three or four strong folds on the columella and about eight large teeth on the inside of the outer lip. The body whorl is encircled by four rows of large nodules. Greyish white, with black nodules; aperture and apertural teeth purple.
• **REMARK** Easily recognized by its very distinctive purple-tinged aperture.
• **HABITAT** Intertidal reefs.

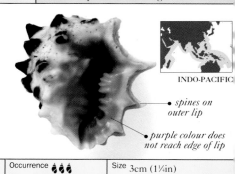

INDO-PACIFIC

spines on outer lip

purple colour does not reach edge of lip

Range Tropical Indo-Pacific	Occurrence 🐚🐚🐚	Size 3cm (1¼in)

Superfamily MURICOIDEA	Family Muricidae	Species *Drupa rubusidaeus* Röding

STRAWBERRY DRUPE

This globose shell has a short, spire but mature examples are almost flat-topped. About five rows of spines encircle body whorl, those nearest the outer lip being open-sided. Creamy yellow; mature examples have a rich-pink columella.
• **HABITAT** Intertidal reefs.

deep grooves between spines

INDO-PACIFIC

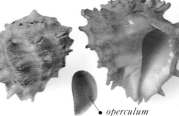

operculum

Range Tropical Indo-Pacific	Occurrence 🐚🐚	Size 5cm (2in)

Superfamily MURICOIDEA	Family Muricidae	Species *Drupa ricinus* Linnaeus

PRICKLY PACIFIC DRUPE

This small species has pointed spines near the outer lip that are much longer than those on the rest of the shell. Squarish, blunt teeth on the columella and others lining the outer lip severely restrict the aperture. Whitish, with black-ended spines; aperture ringed with orange.
• **REMARK** The orange coloration around the aperture is often absent.
• **HABITAT** Intertidal reefs.

black tips to spines

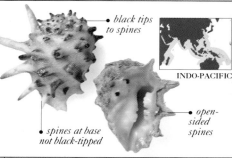

INDO-PACIFIC

open-sided spines

spines at base not black-tipped

Range Tropical Indo-Pacific	Occurrence 🐚🐚🐚🐚	Size 3cm (1¼in)

THORN DRUPES

T HESE THICK-SHELLED species are found on inshore rocks along the estern coasts of the Americas. The irface may be smooth, knobbed, or scaly. The prominent or inconspicuous tooth at the base of the aperture enables the animal to force open the shells of the bivalves it preys upon.

uperfamily MURICOIDEA	Family Muricidae	Species *Acanthina monodon* Pallas

ROUGH THORN DRUPE

A low-spired shell with projecting basal tooth. Its surface is covered with scaly spiral ridges. Pale reddish brown; aperture and columella white.
• **REMARK** Strong teeth are common within the outer lip of this species.
• **HABITAT** Inshore rocks.

MAGELLANIC

strongly keeled early spiral ridges

reddish brown inner edge of outer lip

broad basal ridge

straight, smooth columella

ange Peru to Argentina, Falklands	Occurrence 🌑🌑🌑🌑	Size 5cm (2in)

FALSE TRITONS

T HERE MAY WELL BE only two living species in this group, and little is nown about their habitat and diet. ike miniature versions of the larger triton shells, they have a thin shell with prominent varices and a flaring aperture. The early whorls are usually missing from mature examples.

uperfamily MURICOIDEA	Family Muricidae	Species *Phyllocoma convoluta* Broderip

CONVOLUTED FALSE TRITON

This thin, tall-spired shell has a well-impressed suture and a large body whorl with a flaring aperture. Early whorls are absent from mature examples but later whorls have two thin, evenly spaced varices and strong, flat spiral ribs. The smooth columellar lip is strongly reflected. Yellowish white in colour, with paler aperture.
• **REMARK** The outer lip may sometimes have a saw-tooth edge to it.
• **HABITAT** Offshore.

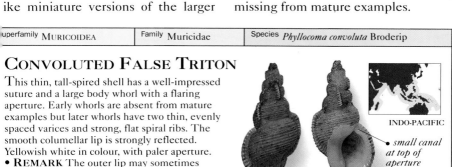

INDO-PACIFIC

small canal at top of aperture

short, reflected siphonal canal

ange Tropical Indo-Pacific	Occurrence 🌑	Size 3cm (1¼in)

CORAL SHELLS

S OME OF THESE SMALL to moderate-sized shells are curiously coiled and ornamented with elaborate spines and frills. They live mostly among corals or sea-fans; the specialized nature of th habitat ensures a degree of variation shell shape and sculpture. They are mo numerous in shallow tropical waters.

Superfamily MURICOIDEA	Family Coralliophilidae	Species *Coralliophila meyendorffi* Calcara

LAMELLOSE CORAL SHELL

Solid, compact, high-spired shell with a deeply-impressed suture. Broad, obliquely vertical ribs are crossed by crowded spiral ribs which are scaly, especially near outer lip. Columella is straight and smooth. Dirty white, grey, or yellowish brown in colour; aperture rosy in fresh examples.
• **HABITAT** Offshore.

MEDITERRANEAN

• *edge of lip finely toothed*

• *short, open siphonal canal*

Range Mediterranean	Occurrence 🐚🐚🐚	Size 3cm (1¼in)

Superfamily MURICOIDEA	Family Coralliophilidae	Species *Coralliophila neritoidea* Lamarck

VIOLET CORAL SHELL

A very thick, usually squat, and bulbous shell with a short or almost non-existent spire and a large body whorl. The suture of taller examples is impressed. Columella is straight and smooth. Fine spiral riblets sometimes visible. Aperture ovate; outer lip sharp-edged. Sometimes a small umbilicus. Siphonal canal is short and narrow. Dirty white, sometimes tinged pale violet; aperture dark violet.
• **REMARK** Outline of species varies and surface is often eroded or coral-encrusted, but violet aperture is a constant feature.
• **HABITAT** Under coral rocks.

• *fine spiral ridges in aperture*

INDO-PACIFIC

• *kink at end of columella*

Range Indo-Pacific	Occurrence 🐚🐚🐚🐚	Size 2.5cm (1in)

Superfamily MURICOIDEA	Family Coralliophilidae	Species *Coralliophila erosa* Röding

SOUTHERN CORAL SHELL

Biconic shell, with similar outline top and bottom; widest point at shoulder of body whorl. Well-impressed suture. Columella is straight and smooth; edge of outer lip is wrinkled. Close-set spiral ribs are ornamented with tiny scales. Small, shallow umbilicus. Dirty white.
• **HABITAT** Hard corals.

INDO-PACIFIC

• *short, curved siphonal canal is open*

Range Indo-Pacific	Occurrence 🐚🐚🐚	Size 3cm (1¼in)

RAPA WHELKS

T HE FEW MEMBERS of this group are mostly globular, thin and fragile, colourless and translucent. They have a thin, corneous operculum which is too small to close the large aperture. A few occur at considerable depths but most inhabit soft corals in warm tropical seas where they may be plentiful locally.

Superfamily MURICOIDEA	Family Muricidae	Species *Rapa rapa* Linnaeus

RAPA SNAIL

Resembling a turnip with a flattened top, this fragile shell has a short spire with a pointed apex almost submerged in the body whorl. The columella is straight and smooth, its lower half broadly expanded and forming a thin plate quite separate from the body whorl. The siphonal canal is broad and wide-open, either straight or strongly bent to one side. Strong spiral ridges cover the shell and give a saw-tooth edge to the outer lip. The ribs, seen from above, are separated by wide channels filled with thin, vertical ridges; around the wide, top-most channel of the body whorl these ridges are more numerous and wrinkled. Uniformly white.
• **REMARK** This species is the largest of the rapa whelks.
• **HABITAT** Soft corals.

APERTURAL VIEW

crescent-shaped grooves between saw teeth

• *layered structure of shell*

TOP VIEW

• *crowded, wrinkled ridges found in largest spiral channel*

INDO-PACIFIC

Range W. Pacific	Occurrence 🌢🌢🌢	Size 7.5cm (3in)

LATIAXIS SHELLS

S HELLS IN THIS GROUP of small, tall-spired shells are ornamented with well-developed spines and scales which sometimes combine to make these shells objects of remarkable beauty. They have a dark brown corneous operculum. Most of the species occur in warm seas, usually offshore and sometimes at great depths.

Superfamily MURICOIDEA	Family Coralliophilidae	Species *Latiaxis mawae* Griffith & Pidgeon

MAWE'S LATIAXIS

The whorls of this extraordinary shell are almost separated from one another. Early whorls of spire are flattened; upper half of body whorl is slightly raised, its lower surface rounded. Shoulder of body whorl has a curled-over, deeply notched flange. Exterior of shell is covered in fine spiral grooves. It has a wide, deep umbilicus, with a roughly serrated edge. Whitish.
• **REMARK** One of the first latiaxis shells to be made known to science.
• **HABITAT** Offshore.

JAPONIC
INDO-PACIFIC

hollow flange

strongly recurved siphonal canal

Range Japan to Philippines	Occurrence 🐚🐚	Size 4.5cm (1¾in)

Superfamily MURICOIDEA	Family Coralliophilidae	Species *Latiaxis pagodus* A. Adams

PAGODA LATIAXIS

A small, very thin shell with a tall, pointed spire, a large body whorl, and a moderately long siphonal canal. Deep umbilicus. Spines are broad at their base, open at one side, and pointed. Yellowish white or greyish, with pink or brownish blotches.
• **HABITAT** Offshore.

longest spines at periphery of body whorl

JAPONIC
INDO-PACIFIC

spines curve upwards

Range Japan to Philippines	Occurrence 🐚🐚🐚	Size 3cm (1¼in)

Superfamily MURICOIDEA	Family Coralliophilidae	Species *Latiaxis winckworthi* Fulton

WINCKWORTH'S LATIAXIS

Small, thin, but sturdy shell with a large, inflated body whorl and a fairly tall, stepped spire. Spines in a spiral row at periphery of body whorl; low vertical ribs. Aperture large, columella straight and smooth. Ridge surrounds umbilicus. Yellowish; aperture white.
• **HABITAT** Offshore.

JAPONIC

saw-tooth edge to outer lip

Range Japan	Occurrence 🐚🐚🐚	Size 3cm (1¼in)

TYPHIS SHELLS

T HESE SMALL SHELLS are curiously ornamented but not very colour-ul. Most of them have strong varices earing well-developed flanges and tubular extensions open at their ends. The shells are found in warm seas; some of them are intertidal, others live at considerable depths.

Superfamily MURICOIDEA	Family Muricidae	Species *Typhisala grandis* A. Adams

GRAND TYPHIS

Underneath its ornamental features, this shell has a large body whorl and a short spire. The varices bear thin flanges which are folded back at their edges, the last one joining up with the siphonal canal to form a broad shield around the small, circular aperture. The upper edge of the flanges bears small, open tubes. Pale brown and white.
• **REMARK** This shell is notable for the size of its apertural flange.
• **HABITAT** Offshore.

PANAMIC

• *operculum*

• *brown dashes on edge of outer lip*

Range W. Mexico to Panama	Occurrence 🐚🐚	Size 3.5cm (1½in)

Superfamily MURICOIDEA	Family Muricidae	Species *Typhisopsis coronatus* Broderip

CROWNED TYPHIS

The ornamentation of this small species partly conceals a tall spire and elongate body whorl. Broad varices are produced into needle-like spines at their tops; occasional open tubes also project upwards, close to spines. Body whorl has strong spiral cords. Outer lip of circular aperture has a broad flange extending length of body whorl. Yellowish brown.
• **HABITAT** Shallow water.

PANAMIC

• *pointed top to flange*

• *opening of siphonal canal*

Range W. Mexico to Ecuador	Occurrence 🐚🐚	Size 3cm (1¼in)

Superfamily MURICOIDEA	Family Muricidae	Species *Typhina cleryi* Petit

CLERY'S TYPHIS

Elaborate ornamentation suggests the spire is short and squat but it is actually quite tall, the body whorl being only moderately inflated. Well-impressed suture is clearly visible. The flanges are curled over at their tops and next to them are open-ended, downward-pointing tubes. Edge of aperture is flared. Dirty white, flushed with pink.
• **HABITAT** Deep water.

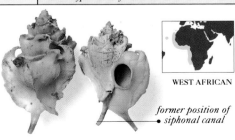

WEST AFRICAN

former position of siphonal canal

Range W. Africa	Occurrence 🐚🐚	Size 2cm (¾in)

TROPHONS

A LARGE GROUP of mainly colourless, dull, and thin shells from cold and temperate waters, some living inshore, others at great depths. Small or medium sized, they have a prominent, ope[n] siphonal canal and a smooth columell[a]. Vertical ridges on some species may [be] well developed or rudimentary.

Superfamily MURICOIDEA	Family Muricidae	Species *Trophon geversianus* Pallas

GEVERS' TROPHON

A thick but brittle shell with a large, inflated body whorl and a short spire with rounded apex. Deep suture is sometimes channelled. The deep umbilicus can be either broad or narrow; broad siphonal canal is slightly recurved. Vertical ridges on all whorls vary in strength, with low, regularly spaced spiral ribs between them; on spire whorls, ridges and ribs may form a lattice pattern. Vertical ridges sometimes absent. Columella and outer lip are smooth. Chalky white; aperture purple-brown.
• **REMARK** This variable, large trophon is washed up on some S. American beaches.
• **HABITAT** Offshore.

no spiral ribs above shoulder of body whorl

MAGELLANIC

ridges strongly developed at top of body whorl

rim around umbilicus

very thin outer lip

Range S. Chile, S. Argentina	Occurrence 🐚🐚🐚🐚	Size 7.5cm (3in)

Superfamily MURICOIDEA	Family Muricidae	Species *Trophon beebei* Hertlein & Strong

BEEBE'S TROPHON

A thin, lightweight, and fragile shell with loosely coiled whorls; spire less than half the total height. Apex and early whorls eroded, indicating lack of calcium carbonate in the shell. Long, broad siphonal canal is wide open. Aperture is rounded; smooth columella is nearly straight. Only ornament is occasional upright spine or the beginning of one at shoulder of whorls. Pale brown or tan; aperture paler.
• **REMARK** This most elegant species is named after American naturalist, William Beebe.
• **HABITAT** Offshore.

upper half of whorl is shelf-like

rudimentary spines on shoulder of whorl

PANAMIC

isolated spine

smooth surface of shell

siphonal canal slightly curved

operculum

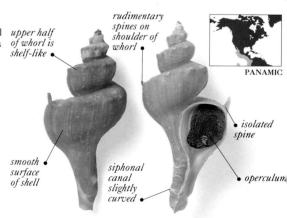

Range Gulf of California	Occurrence 🐚🐚🐚	Size 4cm (1½in)

PAGODA SHELLS

E ACH MEMBER of this small but distinctive group of appropriately named shells has a high spire, a pear-shaped, corneous operculum, and a long siphonal canal. The whorls usually have a strongly keeled periphery decorated with knobs, spines, or scales. Most occur on mud in deep water in tropical seas.

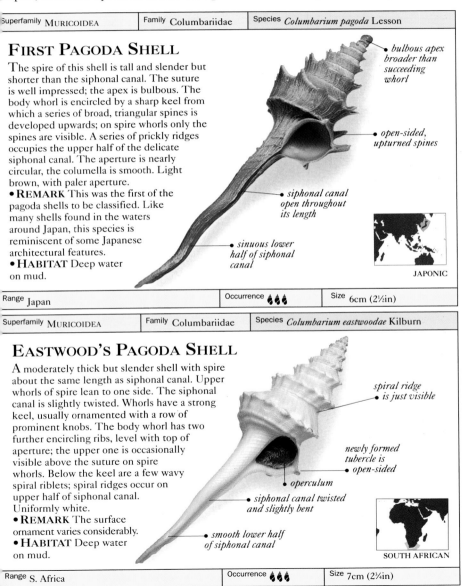

Superfamily MURICOIDEA	Family Columbariidae	Species *Columbarium pagoda* Lesson

FIRST PAGODA SHELL

The spire of this shell is tall and slender but shorter than the siphonal canal. The suture is well impressed; the apex is bulbous. The body whorl is encircled by a sharp keel from which a series of broad, triangular spines is developed upwards; on spire whorls only the spines are visible. A series of prickly ridges occupies the upper half of the delicate siphonal canal. The aperture is nearly circular, the columella is smooth. Light brown, with paler aperture.
• **REMARK** This was the first of the pagoda shells to be classified. Like many shells found in the waters around Japan, this species is reminiscent of some Japanese architectural features.
• **HABITAT** Deep water on mud.

• *bulbous apex broader than succeeding whorl*

• *open-sided, upturned spines*

• *siphonal canal open throughout its length*

• *sinuous lower half of siphonal canal*

JAPONIC

Range Japan	Occurrence ♦♦♦	Size 6cm (2½in)

Superfamily MURICOIDEA	Family Columbariidae	Species *Columbarium eastwoodae* Kilburn

EASTWOOD'S PAGODA SHELL

A moderately thick but slender shell with spire about the same length as siphonal canal. Upper whorls of spire lean to one side. The siphonal canal is slightly twisted. Whorls have a strong keel, usually ornamented with a row of prominent knobs. The body whorl has two further encircling ribs, level with top of aperture; the upper one is occasionally visible above the suture on spire whorls. Below the keel are a few wavy spiral riblets; spiral ridges occur on upper half of siphonal canal. Uniformly white.
• **REMARK** The surface ornament varies considerably.
• **HABITAT** Deep water on mud.

spiral ridge • is just visible

newly formed tubercle is • open-sided

• *operculum*

• *siphonal canal twisted and slightly bent*

• *smooth lower half of siphonal canal*

SOUTH AFRICAN

Range S. Africa	Occurrence ♦♦♦	Size 7cm (2¾in)

DOVE SHELLS

THESE SMALL, and mostly spindle-shaped, shells comprise over 30 genera. The columella usually has a few folds and there are teeth on the inner edge of the outer lip. Colour and patter vary greatly within a species. Dove shel are widely distributed in warm seas; th animals are carnivorous scavengers.

Superfamily MURICOIDEA	Family Columbellidae	Species *Strombina elegans* Sowerby

ELEGANT STROMBINA

A small shell whose fragile, tapering early whorls become progressively more solid and more shouldered; the body whorl is gently rounded and ends in a narrow siphonal notch. The first nine or ten whorls are smooth and silky, the later ones are shouldered and vertically ribbed. The columella is straight. White ground colour, with vertical, sometimes fused, brown streaks.
• **REMARK** The uncoloured early whorls of this shell taper to a sharp point; they contrast strikingly with the boldly patterned later whorls.
• **HABITAT** Offshore.

PANAMIC

top of outer lip thickened

strong, blunt teeth

Range W. coast of Central America	Occurrence 🐚🐚🐚	Size 3cm (1¼in)

Superfamily MURICOIDEA	Family Columbellidae	Species *Mazatlania aciculata* Lamarck

FALSE AUGER SHELL

A small, delicate, elongate shell with a pointed apex and a shiny surface. The vertical ribs on the early spire whorls become a double row of very smooth tubercles on the later ones. The spire is considerably taller than the body whorl. Creamy yellow to pale brown, encircled by a single spiral brown band.
• **REMARK** Once thought to occur in the Bay of Naples, but this has not been confirmed.
• **HABITAT** Sand offshore.

CARIBBEAN

tubercles interrupt brown band

brown band visible within aperture

Range W. Indies, Brazil	Occurrence 🐚🐚🐚	Size 2cm (¾in)

Superfamily MURICOIDEA	Family Columbellidae	Species *Parametaria macrostoma* Reeve

CONE-LIKE DOVE SHELL

This species resembles a cone shell, with its short spire. The suture is well impressed and the lower half of the body whorl is spirally grooved. Purplish brown, mottled with greyish white; aperture deep violet.
• **REMARK** The thickened lip and the spiral ridges within the aperture show that the resemblance to a cone shell is superficial.
• **HABITAT** Intertidal under stones.

PANAMIC

spiral ridges inside outer lip

Range W. Mexico to Panama	Occurrence 🐚🐚	Size 2cm (¾in)

Superfamily MURICOIDEA	Family Columbellidae	Species *Pyrene scripta* Lamarck

DOTTED DOVE SHELL

This glossy shell has a large body whorl which is roundly angled at the shoulder. The outer lip is angled at the top and bottom, but it is straight in between; it has up to 14 teeth on its inner side. There are folds on the columella. The spiral ridges on the body whorl become prominent towards the base. Creamy, with pale brown blotches and spiral rows of darker brown dots.
• **HABITAT** Shallow water.

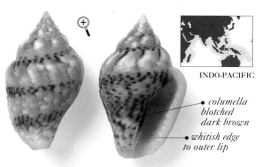

INDO-PACIFIC

• *columella blotched dark brown*

• *whitish edge to outer lip*

Range Tropical Pacific	Occurrence 👣👣👣👣	Size 2cm (¾in)

Superfamily MURICOIDEA	Family Columbellidae	Species *Pyrene flava* Bruguière

YELLOW DOVE SHELL

The whorls of this spindle-shaped shell are slightly telescoped into each other; the deep suture contributes to this effect. The narrow aperture is slightly more than half the height of the body whorl; riblets encircle lower half of body whorl. Colour variable, but usually pale brown patterned with white blotches, spots, and lines; aperture often violet.
• **REMARK** The striking pattern of the left-hand example is rare.
• **HABITAT** Intertidal.

INDO-PACIFIC

• *teeth on inside edge of outer lip*

Range Tropical Indo-Pacific	Occurrence 👣👣👣	Size 2.5cm (1in)

Superfamily MURICOIDEA	Family Columbellidae	Species *Pyrene punctata* Bruguière

TELESCOPED DOVE SHELL

A smooth shell, apart from the ribs encircling the lower half of the body whorl. Early whorls are telescoped into each other, making the body whorl much longer than the spire. The aperture is narrow and the outer lip has teeth on its inner edge. Reddish brown, with white mottling and dark brown blotches, zigzags, and spots.
• **REMARK** The telescoped appearance of the early whorls is the hallmark of this species.
• **HABITAT** Offshore.

INDO-PACIFIC

upper end of outer lip
• *thickened*

• *lower part of outer lip lacks teeth*

Range Tropical Indo-Pacific	Occurrence 👣👣👣	Size 2.5cm (1in)

Superfamily MURICOIDEA	Family Columbellidae	Species *Columbella mercatoria* Linnaeus

COMMON DOVE SHELL

A thick shell with short spire and swollen body whorl narrowing sharply toward the base. The suture is distinctly channeled; there are strong, regularly spaced, spiral ribs on all whorls. Upper half of the columella is smooth, the lower half bearing six or eight small folds; entire length of the outer lip is toothed. Brown, white, orange, and pink form varied patterns; teeth and folds white.
• **REMARK** The columella and the inside edge of the outer lip make almost parallel curves, leaving a narrow aperture.
• **HABITAT** Shallow water under rocks.

apex often eroded

CARIBBEAN

canal at top of aperture

Range S.E. Florida to Brazil	Occurrence 🐚🐚🐚🐚🐚	Size 2cm (¾in)

Superfamily MURICOIDEA	Family Columbellidae	Species *Columbella strombiformis* Lamarck

STROMBOID DOVE SHELL

This tall-spired shell has a distinctive jutting-out lip. The swollen body whorl is often keeled at the shoulder. There are small folds on the lower half of the columella. Reddish brown, marked with white spots, blotches, and stripes.
• **REMARK** Lamarck's name suggests a resemblance to the much larger group, the strombs.
• **HABITAT** Intertidal under rocks.

PANAMIC

strong teeth at middle of lip

convex side to outer lip

Range Gulf of California to Peru	Occurrence 🐚🐚🐚🐚	Size 3cm (1¼in)

Superfamily MURICOIDEA	Family Columbellidae	Species *Nitidella ocellata* Gmelin

WHITE-SPOTTED DOVE SHELL

A shiny shell, nearly smooth all over, with a very shallow suture; its body whorl is about the same height as its spire – which is sharply pointed in undamaged examples. A series of large, blunt teeth line the inside of the outer lip; the columella is quite smooth. Pale brown, with chocolate-brown spiral bands overlain with large, rounded, milky white spots.
• **REMARK** It is normal, and not at all harmful to the animal inside, for the apical whorls of this dove shell to be severely eroded.
• **HABITAT** Shallow water under rocks.

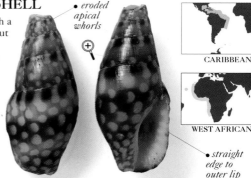

eroded apical whorls

CARIBBEAN

WEST AFRICAN

straight edge to outer lip

Range S.Florida, W. Indies, W. Africa, Canary Is.	Occurrence 🐚🐚🐚🐚	Size 1.2cm (½in)

WHELKS

MOST SHELLS of these cold-water species have a very capacious body whorl and a short, broad, siphonal canal. They vary in size, shape, and ornament. A thick periostracum covers the shell when fresh. Widely distributed in the northern hemisphere, whelk animals scavenge dead fish and other offal.

Superfamily MURICOIDEA	Family Buccinidae	Species *Buccinum zelotes* Dall

SUPERIOR BUCCINUM

Unusually tall-spired and boldly ornamented for a whelk, its well-rounded whorls are separated by a deep suture; the aperture is more than half the height of the body whorl. About five sharp-edged ribs encircle the later whorls, with additional, less prominent ones on the lower half of the body whorl. Dull white or yellowish.
• **REMARK** The name given by William Healey Dall implies that this species is handsomer than related whelks.
• **HABITAT** Deep water.

uppermost rib is strongest

JAPONIC

fine lattice ornament between ribs

thin flange around edge of outer lip

operculum

Range Japan	Occurrence 🐚🐚	Size 6cm (2½in)

Superfamily MURICOIDEA	Family Buccinidae	Species *Buccinum leucostoma* Lischke

YELLOW-LIPPED BUCCINUM

A thin shell, with well-rounded whorls; it has a deep suture and a spire that is about the same height as the inflated body whorl. The roundly angled outer lip is slightly reflected, as is the siphonal canal. Later whorls are encircled by three or four strong, rounded ribs and many fine riblets; these are crossed by fine, vertical growth lines. The spiral ribs become shiny when worn. White, tinged with yellow; the aperture is white.
• **REMARK** One of several similar whelks described from northern seas; the yellow lip suggested by the popular name is not obvious in these examples.
• **HABITAT** Moderately deep water.

equal spaces between the larger ribs

JAPONIC

spiral ribs shiny when worn

roundly angled outer lip

operculum

Range Japan	Occurrence 🐚🐚🐚	Size 7.5cm (3in)

Superfamily MURICOIDEA	Family Buccinidae	Species *Buccinum undatum* Linnaeus

COMMON NORTHERN WHELK

Thick, ovate shell with tall spire, swollen
body whorl, and impressed suture. Variable
in shape and ornament, it usually has
regularly spaced, low spiral ribs crossed by
finer, vertical growth ridges. Smooth
columella; short siphonal canal. Creamy
or greyish, sometimes with brown band at
suture and middle of body whorl; covered
in greenish periostracum when fresh.
• **REMARK** This species has been eaten
in N.W. Europe since prehistoric times.
Shell may have oblique folds; occurs
rarely with whorls reversed.
• **HABITAT** Sand offshore.

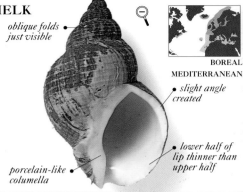

oblique folds
just visible

BOREAL
MEDITERRANEAN

• slight angle
created

• lower half of
lip thinner than
upper half

porcelain-like •
columella

Range N.E. United States, W. Europe	Occurrence 🐚🐚🐚🐚🐚	Size 7.5cm (3in)

Superfamily Muricoidea	Family Buccinidae	Species *Colus gracilis* Costa

SLENDER COLUS

This spindle-shaped shell has straight sides
and bulbous, almost flat-topped apex. Body
whorl is slightly longer than spire; all whorls
gently rounded; suture well impressed.
Narrow aperture descends from pointed top
to short, broad, strongly recurved siphonal
canal. Regularly spaced, low spiral ribs are
crossed by fine growth lines. Yellow-white,
with white aperture and columella.
• **REMARK** Yellowish brown periostracum
on fresh examples will flake off.
• **HABITAT** Sand or mud offshore.

BOREAL

• suture is
slightly
channelled

• operculum

• sharp-edged li,

Range N.W. Europe	Occurrence 🐚🐚🐚	Size 7cm (2¾in)

Superfamily MURICOIDEA	Family Buccinidae	Species *Volutharpa perryi* Jay

VELVETY BUCCINUM

Thin, fragile shell with globular body
whorl and short spire with flat-topped
apex. Very wide siphonal canal with
columella ending abruptly to one
side. Shallow suture. Smooth, with
faint spiral lines covered by a
velvety periostracum. Creamy,
streaked with brown; the
aperture is purplish brown.
• **REMARK** Paper-thin operculum is tiny or absent.
• **HABITAT** Offshore.

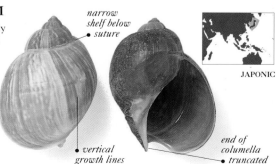

narrow
shelf below
• suture

JAPONIC

• vertical
growth lines

end of
columella
• truncated

Range Japan, Bering Sea	Occurrence 🐚🐚🐚	Size 4.5cm (1¾in)

NEPTUNES

THESE MEDIUM to large shells are found offshore in temperate or very cold waters of the northern hemisphere, some at great depths. Most are sombre in colour and are thick and heavy, with rounded whorls and a large aperture. Usually the siphonal canal is short, broad, and recurved. Most species have spiral ribs but some are smooth or have vertical folds or ridges. Many new species are nothing more than varieties of other common and variable members of the group. Most have a thin periostracum when fresh.

Superfamily MURICOIDEA	Family Buccinidae	Species *Neptunea tabulata* Baird

TABLED NEPTUNE

Thick, elongate shell with tall spire and slightly longer body whorl. Whorls have concave sides, topped by a broad shelf bearing a rampart-like, scaly ridge around its edge, features distinguishing it from all other neptunes. Elongate aperture ends in moderately long, wide, open siphonal canal; columella gently curved and smooth. Regular spiral ribs cover all whorls. Uniformly yellowish white colour.
• **REMARK** The name refers to the broad, flat shelf below the suture.
• **HABITAT** Deep water.

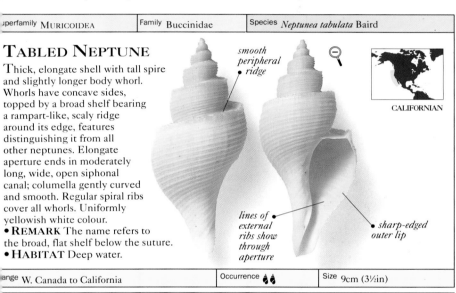

smooth peripheral ridge

CALIFORNIAN

lines of external ribs show through aperture

sharp-edged outer lip

Range W. Canada to California	Occurrence	Size 9cm (3½in)

Superfamily MURICOIDEA	Family Buccinidae	Species *Neptunea contraria* Linnaeus

LEFT-HANDED NEPTUNE

A thick, heavy shell with very rounded whorls which are coiled anti-clockwise; the body whorl is taller than the spire. Suture is impressed and apex well-rounded. Aperture long and narrow; columella gently curved and smooth; siphonal canal short. All whorls have regular spiral ribs which may be low or prominently raised. White or pale brown in colour; aperture white.
• **REMARK** The only neptune which is normally coiled in a left-handed spiral, occasionally it has been found with a right-handed spiral.
• **HABITAT** Offshore.

corneous operculum pointed at one end

MEDITERRANEAN

whorls may be more inflated than those shown here

siphonal canal gently curved

Range Mediterranean, E. Atlantic	Occurrence	Size 9cm (3½in)

Superfamily MURICOIDEA	Family Buccinidae	Species *Siphonalia trochulus* Reeve

HOOPED WHELK

A thick, tall-spired shell with an inflated body whorl. The elongate aperture ends in a broad, recurved siphonal canal. Spire whorls have low vertical folds; all whorls have regular spiral riblets. Brown with larger riblets white.
• **REMARK** Inside of outer lip and columella maybe purple.
• **HABITAT** Offshore.

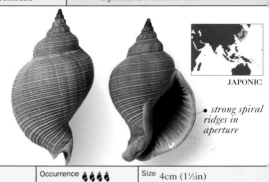

JAPONIC

strong spiral ridges in aperture

Range Japan	Occurrence ♦♦♦♦	Size 4cm (1½in)

Superfamily MURICOIDEA	Family Buccinidae	Species *Metula amosi* Vanatta

PINK METULA

Fairly thick, elongate shell with almost straight sides; body whorl over half the total height. Suture shallow, apex blunt. Aperture long and thin; columella smooth. Later whorls have vertical and spiral ribs, giving lattice effect. Brown, with whitish bands on body whorl.
• **REMARK** Distinctive narrow body whorl and lattice ornament.
• **HABITAT** Deep water.

PANAMIC

wrinkled edge to lip

elongate teeth just inside lip

Range Panama	Occurrence ♦♦	Size 4cm (1½in)

Superfamily MURICOIDEA	Family Buccinidae	Species *Kelletia kelleti* Forbes

KELLET'S WHELK

Thick, heavy, high-spired shell with large body whorl and finely incised, wavy suture. Apex is always eroded. Columella concave and smooth. Siphonal canal moderately long and broad; small umbilicus present. Sides are straight but for prominent vertical folds and knobs. Irregular spiral grooves cover all whorls; usually eroded on spire. Edge of outer lip has low serrations. Yellow-white; aperture and columella white.
• **REMARK** The only member of its genus now living; always looks worn and grubby.
• **HABITAT** Offshore.

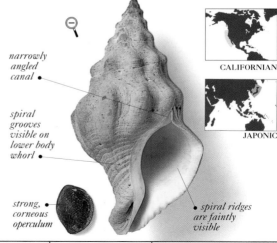

narrowly angled canal

spiral grooves visible on lower body whorl

strong, corneous operculum

CALIFORNIAN

JAPONIC

spiral ridges are faintly visible

Range California to Mexico, Japan	Occurrence ♦♦♦	Size 11cm (4½in)

Superfamily MURICOIDEA	Family Buccinidae	Species *Cominella adspersa* Bruguière

SPECKLED WHELK

A thick shell with short, pointed spire and large body whorl. Large aperture has a narrow canal at its upper corner and ends in a short, broad siphonal canal; concave, smooth columella. Umbilicus obscured by reflected columellar lip. Broad and low vertical ribs on spire whorls; strong spiral ribs on all whorls. Creamy yellow in colour , with rows of small brown squares.
• **REMARK** Unknown to scientists before Captain Cook's exploratory voyages in the 18th century.
• **HABITAT** Sand and rocks inshore.

body whorl angled at periphery

NEOZELANIC

upper half of whorl bowing outwards

oval outline to corneous operculum

Range New Zealand	Occurrence 🐾🐾🐾🐾	Size 5cm (2in)

Superfamily MURICOIDEA	Family Buccinidae	Species *Northia pristis* Deshayes

NORTH'S LONG WHELK

Thick, sturdy, high-spired shell with a large body whorl. The early whorls have strong vertical ribs crossed by fine spiral riblets; later whorls are smooth, except for growth lines. Below the shallow suture, the penultimate body whorls are angled sharply. Columella is straight and smooth; siphonal canal is short and broad. Brown or greenish brown; inside edge of outer lip and columella paler.
• **HABITAT** Shallow water.

PANAMIC

whorl bulges behind the outer lip

spiral ridges inside aperture

Range W. Mexico to Ecuador	Occurrence 🐾🐾🐾	Size 5cm (2in)

Superfamily MURICOIDEA	Family Buccinidae	Species *Burnupena cincta* Röding

GIRDLED BURNUPENA

Thick, high-spired shell with an elongate body whorl which has a broad channel above the shoulder, resulting in a narrow canal at top of aperture. The outer lip is thin; the columella gently curved and smooth. Broad, flat-topped spiral ribs cover all whorls. Brown, with paler vertical streaks; columella white; aperture white or violet.
• **REMARK** Surface features of fresh shells are completely covered by thick, rough periostracum.
• **HABITAT** Rock pools.

early whorls often encrusted

SOUTH AFRICAN

swelling at top of aperture

spiral grooves between ribs

operculum fills aperture

Range S. Africa	Occurrence 🐾🐾🐾🐾	Size 6cm (2½in)

Superfamily MURICOIDEA	Family Buccinidae	Species *Phos senticosus* Linnaeus

THORNY PHOS

A tall-spired shell, with an aperture more than
half the height of the large body whorl. About
twelve vertical ribs, some varix-like. Strong
ribs encircle whole shell producing sharp
points where they cross the vertical ribs.
Strong spiral ridges inside the aperture;
two to four indistinct folds at lower end
of columella. Cream or white, sometimes
pinkish, with brown spiral bands;
aperture white or lavender.
• **REMARK** As its name suggests,
this shell is prickly to the touch.
• **HABITAT** Shallow water on sand.

deep suture

INDO-PACIFIC

prickly-
edged ribs

short
siphonal canal

Range Tropical Pacific	Occurrence 🐚🐚	Size 3cm (1¼in)

Superfamily MURICOIDEA	Family Buccinidae	Species *Nassaria magnifica* Lischke

MAGNIFICENT PHOS

The whorls of this tall shell seem keeled because
each spire whorl has two rows of prominent,
vertically aligned nodules at the periphery. These
nodules are linked by low spiral ridges; there is
an extra row of nodules on the body whorl.
Rounded outer lip ends in a recurved siphonal
canal; columella is sinuous and smooth.
Cream, with pale brown spiral lines.
• **REMARK** This shell varies considerably
both in shape and in the strength and
arrangement of its surface features.
• **HABITAT** Offshore.

JAPONIC

pale brown
periostracum

sharp-edged
outer lip

operculum

Range S. Japan	Occurrence 🐚🐚	Size 4cm (1½in)

Superfamily MURICOIDEA	Family Buccinidae	Species *Buccinulum corneum* Linnaeus

SPINDLE EUTHRIA

A thick, heavy, elongate-oval shell, with body
whorl slightly longer than spire. The early whorls
have smooth, low tubercles, the remaining
whorls being smooth; a well-impressed suture
separates all whorls. The body whorl is roundly
angled at the shoulder and its lower half has
low spiral riblets. Thin-edged outer lip is
spirally ridged within. Cream, mottled and
lined with brown patterning.
• **REMARK** Most of the related species
come from New Zealand and elsewhere
in the southern hemisphere.
• **HABITAT** Offshore.

MEDITERRANEAN

deep canal
at top of
aperture

outer lip
edged with
brown
markings

Range Mediterranean	Occurrence 🐚🐚	Size 5cm (2in)

Superfamily MURICOIDEA	Family Buccinidae	Species *Pisania pusio* Linnaeus

SMALL TRITON-TRUMPET

A sturdy, spindle-shaped shell whose early whorls are almost straight-sided; its penultimate whorl and body whorl are gently rounded. Fine growth lines encircle the whole shell. The smooth columella has a downward-pointing fold at its lower end; there is a tooth at the top of the aperture. Purplish brown, marked with dark and light spots, blotches, and streaks.
• **REMARK** The popular name highlights the resemblance of this species to the large triton shells.
• **HABITAT** Near coral reefs.

beaded early whorls

CARIBBEAN

cluster of small teeth

weak spiral ridges within aperture

operculum

Range S.E. Florida to Brazil	Occurrence 🐚🐚🐚	Size 4cm (1½in)

Superfamily MURICOIDEA	Family Buccinidae	Species *Pisania truncata* Hinds

TRUNCATE PISANIA

When complete, this shell has a tall, pointed spire of about ten gently rounded whorls. Strong vertical ribs are topped by spiral rows of elongated ridges. There is a tooth at each end of the columella. Orange, with brown blotches and spiral white bands.
• **REMARK** Mature examples, such as those shown here, rarely retain early spire whorls.
• **HABITAT** Shallow water.

INDO-PACIFIC

teeth on inner side of outer lip

Range Tropical Pacific	Occurrence 🐚🐚	Size 2cm (¾in)

Superfamily MURICOIDEA	Family Buccinidae	Species *Macron aethiops* Reeve

DUSKY MACRON

This massive shell, which is remarkable for its thick periostracum, has a large body whorl and a comparatively short spire of about six whorls. The shell appears turreted because the later whorls are strongly shouldered and separated from each other by a deep and broad suture. A series of broad, flattened ribs encircles the whorls, which are separated from each other by deep, narrow grooves. The undulating edge of the outer lip shows these features in cross-section. By contrast, the inside of the aperture and the columella are smooth. Underneath the greenish brown periostracum, the shell is porcelain-white.
• **REMARK** The ribs, which vary in number and width, are sometimes absent altogether.
• **HABITAT** Intertidal.

CALIFORNIAN PANAMIC

small canal at top of aperture

operculum

narrow, deep siphonal canal

Range W. Mexico	Occurrence 🐚🐚🐚🐚	Size 6cm (2½in)

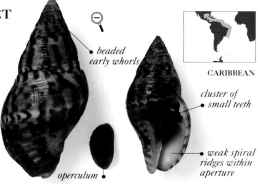

GOBLET WHELKS

T HIS GROUP of small to medium-sized solid shells is abundant in the shallow waters of tropical and warm seas, where it hides under rocks and dead coral. The well-rounded whorl usually have prominent vertical fold and strong spiral ribs. The margin of th shell's outer lip may be boldly coloured.

Superfamily MURICOIDEA	Family Buccinidae	Species *Canatharus undosus* Linnaeus

WAVED GOBLET

A sturdy shell with a fairly tall, almost straight-sided spire, a large body whorl with a thickened outer lip, and a short, broad siphonal canal. Spiral cords are especially conspicuous at widest part of body whorl; vertical grooves between ribs. Columella has folds. Fresh shells have a thick, brown periostracum. Whitish; purple-brown ribs.
• **HABITAT** Rocks and under coral.

INDO-PACIFIC

• *strong teeth inside outer lip*

• *edge of apertural lip bright orange*

Range Tropical Pacific	Occurrence 🐚🐚🐚🐚🐚	Size 3cm (1¼in)

Superfamily MURICOIDEA	Family Buccinidae	Species *Cantharus erythrostomus* Reeve

RED-MOUTH GOBLET

The spire of this solid shell is less than half the height of swollen body whorl. Upper half of outer lip thickened; concave columella has three or four folds. The suture is well impressed. Strong vertical folds on all whorls crossed by spiral ribs. A silky periostracum covers fresh examples. Yellowish brown, dark brown folds; aperture white, outer lip reddish.
• **HABITAT** Under stones and coral.

INDO-PACIFIC

• *teeth strongest on upper half of outer lip*

• *short, broad siphonal canal*

Range Tropical Pacific	Occurrence 🐚🐚🐚🐚	Size 4cm (1½in)

Superfamily MURICOIDEA	Family Buccinidae	Species *Solenosteira pallida* Broderip & Sowerb'

PALE GOBLET

A thick, biconic shell with strong shouldered body whorl. Concave columella; siphonal canal broad and recurved. Strong vertical folds, varying in strength and number, are pointed at periphery of whorls and crossed by broad, flat-topped ribs. Surface yellowish under a thick, pale-brown periostracum; aperture white.
• **HABITAT** Intertidal and offshore.

CALIFORNIAN
PANAMIC

• *upper half of body whorl slopes strongly*

Range California to Ecuador	Occurrence 🐚🐚🐚🐚	Size 4cm (1½in)

BABYLON SHELLS

T HIS SMALL GROUP has thick, glossy, often plump shells blotched with rown. The columella is smooth, the uter lip sharp-edged, and the siphonal canal short and broad. There is a thin, flexible, corneous operculum. Most species are from the tropical Indo-Pacific and live in shallow water on sand or mud.

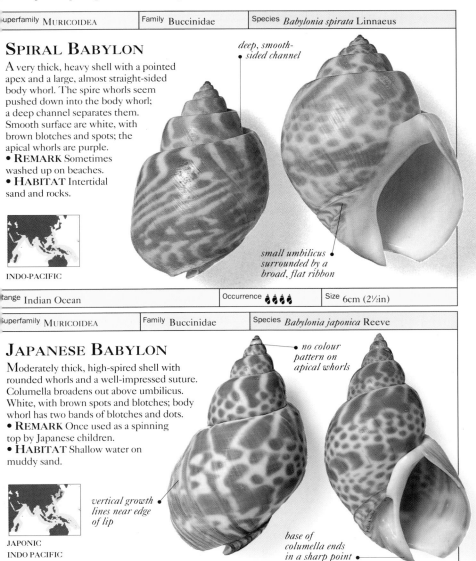

Superfamily MURICOIDEA	Family Buccinidae	Species *Babylonia spirata* Linnaeus

SPIRAL BABYLON

A very thick, heavy shell with a pointed apex and a large, almost straight-sided body whorl. The spire whorls seem pushed down into the body whorl; a deep channel separates them. Smooth surface are white, with brown blotches and spots; the apical whorls are purple.
• **REMARK** Sometimes washed up on beaches.
• **HABITAT** Intertidal sand and rocks.

INDO-PACIFIC

deep, smooth-sided channel

small umbilicus surrounded by a broad, flat ribbon

Range Indian Ocean	Occurrence 🐚🐚🐚🐚	Size 6cm (2½in)

Superfamily MURICOIDEA	Family Buccinidae	Species *Babylonia japonica* Reeve

JAPANESE BABYLON

Moderately thick, high-spired shell with rounded whorls and a well-impressed suture. Columella broadens out above umbilicus. White, with brown spots and blotches; body whorl has two bands of blotches and dots.
• **REMARK** Once used as a spinning top by Japanese children.
• **HABITAT** Shallow water on muddy sand.

JAPONIC
INDO PACIFIC

no colour pattern on apical whorls

vertical growth lines near edge of lip

base of columella ends in a sharp point

Range Japan, Taiwan	Occurrence 🐚🐚🐚🐚	Size 7cm (2¾in)

DWARF TRITONS

T HIS FAMILY of rock dwellers lives in warm seas and can be found between the tide lines. The swollen whorls of the elongate shells have thick varices and are boldly ornamented None of the few species is common Recent studies show that dwarf triton may belong to the family Fasciolariidae

Superfamily MURICOIDEA	Family Buccinidae	Species *Colubraria tortuosa* Reeve

TWISTED DWARF TRITON

Small, thick shell with a lop-sided spire, blunt apex, and shallow suture. The shell is slightly twisted about its axis, making later spire whorls lean over. The twisting is exaggerated by the irregular positioning of the varices. Whole shell is ornamented with spiral rows of square-sided pimples. White, with brown blotches; aperture white.
• **REMARK** Twisted spire is normal.
• **HABITAT** Rocks offshore.

early whorls are upright

INDO-PACIFIC

blunt teeth on outer lip

brown blotches arranged in spiral bands

narrow siphonal canal

Range W. Pacific	Occurrence 🐚🐚	Size 4cm (1½in)

Superfamily MURICOIDEA	Family Buccinidae	Species *Colubraria soverbii* Reeve

SOWERBY'S DWARF TRITON

A solid, tall-spired shell with gently rounded whorls and a pointed apex. Each whorl has two broad varices; the final one forms a thick edge to the outer lip, which is bluntly toothed on the inner side. The shallow suture is wavy at positions of varices. Sinuously curved columella, with minor folds at base. Narrow aperture has a canal at its upper corner. Vertical ribs crossed by fine, irregular spiral grooves produce rectangular pimples. Creamy, with pale and dark brown blotches and darker brown spiral bands; aperture golden yellow.
• **REMARK** The early whorls are slightly distorted.
• **HABITAT** Rocks offshore.

varix has conspicuous white bars

dull-coloured early whorls

fine brown spiral lines

INDO-PACIFIC

broad columellar shield

Range Philippines	Occurrence 🐚🐚	Size 5.7cm (2¼in)

MELON CONCHS

T HIS GROUP, represented in the shallow waters of tropical and temperate seas, includes some of the world's largest shells. Their apertures are capacious and siphonal canals long, while the whorls are smooth or spiny. Most species occur in brackish water, on mud or sand. All animals are carnivorous.

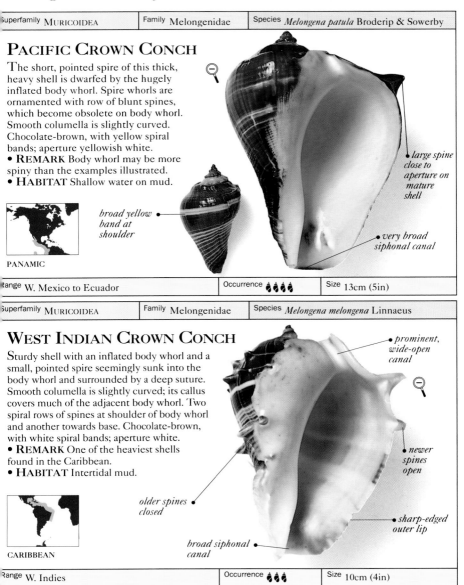

| Superfamily MURICOIDEA | Family Melongenidae | Species *Melongena patula* Broderip & Sowerby |

PACIFIC CROWN CONCH

The short, pointed spire of this thick, heavy shell is dwarfed by the hugely inflated body whorl. Spire whorls are ornamented with row of blunt spines, which become obsolete on body whorl. Smooth columella is slightly curved. Chocolate-brown, with yellow spiral bands; aperture yellowish white.
• **REMARK** Body whorl may be more spiny than the examples illustrated.
• **HABITAT** Shallow water on mud.

large spine close to aperture on mature shell

broad yellow band at shoulder

very broad siphonal canal

PANAMIC

| Range W. Mexico to Ecuador | Occurrence ♦♦♦♦ | Size 13cm (5in) |

| Superfamily MURICOIDEA | Family Melongenidae | Species *Melongena melongena* Linnaeus |

WEST INDIAN CROWN CONCH

Sturdy shell with an inflated body whorl and a small, pointed spire seemingly sunk into the body whorl and surrounded by a deep suture. Smooth columella is slightly curved; its callus covers much of the adjacent body whorl. Two spiral rows of spines at shoulder of body whorl and another towards base. Chocolate-brown, with white spiral bands; aperture white.
• **REMARK** One of the heaviest shells found in the Caribbean.
• **HABITAT** Intertidal mud.

prominent, wide-open canal

newer spines open

older spines closed

sharp-edged outer lip

broad siphonal canal

CARIBBEAN

| Range W. Indies | Occurrence ♦♦♦ | Size 10cm (4in) |

Superfamily MURICOIDEA	Family Melongenidae	Species *Pugilina morio* Linnaeus

GIANT MELONGENA

A heavy, tall-spired shell with a large body whorl and a long, open siphonal canal. Each spire whorl has an almost flat-sided lower half, and is prominently shouldered, then rises steeply to the suture, giving the spire a stepped appearance. Weak vertical growth ridges cover the shell with spiral ribs on all whorls. There are nodules at the shoulders, tending to become obsolete on the body whorl. The columella is smooth and straight. Chocolate-brown with a few yellowish spiral bands.
• **REMARK** Fresh examples are covered by thick green periostracum.
• **HABITAT** Mud, among mangroves.

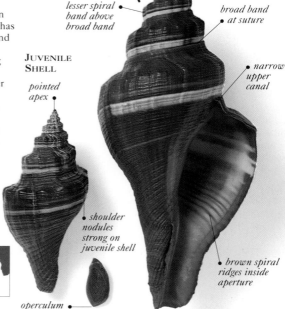

ADULT SHELL

lesser spiral band above broad band

broad band at suture

narrow upper canal

JUVENILE SHELL

pointed apex

shoulder nodules strong on juvenile shell

brown spiral ridges inside aperture

WEST AFRICA   CARIBBEAN

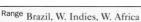

operculum

Range Brazil, W. Indies, W. Africa	Occurrence 🐚🐚🐚	Size 11cm (4½in)

Superfamily MURICOIDEA	Family Melongenidae	Species *Volema paradisiaca* Röding

PEAR MELONGENA

Thick, low-spired shell with a large body whorl. The whorls have a slightly concave upper half. The suture is well defined but shallow. There is a narrow canal at the top of the aperture. The columella is smooth and the aperture has faint spiral ridges. The shallow spiral grooves are crossed by fine growth lines. The colour is yellowish to reddish brown, sometimes spirally banded; the aperture is orange coloured.
• **REMARK** The animal lays its eggs in disc-shaped capsules strung together in a row.
• **HABITAT** Muddy or sandy flats.

INDO-PACIFIC

operculum

knobs may occur at shoulder

small umbilicus

Range Indian Ocean	Occurrence 🐚🐚🐚🐚	Size 5cm (2in)

BUSYCON WHELKS

T HERE are very few species and forms of busycon whelks; some of these are large, and two normally have a left-handed spiral. Most have a long siphonal canal and a smooth columella. They are limited to southeast Mexico and the eastern and southern coasts of the United States.

Superfamily MURICOIDEA	Family Melongenidae	Species *Busycon contrarium* Conrad

LIGHTNING WHELK

Moderately thick, left-handed shell with short, pointed spire, large body whorl, and long siphonal canal. Columella is smooth; spiral ridges in aperture. Spiral row of broad, pointed knobs occurs at shoulder of body whorl; spiral ribs on rest of shell. White, with greyish brown spiral bands and vertical streaks; aperture reddish brown with paler spiral ridges.
• **REMARK** May also occur without knobs at the shoulder.
• **HABITAT** Sand offshore.

TRANSATLANTIC

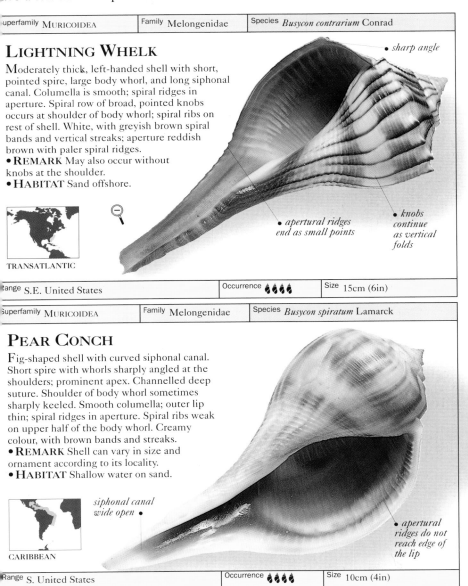

• *sharp angle*

• *apertural ridges end as small points*

• *knobs continue as vertical folds*

Range S.E. United States	Occurrence 🌢🌢🌢🌢	Size 15cm (6in)

Superfamily MURICOIDEA	Family Melongenidae	Species *Busycon spiratum* Lamarck

PEAR CONCH

Fig-shaped shell with curved siphonal canal. Short spire with whorls sharply angled at the shoulders; prominent apex. Channelled deep suture. Shoulder of body whorl sometimes sharply keeled. Smooth columella; outer lip thin; spiral ridges in aperture. Spiral ribs weak on upper half of the body whorl. Creamy colour, with brown bands and streaks.
• **REMARK** Shell can vary in size and ornament according to its locality.
• **HABITAT** Shallow water on sand.

siphonal canal wide open •

CARIBBEAN

• *apertural ridges do not reach edge of the lip*

Range S. United States	Occurrence 🌢🌢🌢🌢	Size 10cm (4in)

FALSE FUSUS SHELLS

T HE SHELLS in this group, though large, are very variable and the differences between species are blurred, so it is sometimes difficult to name them correctly. Most are elongate wit a high spire and long siphonal cana They occur in the offshore waters o Japan and south-east Asia.

Superfamily MURICOIDEA	Family Melongenidae	Species *Hemifusus colosseus* Lamarck

COLOSSAL FALSE FUSUS

A large, elongate shell, thick and strong, with a high spire about one third of the total height. Whorls are rounded and angulated at shoulder and constricted towards the suture. Long and narrow aperture ends in broad siphonal canal. Spiral ribs are crossed by weaker vertical growth ridges. White or creamy; aperture orange-pink.
• **REMARK** Can be used as a trumpet by breaking off apical whorls.
• **HABITAT** Offshore.

JAPONIC
INDO-PACIFIC

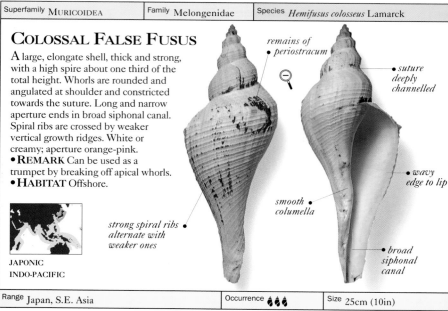

remains of periostracum

suture deeply channelled

wavy edge to lip

smooth columella

strong spiral ribs alternate with weaker ones

broad siphonal canal

Range Japan, S.E. Asia	Occurrence 🐚🐚🐚	Size 25cm (10in)

Superfamily MURICOIDEA	Family Melongenidae	Species *Hemifusus tuba* Gmelin

TUBA FALSE FUSUS

A large, heavy shell which varies considerably in size, shape, and ornament. The spire is broad and moderately high but less than one third of the total height. Columella and siphonal canal are smooth, glossy, and very straight. Strong and weak spiral ribs are crossed by fine, irregular growth ridges; shoulders of whorls are angular and sometimes developed into spiral ridges or rows of triangular knobs. Pinkish white; aperture pinkish with white edge.
• **REMARK** The fresh shell has a thick, soft, and velvety periostracum.
• **HABITAT** Offshore.

deep suture

JAPONIC

end of spiral keel

edge of lip is wrinkled where spiral ribs end

Range Japan	Occurrence 🐚🐚🐚	Size 15cm (6in)

Superfamily MURICOIDEA	Family Melongenidae	Species *Syrinx aruanus* Linnaeus

AUSTRALIAN TRUMPET

The world's largest gastropod, this shell has a very capacious body whorl and a long, solid siphonal canal. Whorls are strongly keeled or rounded; lower half of body whorl often has a second, less prominent keel; the suture is deep. The columella is smooth; the umbilicus has a deep slit; the outer lip is thin and often jagged. All whorls have weak spiral ribs of varying widths, crossed by weak vertical ridges. Column-like spire of embryonic shell is retained for a time on top of the juvenile, then breaks off. The shell's apricot colour is hidden by a thick, brown periostracum which is easily removed.

• **REMARK** In the central Pacific, this shell is used as a water carrier.

• **HABITAT** Intertidal flats.

INDO-PACIFIC

ADULT SHELL

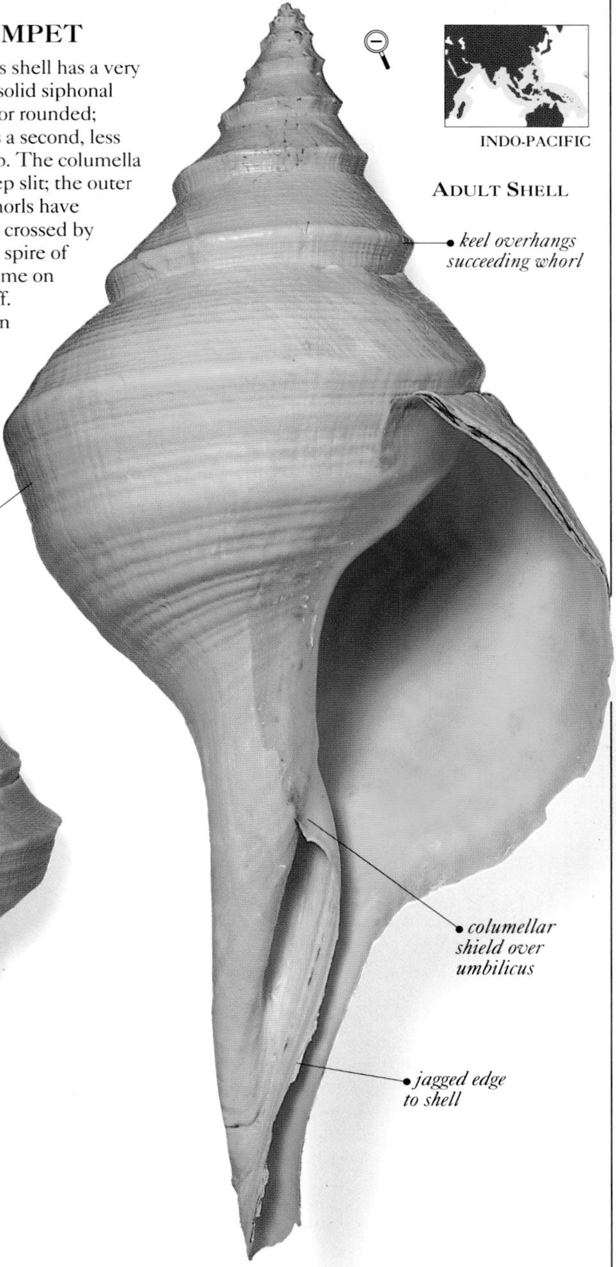

keel overhangs succeeding whorl

secondary keel

JUVENILE SHELL

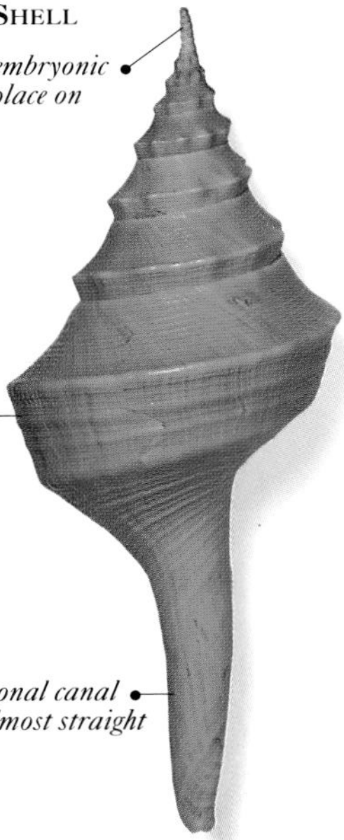

spire of embryonic shell in place on juvenile

whorls are concave either side of keel

siphonal canal is almost straight

columellar shield over umbilicus

jagged edge to shell

Range N. Australia, New Guinea	Occurrence	Size 75cm (30in)

BULLIAS

T HE ANIMALS of this shiny, smooth-shelled group are all blind, and scavenge for food in sandy places. The tall-spired shell frequently has a thick callus above the aperture and a thin corneous operculum. Bullias are well represented in the Indian Ocean and along the east coast of S. America.

Superfamily MURICOIDEA	Family Nassariidae	Species *Bullia mauritiana* Gray

MAURITIAN BULLIA

A tall, pointed shell; columella callused and smooth; siphonal canal short and broad. Each whorl angled at top with thick, smooth, spiral band just above the suture. Whorls have shallow grooves crossed by growth ridges. White, yellowish, or pinkish; aperture reddish brown.
• **REMARK** The spiral grooves are sometimes absent.
• **HABITAT** Intertidal sand.

INDO-PACIFIC

• *thick callus pad*

• *pale edge to lip*

Range Indian Ocean	Occurrence 🐚🐚🐚🐚	Size 5cm (2in)

Superfamily MURICOIDEA	Family Nassariidae	Species *Bullia callosa* Wood

CALLUSED BULLIA

A small, thick shell with variable callus thickening which modifies its shape considerably. Callus continues up the spire whorls as a thick rib above the suture. Smooth or vertically ribbed. Whitish to dark brown.
• **REMARK** Examples from S. Africa are usually more callused and fatter.
• **HABITAT** Shallow water on sand.

SOUTH AFRICAN

• *narrow canal just below callus*

Range S. Africa, N. Indian Ocean	Occurrence 🐚🐚🐚	Size 4cm (1½in)

Superfamily MURICOIDEA	Family Nassariddae	Species *Bullia tranquebarica* Röding

LINED BULLIA

Elongate shell with rounded, silky whorls. Columella and outer lip smooth; siphonal canal short and broad. Thick callus pad at top of aperture is continued on spire as a smooth, rounded rib above the suture. Spiral grooves strongest on body whorl. Greyish brown to pale brown, with vertical brown streaks.
• **REMARK** Fine vertical growth ridges are occasionally very thick on body whorl.
• **HABITAT** Intertidal sand.

narrow canal just below callus •

INDO-PACIFIC

• *strong kink at end of columella*

Range Indian Ocean	Occurrence 🐚🐚🐚🐚	Size 4cm (1½in)

NASSA MUD SNAILS

A N EXTREMELY LARGE and very widely distributed group of small species which scavenge for food in sandy and muddy places; it is well represented in the tropics. Many species show variation in size, ornament, and coloration. There are strong vertical ridges and spiral ribs.

Superfamily MURICOIDEA	Family Nassariidae	Species *Nassarius coronatus* Bruguière

CROWNED NASSA

The large, rounded body whorl of this glossy shell gives it a squat appearance. Outer lip is very thick; columella has a few folds and a broadly extended callus, thickest at base and top. Early whorls have vertical ridges; later whorls have faint spiral grooves with humps below the suture. Creamy or brownish, sometimes banded.
• **REMARK** The operculum has sharp points along one side.
• **HABITAT** Intertidal sand and mud flats.

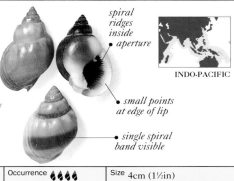

spiral ridges inside aperture

INDO-PACIFIC

small points at edge of lip

single spiral band visible

Range Tropical Indo-Pacific	Occurrence ♦♦♦	Size 4cm (1½in)

Superfamily MURICOIDEA	Family Nassariidae	Species *Nassarius dorsatus* Röding

CHANNELLED NASSA

A thick shell with silky surface. Its spire has almost straight sides and a sharp, vertically ridged apex (missing from illustrated specimens). Columella has weak folds; inside of outer lip is ridged. Blue, greyish green, or brown; aperture purplish brown, edge of outer lip white.
• **HABITAT** Shallow water on sand.

INDO-PACIFIC

sharp points at lower edge of outer lip

Range N. Australia	Occurrence ♦♦♦	Size 3cm (1¼in)

Superfamily MURICOIDEA	Family Nassariidae	Species *Nassarius reticulatus* Linnaeus

NETTED NASSA

This thick, high-spired shell has almost straight sides and varies in ornamentation. Vertical folds crossed by low spiral ridges produce a lattice pattern or beaded folds. Callus projects above aperture. Columella has small folds at base. Sand-coloured; occasional brown bands; aperture white.
• **REMARK** Colour resembles sand in which animal dwells.
• **HABITAT** Sand offshore.

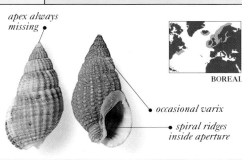

apex always missing

BOREAL

occasional varix

spiral ridges inside aperture

Range W. Europe, Mediterranean	Occurrence ♦♦♦♦	Size 2.5cm (1in)

Superfamily MURICOIDEA	Family Nassariidae	Species *Nassarius trivittatus* Say

NEW ENGLAND NASSA

A thin, ovate, high-spired shell
with stepped whorls. The apex is
smooth but the rest of the shell is
ornamented with strong vertical
ridges crossed by deep grooves,
producing a lattice appearance.
Below suture, the whorls have a flat ramp.
Aperture has distinct spiral ridges inside.
Yellowish, with reddish bands.
• **HABITAT** Shallow water.

lattice ornament begins here

top of whorl has beaded appearance

TRANSATLANTIC

apertural ridges absent from this immature specimen

Range E. United States	Occurrence 🐚🐚🐚🐚	Size 2cm (¾in)

Superfamily MURICOIDEA	Family Nassariidae	Species *Nassarius fossatus* Gould

GIANT WESTERN NASSA

A high-spired shell with smooth apex;
body whorl is about same height as
spire. Upper corner of aperture is
constricted by in-turned outer lip.
Early whorls have rows of evenly
spaced beads; later whorls have
oblique vertical folds and lesser
spiral ribs. Spiral groove at body
whorl base. Shades of brown.
• **REMARK** Largest nassa
mud snail on the Pacific coast
of N. America.
• **HABITAT** Intertidal mud
and sand.

channelled suture

CALIFORNIAN

folds on columella

tubercles in aperture

Range W. United States	Occurrence 🐚🐚🐚🐚	Size 4cm (1½in)

Superfamily MURICOIDEA	Family Nassariidae	Species *Nassarius arcularius* Linnaeus

CASKET NASSA

A thick, fat shell best viewed dorsally
because of the extensive callus around
the aperture. Spire varies, and can be
low or high; the apex is smooth, but all
later whorls have thick vertical folds
which may have prominent, rounded
tubercles at the shoulder. Strong spiral
grooves at base of the body whorl. There
is a massive callus around aperture.
Creamy, silver greyish, or pale brown,
with occasional brown spot markings.
• **REMARK** Thin, brown operculum
has serrations along one side.
• **HABITAT** Inshore sand and mud.

edge of whorl is flat-topped

INDO-PACIFIC

spiral ridges in the aperture

brown spots between the vertical folds

Range E. Indian Ocean, Pacific	Occurrence 🐚🐚🐚🐚	Size 3cm (1¼in)

Superfamily MURICOIDEA	Family Nassariidae	Species *Nassarius distortus* A. Adams

NECKLACE NASSA

A glossy shell whose body whorl is about the same height as its spire. The columella is smooth; the aperture has a rounded tooth at the top. All the whorls have strong folds. Whitish; greenish brown spiral bands; columella and outer lip white.
• **REMARK** A few short spines at edge of outer lip.
• **HABITAT** Shallow water on sand.

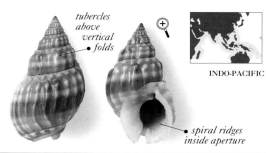

tubercles above vertical folds

INDO-PACIFIC

spiral ridges inside aperture

Range E. Indian Ocean, Pacific	Occurrence 🐚🐚🐚🐚	Size 2.5cm (1in)

Superfamily MURICOIDEA	Family Nassariidae	Species *Nassarius glans* Linnaeus

GLANS NASSA

A tall-spired, glossy shell with well-rounded whorls and a short, broad siphonal canal. The suture is well impressed; the columella is smooth and straight. Shell's aperture has distinct canal at upper corner; its outer lip has widely spaced points. Early whorls have vertical ribs crossed by fine spiral ridges. Cream, with brown blotches and thin, dark brown spiral lines.
• **REMARK** The outer lip of the left-hand specimen is not completely developed.
• **HABITAT** Offshore, intertidal.

purple apex

INDO-PACIFIC

brown lines show through the aperture

lip edge not fully developed

points at edge of the aperture

Range Tropical Indo-Pacific	Occurrence 🐚🐚🐚	Size 4.5cm (1¾in)

Superfamily MURICOIDEA	Family Nassariidae	Species *Nassarius papillosus* Linnaeus

PIMPLED NASSA

A thick, heavy, high-spired shell with straight sides, well-impressed suture, and pointed apex; body whorl slightly more than half total height. Columella smooth; outer lip has sharp points; distinct canal in upper corner of aperture. All whorls have spiral rows of large tubercles covered by a thin callus on apertural side. Cream, blotched with a sandy colour, darkening to a brown.
• **REMARK** The operculum has a ragged, toothed edge.
• **HABITAT** Sand under coral.

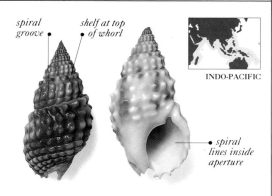

spiral groove

shelf at top of whorl

INDO-PACIFIC

spiral lines inside aperture

Range Tropical Indo-Pacific	Occurrence 🐚🐚🐚	Size 4.5cm (1¾in)

Superfamily MURICOIDEA	Family Nassariidae	Species *Nassarius marmoreus* A. Adams

MARBLED NASSA

A high-spired, glossy shell with rounded apex and whorls. The body whorl is more than half the shell's total height and the aperture about half the height of the body whorl; suture is moderately impressed. The smooth columella with transparent callus is truncated just above the siphonal canal. Early whorls have vertical riblets; later whorls smooth except for fine growth lines and a few spiral grooves at base. Elongated teeth inside outer lip. White or pale violet, with greyish brown or purplish dots.
• **HABITAT** Offshore and intertidal.

healed break

INDO-PACIFIC

narrow canal at upper corner of aperture

sharp-edged outer lip

Range N. Indian Ocean	Occurrence 🐚🐚🐚	Size 3cm (1¼in)

Superfamily MURICOIDEA	Family Nassariidae	Species *Ilyanassa obsoleta* Say

EASTERN MUD SNAIL

This thick, squat shell is usually eroded. Whorls well rounded; suture well impressed. Columella is smooth with distinctive spiral ridge at base. Weak vertical folds crossed by weak spiral grooves. Reddish or brown, occasionally with whitish spiral band.
• **REMARK** Usually covered by mud and algae.
• **HABITAT** Mud flats.

TRANSATLANTIC BOREAL (U.S.)

mended break

broad siphonal canal

Range E. and W. United States	Occurrence 🐚🐚🐚🐚🐚	Size 2.5cm (1in)

Superfamily MURICOIDEA	Family Nassariidae	Species *Demoulia ventricosa* Lamarck

BLUNT DEMOULIA

Lightweight shell; spire looks pushed down into body whorl. Apical whorls pointed (usually broken off); penultimate whorl almost straight-sided, like body whorl, which is taller than the spire; suture very deep. The small aperture narrows at its upper end into a deep canal. Columella smooth. Shallow spiral grooves on all whorls. White, reddish or brown blotches and dashes; aperture white.
• **REMARK** Difficult to find mature examples with apex intact.
• **HABITAT** Sand offshore.

suture above body whorl slopes steeply downwards

SOUTH AFRICAN

spiral ridges in aperture

Range S. Africa	Occurrence 🐚🐚🐚🐚	Size 2.5cm (1in)

HORSE CONCHS

THESE HEAVY SHELLS include some of the world's largest gastropods. They are high-spired, have a smooth columella, a long siphonal canal, and a thick and corneous operculum. When fresh, they have a thick, brown periostracum. The animals are carnivorous and mainly consume other molluscs.

Superfamily MURICOIDEA	Family Fasciolariidae	Species *Pleuroploca trapezium* Linnaeus

TRAPEZIUM HORSE CONCH

Tall-spired shell with large body whorl; apex usually eroded. Shallow suture; large aperture; columella smooth. Spiral rows of large tubercles at periphery of spire whorls and shoulder of body whorl; spiral lines are arranged in pairs. Strong growth ridges; occasional mended breaks. Reddish and cream.
• **REMARK** Best-known member of group.
• **HABITAT** Shallow water near coral.

INDO-PACIFIC

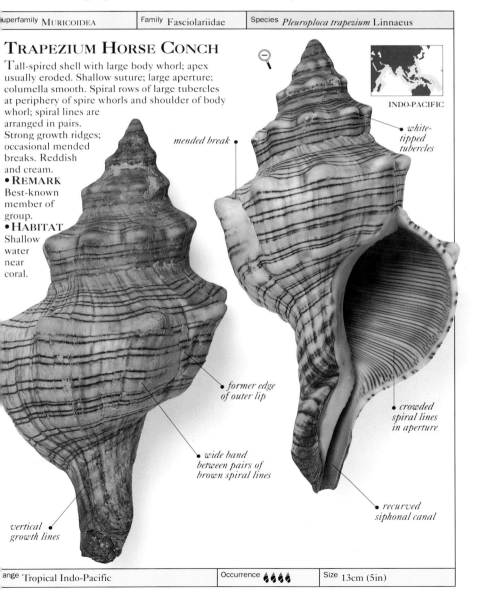

mended break

white-tipped tubercles

former edge of outer lip

wide band between pairs of brown spiral lines

crowded spiral lines in aperture

vertical growth lines

recurved siphonal canal

Range Tropical Indo-Pacific	Occurrence 🌢🌢🌢🌢	Size 13cm (5in)

TULIP SHELLS

T HE FEW SPECIES in this group of shells include some attractively patterned varieties. They may have a long or a short siphonal canal. A thick, corneous operculum is present. Tulip shells are limited to shallow and deeper waters in the Gulf of Mexico and the east coast of the United States

Superfamily MURICOIDEA	Family Fasciolariidae	Species *Fasciolaria tulipa* Linnaeus

TRUE TULIP

This high-spired shell is consistently spindle-shaped, with well-rounded whorls, a pointed apex, and a long siphonal canal. The suture is shallow and puckered; the colu-mella is smooth and gently curved. The broad columellar callus is usually thin and transparent. Spiral grooves are weak except just below the suture and at the base; irregular vertical growth lines. White or pink in colour, with brown blotches and dashes forming three or four bands on the body whorl; edge of the aperture reddish orange.
• **REMARK** Examples twice as long as the average have been found. A bright orange variety is sometimes fished up.
• **HABITAT** Shallow water and offshore.

edge of callus

CARIBBEAN

sharp points to edge of outer lip

fine spiral lines inside aperture

inconspicuous fold at base of columella

dark brown inside siphonal canal

Range S. United States, W. Indies, Brazil	Occurrence 🌢🌢🌢	Size 13cm (5in)

Superfamily MURICOIDEA	Family Fasciolariidae	Species *Fasciolaria lilium* G. Fischer

BANDED TULIP

The spire of this shell is much shorter than the inflated body whorl; siphonal canal short and broad. Smooth from top to bottom, except for low spiral ridges at base. Little columella callus. Dull yellow, with greyish streaks; thin, brown spiral lines on body whorl.
• **REMARK** There are several named forms of this shell.
• **HABITAT** Sand and rocks.

rounded apex

spire whorls are entirely smooth

TRANSATLANTIC
CARIBBEAN

siphonal canal without spiral brown lines

Range E. and S. United States	Occurrence 🌢🌢🌢	Size 9cm (3½in)

LATIRUS SHELLS

MEMBERS OF THIS LARGE group have small, solid, elongate shells rna- mented with tubercles or knobs spiral rows. Some are brightly pat- terned. The columella often has folds at its base. The animals prey on various invertebrates and hide among rocks and corals in warm tropical seas.

uperfamily MURICOIDEA	Family Fasciolariidae	Species *Latirus belcheri* Reeve

BELCHER'S LATIRUS

This biconic shell has a high spire and a long, slightly recurved siphonal canal. The columella has three or four folds; outer lip has two sharp angles. Spire whorls have spiral row of large tubercles above suture; two rows of tubercles and low spiral ribson body whorl. White with brown or black blotches and spots.
• **REMARK** Named after Sir Edward Belcher, a keen shell collector.
• **HABITAT** Offshore.

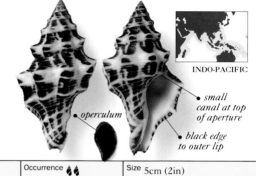

INDO-PACIFIC

operculum

• *small canal at top of aperture*

• *black edge to outer lip*

ange W. Pacific	Occurrence	Size 5cm (2in)

uperfamily MURICOIDEA	Family Fasciolariidae	Species *Latirus cariniferus* Lamarck

TROCHLEAR LATIRUS

A high-spired shell with a broad siphonal canal. Its aperture is small in relation to the body whorl. The suture is shallow; the columella is straight. Vertical ribs are prominent at shoulder of body whorl; widely spaced spiral riblets connect ribs. Creamy or yellowish brown, with brown blotches or stripes between ribs.
• **HABITAT** Coral and rocks.

early whorls lack brown markings

CARIBBEAN

• *outer lip and siphonal canal not fully developed*

ange W. Indies S. United States	Occurrence	Size 5cm (2in)

uperfamily MURICOIDEA	Family Fasciolariidae	Species *Latirus mediamericanus* Hertlein & Strong

CENTRAL AMERICAN LATIRUS

High-spired shell with long straight siphonal canal. Wavy suture well impressed; apex usually eroded. Aperture small in relation to body whorl; widely spaced spiral ridges inside. Columella has three or four folds. Yellowish brown; aperture white.
• **REMARK** A thick, brown periostracum is found on fresh specimens.
• **HABITAT** Offshore.

spiral riblets on siphonal canal •

PANAMIC

• *small tooth at top of aperture*

ange W. Mexico to Ecuador	Occurrence	Size 6cm (2½in)

Superfamily MURICOIDEA	Family Fasciolariidae	Species *Latirus infundibulum* Gmelin

BROWN-LINED LATIRUS

A very thick, elongate, high-spired shell with a long, straight siphonal canal and a funnel-shaped umbilicus. The suture is shallow. Thick, bulging vertical nodules occur in alternating positions on all the whorls. Crossing all of these nodules are a series of well-defined, sharp-edged spiral riblets; each spire whorl has three or four strong riblets and two or three minor ones. There are three inconspicuous folds on the columella. The shell is pale brown in colour, with darker brown spiral riblets; the aperture is white.
• **REMARK** Umbilicus may be broader than in illustrated example of the shell.
• **HABITAT** Shallow water.

CARIBBEAN

small tooth at top of aperture

blunt teeth on outer lip

Range W. Indies to Brazil, S. Florida	Occurrence 🐚🐚	Size 7.5cm (3in)

Superfamily MURICOIDEA	Family Fasciolariidae	Species *Latirus gibbulus* Gmelin

HUMPED LATIRUS

Heavy, thick, high-spired shell with shallow suture and moderately long, broad siphonal canal. Elongate aperture; outer lip thin, with small teeth. Smooth columella ; small umbilicus. Large, low tubercles crossed by low spiral ribs. Brownish orange with dark brown spiral ribs; aperture pinkish orange.
• **REMARK** Shells often encrusted with algae and coral.
• **HABITAT** Near coral reefs.

operculum is sharply pointed

INDO-PACIFIC

body whorl constricted at suture

small canal at top of aperture

teeth not yet developed on outer lip

Range Indo-W. Pacific	Occurrence 🐚🐚	Size 7.5cm (3in)

Superfamily MURICOIDEA	Family Fasciolariidae	Species *Opeatostoma pseudodon* Burrow

THORN LATIRUS

A solid, squat shell with a moderately low spire and inflated body whorl. Outer lip, angled at the top, bears either a short or long spine at bottom. The strongly curved columella has two or three folds. Low spiral ribs are present on all whorls. White, with black and brown spiral bands; aperture white.
• **HABITAT** Rocks offshore.

PANAMIC

thick periostracum covers shell

operculum

short, broad siphonal canal

Range W. Mexico to Peru	Occurrence 🐚🐚🐚🐚	Size 4cm (1½in)

Superfamily MURICOIDEA	Family Fasciolariidae	Species *Peristernia nassatula* Lamarck

FINE-NET PERISTERNIA

A solid, moderately high-spired shell whose
aperture ends in a short siphonal canal.
The whorls are almost straight sided; the
suture impressed. Strongly curved
columella; slight angulation of the outer
lip corresponds with the shoulder of the
body whorl. Broad, low, vertical folds on
all the whorls, crossed by crowded
spiral ribs. Rose-pink or brown; white
folds; aperture light purple.
• **REMARK** There is often evidence
of mended breaks on these shells,
which are usually encrusted with coral.
• **HABITAT** Coral reefs.

*sharply
pointed apex*

INDO-PACIFIC

*canal at top
of aperture*

*inconspicuous
folds at base of
columella*

mended breaks

Range Tropical Pacific	Occurrence 🐚🐚🐚🐚	Size 3.5cm (1¼in)

Superfamily MURICOIDEA	Family Fasciolariidae	Species *Peristernia philberti* Récluz

PHILBERT'S PERISTERNIA

The moderately tall spire of this elegant shell is
less than half the total height. Aperture ends in
a short, broad siphonal canal; umbilicus is a mere
chink. Thick vertical folds are crossed by strong,
crowded spiral ribs; ribs are bluntly pointed and
slightly upturned at periphery of body whorl,
where they cross folds. Reddish brown,
with alternate, thin, black-and-white bands
at periphery of whorls; aperture violet.
• **REMARK** The black-and-white spiral bands
against the reddish brown background makes this
one of the most striking shells in its group.
• **HABITAT** Near coral reefs.

*ornament
eroded on
early whorls*

INDO-PACIFIC

*teeth inside
outer lip*

*inconspicuous
folds at base of
columella*

Range S. China Sea, Philippines	Occurrence 🐚🐚	Size 3cm (1¼in)

Superfamily MURICOIDEA	Family Fasciolariidae	Species *Leucozonia ocellata* Gmelin

WHITE-SPOTTED LATIRUS

A small, biconic shell with short, broad
siphonal canal and shallow suture. There
is a spiral row of humps on spire. On the
lower half of the body whorl there is a
secondary row of humps. These humps
may be crossed by spiral ribs. A few
blunt teeth are present on the outer
lip. Dark brown or black; white humps;
edge of outer lip dark brown; columella
flushed violet; aperture white.
• **HABITAT** Intertidal rocks.

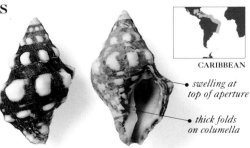

CARIBBEAN

*swelling at
top of aperture*

*thick folds
on columella*

Range S.E. Florida, W. Indies to Brazil	Occurrence 🐚🐚🐚🐚	Size 2cm (¾in)

SPINDLES

SPINDLE-SHAPED APTLY describes the elegant shells of most of the species in this extensive group. All are elongate, with a many-whorled spire, a straight, long siphonal canal, and a smooth columella. Ornamental features include strong tubercles and vertical folds; spiral ribs, and spiral ridges inside the aperture. A few species are long, thick, and heavy. Some have a left-handed spiral. All have a corneous operculum with a nucleus at one end. The carnivorous animals live in warm seas among rocks and coral debris.

Superfamily MURICOIDEA	Family Fasciolariidae	Species *Fusinus salisburyi* Fulton

SALISBURY'S SPINDLE

Large, solid shell with spire about same length as siphonal canal; deep suture. Vertical folds on early whorls become shorter and bluntly pointed on later whorls. Spiral ridges on all whorls. Aperture ovate; columella has distinct rim and a few folds; edge of outer lip and along siphonal canal serrated. Small, deep umbilicus. Thick, yellowish periostracum when fresh.
• **REMARK** Named after British conchologist, Albert Salisbury.
• **HABITAT** Deep water.

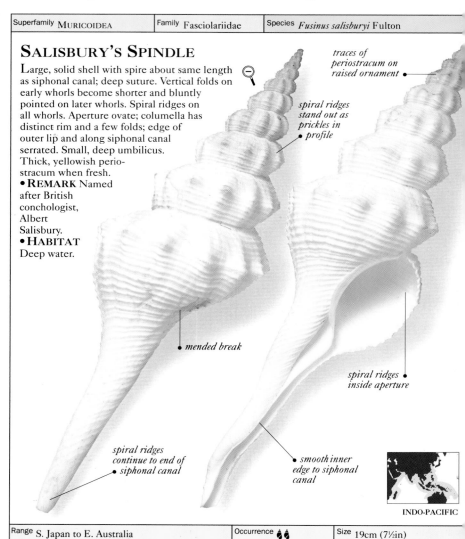

traces of periostracum on raised ornament

spiral ridges stand out as prickles in profile

mended break

spiral ridges inside aperture

spiral ridges continue to end of siphonal canal

smooth inner edge to siphonal canal

INDO-PACIFIC

Range S. Japan to E. Australia	Occurrence	Size 19cm (7½in)

Superfamily MURICOIDEA	Family Fasciolariidae	Species *Fusinus dupetitthouarsi* Kiener

DU PETIT'S SPINDLE

This long, solid shell has a spire which is slightly longer than the siphonal canal, a deep suture and an aperture longer than it is broad. The early whorls are narrow and ornamented with very thick vertical ribs; on succeeding whorls the ribs start to diminish sometimes becoming obsolete. All the whorls have spiral ridges which are sharp-edged on the lower whorls and most developed at the periphery, where they sometimes have several nodular swellings. The aperture leads into a broad, open, and occasionally sinuous siphonal canal. The columella is smooth except for the impression of spiral ridges. The shell is white in colour, with occasional pale or light brown-coloured streaks.
• **REMARK** Covered with a greenish brown periostracum when fresh.
• **HABITAT** Intertidal and offshore.

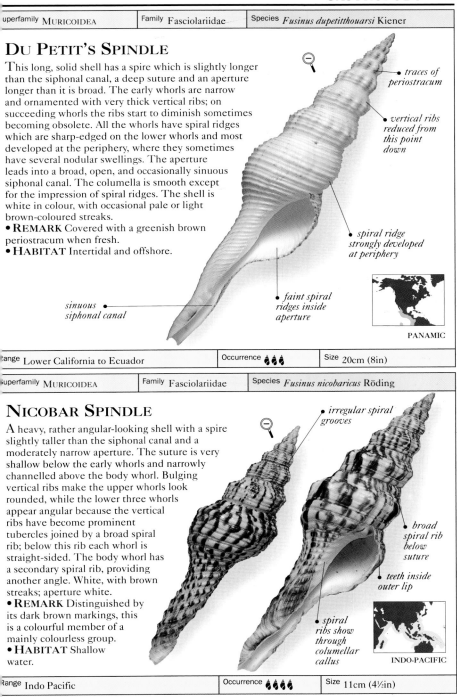

traces of periostracum

vertical ribs reduced from this point down

spiral ridge strongly developed at periphery

sinuous siphonal canal

faint spiral ridges inside aperture

PANAMIC

Range Lower California to Ecuador	Occurrence	Size 20cm (8in)

Superfamily MURICOIDEA	Family Fasciolariidae	Species *Fusinus nicobaricus* Röding

NICOBAR SPINDLE

A heavy, rather angular-looking shell with a spire slightly taller than the siphonal canal and a moderately narrow aperture. The suture is very shallow below the early whorls and narrowly channelled above the body whorl. Bulging vertical ribs make the upper whorls look rounded, while the lower three whorls appear angular because the vertical ribs have become prominent tubercles joined by a broad spiral rib; below this rib each whorl is straight-sided. The body whorl has a secondary spiral rib, providing another angle. White, with brown streaks; aperture white.
• **REMARK** Distinguished by its dark brown markings, this is a colourful member of a mainly colourless group.
• **HABITAT** Shallow water.

irregular spiral grooves

broad spiral rib below suture

teeth inside outer lip

spiral ribs show through columellar callus

INDO-PACIFIC

Range Indo Pacific	Occurrence	Size 11cm (4½in)

Superfamily MURICOIDEA	Family Fasciolariidae	Species *Fusinus colus* Linnaeus

DISTAFF SPINDLE

A solid shell reminiscent of a pagoda, with the first seven or eight very narrow whorls bearing strong vertical ribs. The later, more expansive whorls are angled at the periphery, where the ribs become bluntly pointed tubercles. Spiral grooves cover all whorls, deeply incised on lower half of body whorl; suture is well impressed. Aperture is moderately large; columella is straight or gently sinuous. White, with brown dots between vertical ribs, brown blotches between tubercles, and traces of brown may be visible on edges of siphonal canal and outer lip.
• **REMARK** A taller, more slender form occurs in which the later rows of nodules are subdued or absent.
• **HABITAT** Intertidal and offshore.

vertical ribs on the early whorls are aligned

spiral ridges inside aperture

thin edge of columellar lip

body-whorl ridges show through to columella

strong spiral rib below tubercles

INDO-PACIFIC

Range Tropical Pacific	Occurrence 🐚🐚🐚	Size 13cm (5in)

Superfamily MURICOIDEA	Family Fasciolariidae	Species *Sinistralia gallagheri* Smythe & Chatfiel

GALLAGHER'S SPINDLE

This thick shell has a left-handed spire less than half the shell's total height. Shallow suture. The aperture is narrow and rather small, its base ending in a short, broad, oblique siphonal canal; the inside of the outer lip is smooth. There is a spiral row of large nodules at the periphery of each whorl; indistinct spiral ridges on all whorls. The shell is dark brown in colour, with white nodules and base.
• **REMARK** One of several unusual shells from the small island of Masirah off the coast of Oman.
• **HABITAT** Rocks and coral.

apex smooth and round

INDO-PACIFIC

upper part of nodules tinged with yellow

purple-brown inside aperture

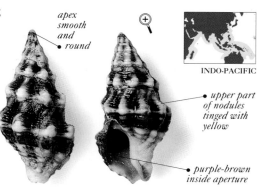

Range Masirah Island, Oman	Occurrence 🐚🐚	Size 2cm (¾in)

OLIVE SHELLS

T HE SHELLS of this sand-dwelling group of carnivorous molluscs ow a variety of colour and pattern, ut a uniformity of shape and orna- ent. Each has a short spire with a annelled suture, long aperture, and callused columella with prominent folds. The smooth surface results from the animal virtually polishing its shell with expanded fleshy lobes. There is no periostracum or operculum. They are widely distributed in tropical seas.

Superfamily MURICOIDEA	Family Olividae	Species *Oliva annulata* Gmelin

AMETHYST OLIVE

A thick, glossy shell with a moderately elevated, conical spire, a deeply channelled suture, slightly convex sides, and a broad siphonal notch. Thick outer lip. Strong folds on columella lengthen towards base. Colour and pattern variable, often yellowish pink with brownish spots.
• **REMARK** These examples have a noticeably angled shoulder.
• **HABITAT** Shallow water on sand.

INDO-PACIFIC

orange aperture

straight inside edge to outer lip

Range Tropical Indo-Pacific	Occurrence ♦♦♦♦	Size 4cm (1½in)

Superfamily MURICOIDEA	Family Olividae	Species *Oliva bulbosa* Röding

INFLATED OLIVE

A low-spired shell with thick callus bordering deep suture. Another callus extends obliquely downwards from columella. Creamy, golden, grey, or nearly black, with brownish or greyish streaks, zigzags, and blotches.
• **REMARK** Older shells are in- variably heavier and more swollen.
• **HABITAT** Sand at low tide.

INDO-PACIFIC

small folds on columella

Range Tropical Indo-Pacific	Occurrence ♦♦♦♦	Size 4cm (1½in)

Superfamily MURICOIDEA	Family Olividae	Species *Oliva oliva* Linnaeus

COMMON OLIVE

Small, elongate shell with short spire. A thick callus borders the deep suture. Columella has small, flat-topped folds; callus extends downwards from columella along edge of outer lip. Creamy to brown; variously patterned.
• **REMARK** The identity of this endlessly varied species long puzzled specialists.
• **HABITAT** Intertidal sand.

INDO-PACIFIC

aperture usually brown

Range Tropical Indo-Pacific	Occurrence ♦♦♦♦	Size 3cm (1¼in)

Superfamily MURICOIDEA	Family Olividae	Species *Oliva porphyria* Linnaeus

TENT OLIVE

This impressive, heavy, low-spired shell is easily the largest of all the olives. It has a deeply channelled suture and broad siphonal notch. The pointed apex is almost as tall as the rest of the spire. Viewed from the side, the outer lip appears to be slightly concave, a feature unique among olive shells. The shell has a very thick columellar callus running almost the entire height of the body whorl, with folds all along its length and projecting slightly at the top of the aperture. The columellar callus continues obliquely downwards and partially covers a thinner, broader, oblique callus. Thin, angular lines forming ranks of overlapping triangles on the shell are superimposed on a violet-pink ground colour.

• **REMARK** This shell gets its name from the assemblage of tent-like markings, the fortuitous result of the animal secreting pigments at the edge of its outer lip throughout its growing period.

• **HABITAT** Intertidal sand.

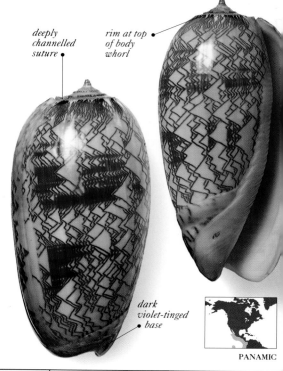

deeply channelled suture

rim at top of body whorl

dark violet-tinged base

PANAMIC

Range Gulf of California to Panama	Occurrence ♦♦♦	Size 9cm (3½in)

Superfamily MURICOIDEA	Family Olividae	Species *Oliva sayana* Ravenel

LETTERED OLIVE

A solid, elongated, almost straight-sided shell with a moderately elevated spire. Deeply channelled suture bordered by a thick callus. The columella has many folds along its length; columellar callus continues downwards and sometimes along edge of outer lip; it partially conceals a broader, thinner callus. Pale brown, tinged with yellow, variegated with dark brown streaks and two bands of zigzags.

• **REMARK** The name stems from the fancied resemblance of the markings to letters of the alphabet; a golden-yellow form occurring rarely off the coast of Florida is prized by collectors.

• **HABITAT** Intertidal sand.

TRANSATLANTIC
CARIBBEAN

violet inside aperture

long folds

Range S.E. United States, Caribbean	Occurrence ♦♦♦♦	Size 5cm (2in)

Superfamily MURICOIDEA	Family Olividae	Species *Oliva incrassata* Lightfoot

ANGLED OLIVE

This low-spired shell is the heaviest of the olives; upper third of body whorl moderately or strongly angled. Spire thickly callused; narrow, deep suture. Outer lip very thick. Thickly callused columella has wide spaced, thin folds. Greyish in colour, with dark spots and zigzag scribbles; aperture and columella rosy or pink.
• **REMARK** Occurs very rarely in black, white or golden forms.
• **HABITAT** Sand at low tide.

callus encircles spire whorls

callus at top of aperture

PANAMIC

zigzags are close to surface of shell

thick folds on continuation of columellar callus

Range W. Mexico to Peru	Occurrence ♦♦♦	Size 6cm (2½in)

Superfamily MURICOIDEA	Family Olividae	Species *Oliva miniacea* Röding

RED-MOUTH OLIVE

This short-spired shell has a deep suture, a long body whorl, and a blunt, rounded apex. Outer lip almost straight, its lower half slightly thickened; columella has many small folds; a callus thickening projects from top of the aperture. Colour and pattern both variable but often creamy ground with dark brown and purplish streaks and bands.
• **REMARK** A reddish orange aperture is a constant feature.
• **HABITAT** Intertidal sand.

spire whorls are slightly convex

INDO-PACIFIC

broad siphonal notch

continuation of columellar callus

Range Tropical Indo-Pacific	Occurrence ♦♦♦♦	Size 6cm (2½in)

Superfamily MURICOIDEA	Family Olividae	Species *Olivancillaria contortuplicata* Reeve

TWISTED PLAIT OLIVE

The short spire of this species is separated from the body whorl by a deeply channelled suture. Thick, lumpy callus on columella and another on upper part of body whorl and spire; upper edge of outer lip divides one callus from the other. White columella strongly twisted. Greyish brown.
• **REMARK** The Brazilian coast is home to several similar species.
• **HABITAT** Shallow water.

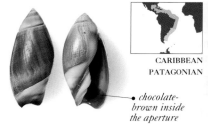

CARIBBEAN
PATAGONIAN

• *chocolate-brown inside the aperture*

Range Brazil to Uruguay	Occurrence ♦♦♦♦	Size 3cm (1¼in)

Superfamily MURICOIDEA	Family Olividae	Species *Olivancillaria gibbosa* Born

SWOLLEN OLIVE

A heavy shell with a short spire and ovate body whorl, swollen in older examples. Spire whorls thickly callused above shallow, channelled suture. Broad columellar callus extends to top of aperture; upper part of callus smooth, lower part has folds. Light or dark brown, with whitish spots and squiggles.
• **REMARK** Has several colour forms, including yellowish green.
• **HABITAT** Shallow water.

edge of body whorl very sharp •

channel • in callus

broad • siphonal notch

• surface colouring visible at inside edge of lip

INDO-PACIFIC

Range Sri Lanka, S. India	Occurrence ♦♦♦♦	Size 5cm (2in)

Superfamily MURICOIDEA	Family Olividae	Species *Olivella biplicata* Sowerby

PURPLE DWARF OLIVE

A sturdy, compact little shell whose short spire sits on top of a much larger body whorl, which may be elongate or swollen. Suture is a narrow, well-defined, but not deep groove. Top of aperture is constricted. Columella is straight and smooth, with a long, thin fold at base. Early spire whorls greyish or brown, rest of shell has brownish or violet streaks.
• **REMARK** This species may swarm on sandy beaches during the summer.
• **HABITAT** Shallow water on sand.

CALIFORNIAN

brown edge to callus band •

• violet aperture

Range British Columbia to Lower California	Occurrence ♦♦♦♦♦	Size 2.5cm (1in)

ANCILLAS

A LARGE GROUP of sand-burrowing, warm-water species with glossy shells. Some have a thick callus which partially or wholly envelops the spire. The columella is smooth and often twisted. The main colours are golden-brown, orange and reddish brown. There is a thin, corneous operculum.

Superfamily MURICOIDEA	Family Olividae	Species *Ancillista velesiana* Iredale

GOLDEN BROWN ANCILLA

A fragile, ovate shell with a blunt, rounded apex, gently convex spire whorls, and a long, narrow aperture. Elongate body whorl has a silky sheen; the spire whorls are thinly covered by a glossy callus. Suture is obliterated by a thin, broad callus; the thin, smooth columella is slightly twisted. Body whorl fawn, its base and penultimate whorl chestnut brown; callus band at suture and early whorls white.
• **REMARK** Distinguished by its large size, light weight, blunt apex, and callused suture.
• **HABITAT** Deep water.

opaque callus
groove in middle of brown band at base
fawn colour spreads over sutural callus

AUSTRALIAN

Range S. Queensland, New South Wales	Occurrence ♦♦♦	Size 7.5cm (3in)

Superfamily MURICOIDEA	Family Olividae	Species *Ancilla lienardi* Bernardi

LIENARD'S ANCILLA

Compact, glossy shell with convex body whorl and straight-sided spire whorls. Sinuous columella; large deep umbilicus; prominent callus above aperture. Dark orange aperture, columellar area and spiral groove on body whorl white.
• **HABITAT** Offshore.

CARIBBEAN
thickened base of columella

Range Brazil	Occurrence ♦♦	Size 2.5cm (1in)

Superfamily MURICOIDEA	Family Olividae	Species *Ancilla albicallosa* Lischke

WHITE BLOTCH ANCILLA

A thick, tall shell with an almost straight-sided spire and convex-sided body whorl. The columella is strongly twisted; the outer lip slightly indented near base. Broad callus band on lower half of body whorl; thick callus above aperture. The spire and base are coloured brown, body whorl paler brown; columella white.
• **HABITAT** Offshore.

callus extends to upper edge of outer lip

JAPONIC

Range S. Japan	Occurrence ♦♦♦	Size 6cm (2½in)

FALSE OLIVES

T HE SMALL sand-burrowing species of this group are common in the Indian Ocean and southern Atlantic. The highly polished shells have a short spire and clear-cut suture. A bar encircles the lower half of the bod whorl while the columella may ha folds spiralling up its entire length.

Superfamily MURICOIDEA	Family Olividae	Species *Agaronia testacea* Lamarck

PANAMA FALSE OLIVE

Elongate shell with straight spire and gently convex body whorl. Deep suture; broad callus band encircles the lower half of the body whorl. The columella has strong folds which spiral into the aperture; outer lip thin. Grey or greyish violet in colour with blotches and zigzag streaks; there is sometimes a pale band above suture; encircling callus band is brownish yellow; columella white.
• **HABITAT** Intertidal sand.

PANAMIC

• *brownish violet aperture*

• *broad siphonal notch*

Range Gulf of California to Peru	Occurrence 🐚🐚🐚	Size 4cm (1½in)

Superfamily MURICOIDEA	Family Olividae	Species *Agaronia nebulosa* Lamarck

BLOTCHY ANCILLA

Slender shell with gently convex body whorl and concave spire whorls. Deep suture; broad spiral callus on body whorl. The columella is mostly straight; short folds on the upper half, long folds on the lower half. Creamy yellow in colour, with brown blotches and zigzags.
• **REMARK** Often eaten in curries.
• **HABITAT** Intertidal sand.

INDO-PACIFIC

• *colour pattern visible at edge of outer lip*

Range Indian Ocean	Occurrence 🐚🐚🐚🐚🐚	Size 5cm (2in)

Superfamily MURICOIDEA	Family Olividae	Species *Agaronia hiatula* Gmelin

OLIVE-GREY ANCILLA

Elongate shell with short pointed spire and inflated body whorl. Outer lip thickened at upper edge. Spire whorls slightly concave; narrow, deep suture; body whorl has broad callus band. Folds on columella spiral into aperture. Yellow or grey, with purple streaks.
• **REMARK** Columellar callus often thicker and more opaque than that shown.
• **HABITAT** Intertidal sand.

WEST AFRICAN

• *brownish violet aperture*

Range W. Africa, Cape Verde Is.	Occurrence 🐚🐚🐚🐚	Size 4cm (1½in)

MITRES

THESE ATTRACTIVELY COLOURED shells are either smooth or ornamented with spiral ribs or vertical folds. All mitres have a narrow aperture, siphonal notch, and folds on the columella; the outer lip may well be smooth, corrugated, or toothed. Many have a thin periostracum; none has an operculum. They are most abundant, colourful, and elaborately ornamented in the tropical Indo-Pacific. Most inhabit the intertidal zone among coral, under stones, or in sand. The animals are predatory or scavenge for food.

Superfamily MURICOIDEA	Family Mitridae	Species *Mitra mitra* Linnaeus

EPISCOPAL MITRE

This solid, heavy shell has a spire which is shorter than the body whorl and a shallow, uneven suture. The spire whorls are gently rounded and smooth, except for indistinct spiral grooves on early whorls and some stronger ones at the base. The constricted aperture ends in a broad siphonal canal. Three to four strong folds on the columella. White, with spiral rows of orange dots and squarish blotches on whorls.
• **REMARK** This shell acquired its common name from a fancied resemblance to a bishop's mitre.
• **HABITAT** Shallow water on sand.

each spire whorl has three rows of markings

SECTIONED SHELL

apical whorls are filled in

columellar folds identical within each whorl

axis of shell

sharp points on outer lip

body whorl has nearly straight sides

narrow chink represents umbilicus

INDO-PACIFIC

Range Tropical Indo-Pacific	Occurrence 🐚🐚🐚	Size 10cm (4in)

Superfamily MURICOIDEA	Family Mitridae	Species *Mitra stictica* Link

PUNCTURED MITRE

This solid shell is easily recognized by its straight-sided, stepped whorls. Each later whorl has upright, blunt tubercles just below the suture; all whorls have spiral rows of tiny, crater-like pits. Columella has three or four folds. White, with orange squares and blotches.
• **REMARK** Popular name refers to the tiny pits found on all the whorls.
• **HABITAT** Rocks and coral.

INDO-PACIFIC

pitted spiral grooves are strongest at base

Range Tropical Indo-Pacific	Occurrence 🐚🐚🐚	Size 6cm (2½in)

| Superfamily MURICOIDEA | Family Mitridae | Species *Mitra puncticulata* Lamarck |

DOTTED MITRE

A solid, compact shell with an aperture about half
the height of the shell; its spire has about six
gently rounded whorls, the later ones stepped at
the suture. Thin, low vertical ridges are crossed
by widely spaced spiral grooves which close
examination reveals are rows of minute pits. The
later whorls are topped by outwardly pointing,
blunt tubercles. There are four or five strong
folds on the columella. Orange, with reddish
brown blotches and white spots.
• **REMARK** The white spots are concentrated around the middle of the body whorl.
• **HABITAT** Shallow water near coral.

INDO-PACIFIC

*• dark brown
spiral grooves*

*• wavy edge
to lip*

| Range S.W. Pacific, S. Japan | Occurrence 🐚🐚 | Size 4.5cm (1¾in) |

| Superfamily MURICOIDEA | Family Mitridae | Species *Mitra nigra* Gmelin |

BLACK MITRE

The body whorl of this thick shell is almost
straight-sided; the aperture is about half
the height of the shell. Spire whorls are
gently rounded and separated by a
shallow suture. Fine spiral lines and
irregular, vertical growth lines. Smooth
outer lip; three or four strong folds on
columella. Bluish grey or pale brown,
with a brown or blackish periostracum.
• **REMARK** Merits its name only when
black periostracum is present.
• **HABITAT** Under stones in
shallow water.

domed apex •

WEST AFRICAN

*• thickened
outer lip*

*• bluish-white
aperture*

| Range W. Africa, Islands in E. Atlantic | Occurrence 🐚🐚 | Size 3cm (1¼in) |

| Superfamily MURICOIDEA | Family Mitridae | Species *Pterygia crenulata* Gmelin |

NOTCHED MITRE

A cylindrical shell whose short, pyramidal
spire has a rounded apex and is dwarfed by
the large body whorl. Regularly spaced
vertical grooves are crossed by equally
regular, pitted spiral grooves producing a
pattern of small, raised squares; the whole
surface is rough to the touch. The lower half
of the columella has up to nine folds. White
with orange-brown blotches; aperture white.
• **REMARK** Several related species have
similar outline and aperture.
• **HABITAT** Shallow water on sand.

INDO-PACIFIC

*• ridged lip
resembling
a file*

*• short, broad
siphonal canal*

| Range Tropical Indo-Pacific | Occurrence 🐚🐚 | Size 3cm (1¼in) |

Superfamily MURICOIDEA	Family Mitridae	Species *Scabricola fissurata* Lamrack

RETICULATE MITRE

This glossy, bullet-shaped shell has a needle-sharp apex and slightly shouldered body whorl almost twice as high as the spire. Aperture is long and narrow; there are four or five folds on the columella. Above the columellar folds are two or three narrow grooves. Encircling the spire whorls and the upper half of the body whorl are broadly spaced rows of punctures. Greyish or pale brown, variegated with white tent-like markings.
• **REMARK** This is the only mitre that has distinctive "tent" markings.
• **HABITAT** Coral sand.

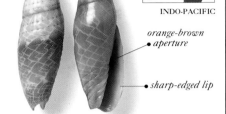

INDO-PACIFIC

*orange-brown
• aperture*

• sharp-edged lip

Range Indian Ocean, Red Sea	Occurrence 🐚🐚	Size 5cm (2in)

Superfamily MURICOIDEA	Family Mitridae	Species *Cancilla praestantissima* Röding

SUPERIOR MITRE

A spindle-shaped shell with a body whorl about the same height as the spire. Its gently rounded whorls have crowded, vertical riblets producing a puckered ridge below the suture. Thin ribs encircle the whorls and override the vertical riblets. There are about five folds on the columella. Coloured white, with reddish brown ribs; the aperture is white.
• **REMARK** Occasionally, there may be additional riblets between the spiral ribs.
• **HABITAT** Shallow water in sand and weed.

*early whorls
• lack spiral ribs*

INDO-PACIFIC

• wavy-edged lip

*• ends of ribs
visible along
inner edge of lip*

Range Tropical Indo-Pacific	Occurrence 🐚🐚	Size 4cm (1½in)

Superfamily MURICOIDEA	Family Mitridae	Species *Neocancilla papilio* Link

BUTTERFLY MITRE

A solid, elongate-ovate shell with well-rounded whorls, a pointed apex, and a moderately impressed suture. Closely spaced vertical grooves are crossed by similarly spaced spiral grooves so that the surface seems to be covered with raised tiles. Spiral grooves are deeper towards base. Columella is almost straight, with four or five folds. Creamy white, variegated with purplish-brown dashes and dots, most of them spirally aligned.
• **REMARK** Colour pattern of left-hand example is less developed than usual.
• **HABITAT** Shallow water on sand.

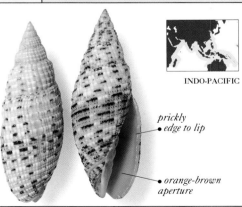

INDO-PACIFIC

*prickly
• edge to lip*

*• orange-brown
aperture*

Range Tropical Indo-Pacific	Occurrence 🐚🐚	Size 5cm (2in)

Superfamily MURICOIDEA	Family Mitridae	Species *Vexillum vulpecula* Linnaeus

LITTLE FOX MITRE

The spire of this glossy shell is shorter than the body whorl. The impressed suture is narrowly channelled above the body whorl; the pointed apex usually broken off. Very narrow aperture; middle portion of the outer lip is slightly concave. Strong or weak vertical folds, most prominent at the shoulder of the body whorl, and deep or shallow spiral grooves. Shell is variously patterned and coloured; most often orange, with red, black, or brown spiral bands.
• **HABITAT** Shallow water on sand.

early whorls straight-sided

spiral grooves on upper part of whorls

INDO-PACIFIC

swelling at top of aperture

very strong upper fold

siphonal canal slightly turned

Range Tropical Pacific	Occurrence 🐚🐚🐚🐚	Size 5cm (2in)

Superfamily MURICOIDEA	Family Mitridae	Species *Vexillum dennisoni* Reeve

DENNISON'S MITRE

A thick, high-spired shell with a well-impressed suture. Whorls are straight-sided or gently convex; apex is acutely pointed. Narrow aperture; outer lip is angled below middle. Broad, low vertical folds crossed by spiral grooves. Pale pink, with orange spiral bands.
• **REMARK** Named after a British collector who amassed many rare shells early in the 19th century.
• **HABITAT** Shallow water on sand.

black dots between folds

INDO-PACIFIC

orange band below suture

narrow canal at top of aperture

four folds on columella

Range W. Pacific	Occurrence 🐚🐚🐚	Size 6cm (2½in)

Superfamily MURICOIDEA	Family Mitridae	Species *Vexillum sanguisugum* Linnaeus

BLOODSUCKER MITRE

A fairly elongate, solid shell with gently convex whorls and impressed suture. Very narrow aperture; columella with three or four folds. Closely spaced vertical folds crossed by deeply incised spiral grooves. Colour varies, usually greyish white or pale brown; red spiral bands in square dots; aperture purple.
• **REMARK** When naming this species, Linnaeus had in mind the livid red wounds inflicted on their human hosts by some blood-sucking insects.
• **HABITAT** Sand near coral reefs.

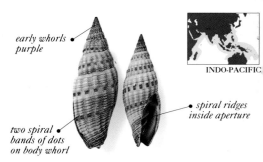

early whorls purple

INDO-PACIFIC

spiral ridges inside aperture

two spiral bands of dots on body whorl

Range Tropical Indo-Pacific	Occurrence 🐚🐚🐚🐚	Size 4cm (1½in)

VASES

MOST SPECIES IN THIS GROUP have thick, heavy shells. The siphonal anal is prominent and the columella as three or four folds. Larger species ave stout tubercles or short spines nd rough spiral ridges; a few are club-shaped and may be ornamented with short or long spines. The operculum can resemble a claw. Widely found, vases are most common on reef flats. The carnivorous animals live in sand and coral debris or sand among rocks.

uperfamily MURICOIDEA	Family Vasidae	Species *Vasum turbinellum* Linnaeus

COMMON PACIFIC VASE

The early whorls of this heavy shell are always eroded. Large body whorl has two rows of blunt spines. Whitish, blotched with brown; aperture yellowish white.
• **REMARK** Example shows a form with depressed spire and upward-curving spines.
• **HABITAT** Intertidal.

INDO-PACIFIC

wavy edge to outer lip

open spines

inconspicuous umbilicus

yellowish orange columella

ange Tropical Indo-Pacific	Occurrence ♦♦♦♦	Size 6cm (2½in)

uperfamily MURICOIDEA	Family Vasidae	Species *Vasum cassiforme* Kiener

HELMET VASE

A heavy shell with a fairly elevated spire, large body whorl, and narrow aperture. Columellar callus spreads out, covering most of shell's apertural side; it is continuous with reflected outer lip of aperture; columella has two or three folds. Spiral rows of long and short open spines encircle whorls. Whitish, with purple-brown callus and outer lip; white inside aperture.
• **REMARK** Greatly extended columellar callus distinguishes this species.
• **HABITAT** Shallow water.

CARIBBEAN

narrow canal at top of aperture

sharp edge to columellar callus

narrow siphonal canal

outer lip deeply wrinkled

ange Brazil	Occurrence ♦♦	Size 9cm (3½in)

Superfamily MURICOIDEA	Family Vasidae	Species *Vasum muricatum* Born

CARIBBEAN VASE

A heavy, squat shell with a very broad body whorl. Moderately broad aperture ends in a narrow siphonal canal; columella has four or five folds. Spiral rows of blunt tubercles on spire. Body whorl has large, blunt tubercles at the shoulder and two or three nodular ribs farther down; it is encircled by coarse, often wavy spiral ribs. Upper edge of outer lip may have a large, blunt spine; lower part of outer lip has a wavy edge. Underneath a dark periostracum, shell is dull white; aperture white; purplish outer lip and blotches on columella.
• **REMARK** The animal feeds on bivalves and worms.
• **HABITAT** Sandy bottoms.

coral-encrusted spire

CARIBBEAN

white shell shows through gap in thick, fibrous periostracum

narrow siphonal canal

pointed lower edge of operculum

Range S. Florida, Caribbean	Occurrence ♦♦♦♦	Size 7.5cm (3in)

Superfamily MURICOIDEA	Family Vasidae	Species *Vasum tubiferum* Anton

IMPERIAL VASE

This solid, ovate, heavy shell is very broad at the shoulder of the body whorl. Early whorls of its moderately tall spire are eroded. Narrow aperture ends in a short siphonal canal; outer lip puckered along its length and angled at its upper end. The almost straight columella has five folds; the central fold is strongest. Small but deep umbilicus. Later spire whorls and body whorl are ornamented with broad vertical folds bearing short and long fluted spines arranged in spiral rows. White, blotched with brown.
• **REMARK** Scientific name emphasizes tube-like character of spines.
• **HABITAT** Shallow water.

brown spines open along one side

canal a͏ angle of outer lip

INDO-PACIFIC

whitish blotch at centre of columella

Range Philippines, Palawan	Occurrence ♦♦♦	Size 9cm (3½in)

Superfamily MURICOIDEA	Family Vasidae	Species *Altivasum flindersi* Verco

FLINDERS' VASE

This highly elegant shell is a delightful combination of robust architecture, harmony of line, and delicate colouring. It has a tall spire and a body whorl of about equal height; the suture is shallow. The small aperture ends in a narrow but very deep siphonal canal. The thin outer lip has a wavy edge; the columella has three strong folds. All the whorls have broad vertical folds crossed by spiral ribs. The ribs and the intervals between them are of equal width. White, yellow, or peachy pink.
• **REMARK** The largest and most spectacular member of the group, this species has always been a collector's favourite, especially when it is as colourful as the example portrayed on this page.
• **HABITAT** Rocks offshore.

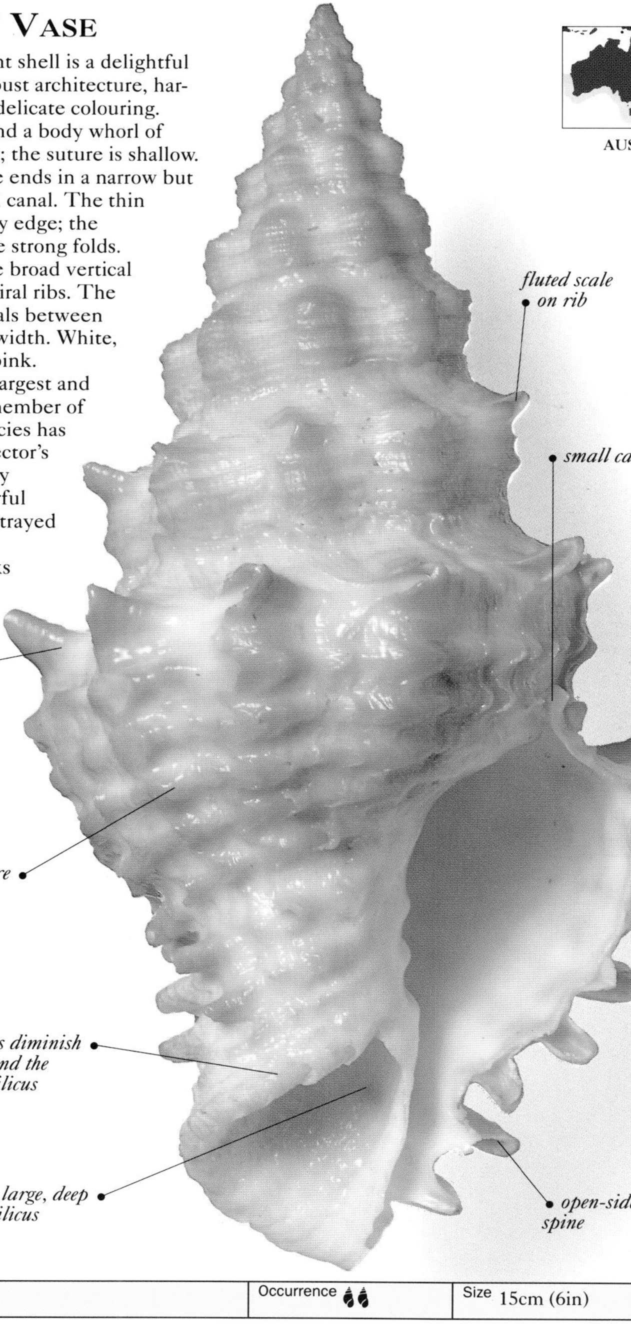

AUSTRALIAN

fluted scale on rib

small canal

scales well developed at shoulder

pink colour more intense on ribs

scales diminish around the umbilicus

very large, deep umbilicus

open-sided spine

Range S. Australia	Occurrence 🐚🐚	Size 15cm (6in)

Superfamily MURICOIDEA	Family Vasidae	Species *Tudivasum armigera* A. Adams

ARMOURED VASE

The body whorl and the very short spire with blunt apex combine with the long, straight siphonal canal to give shell a club shape. Spiral row of upturned spines decorates each later whorl; siphonal canal is also ornamented with long and short spines. Cream or white, with brown spots.
• **REMARK** The folds on the columella confirms that this is not allied to the murex shells which it resembles superficially.
• **HABITAT** Sand offshore.

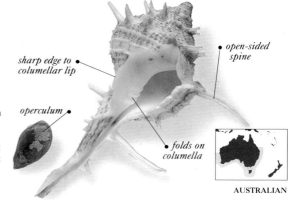

sharp edge to columellar lip

operculum

open-sided spine

folds on columella

AUSTRALIAN

Range S. Australia	Occurrence 🐚🐚🐚	Size 7.5cm (3in)

Superfamily MURICOIDEA	Family Vasidae	Species *Tudicla spirillus* Linnaeus

SPIRAL VASE

A solid shell with a wide, inflated body whorl and a short, compressed spire topped by a large, glossy, and bulbous apex. The suture is a fine line. The body whorl has a sharp keel at the shoulder and shallow spiral grooves below. The long siphonal canal may be curved. Whitish in colour, with brown blotches on the keel.
• **REMARK** A shell chiefly remarkable for the large, rounded apex and the single fold found on the columella.
• **HABITAT** Offshore.

vertical growth line

spiral ridges inside aperture

inconspicuous tooth on columella

INDO-PACIFIC

Range S. India	Occurrence 🐚🐚🐚	Size 6cm (2½in)

Superfamily MURICOIDEA	Family Vasidae	Species *Afer cumingii* Reeve

CUMING'S AFER

APERTURAL VIEW

This sturdy, high-spired shell has a large body whorl and a long, often curved siphonal canal. Apical whorls are smooth; remaining whorls have strong spiral ridges which cross rounded nodules at the shoulder. The outer lip has a serrated edge and ridges just inside. Indistinct folds on the columella are ridges of the body whorl pressing through the columellar callus. Yellowish brown, with darker mottlings; aperture white.
• **REMARK** Named after Hugh Cuming, the most celebrated of all the 19th century shell collectors.
• **HABITAT** Sand offshore.

JAPONIC
INDO-PACIFIC

TOP VIEW

strong tooth at base of the columella

Range Japan to Taiwan	Occurrence 🐚🐚🐚	Size 7cm (2¾in)

CHANKS

T HESE ARE PROBABLY the heaviest shells for their size in the world. They have a large body whorl, a broad siphonal canal and a few prominent folds on the columella. A thick, fibrous periostracum covers them when fresh. Found in the Indian Ocean and the Caribbean, they feed on worms.

Superfamily MURICOIDEA	Family Vasidae	Species *Turbinella pyrum* Linnaeus

INDIAN CHANK

A solid, heavy shell with a very inflated body whorl, a short spire, and a long, broad siphonal canal. The columella has three or four strong folds. The shell is smooth or has low lumps at the shoulder and spiral ridges at the base of the body whorl. Underneath a thick periostracum, the shell is milk-white, often tinged pink.

• **REMARK** Indian chanks are sent to Bengal to be made into jewellery and ornaments.

• **HABITAT** Shallow water on sand.

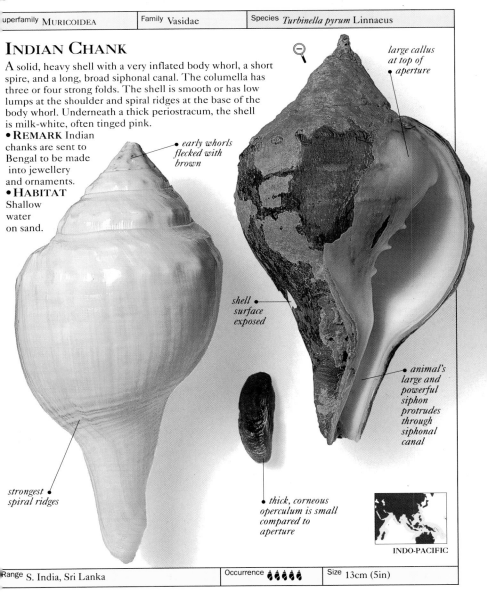

large callus at top of aperture

early whorls flecked with brown

shell surface exposed

animal's large and powerful siphon protrudes through siphonal canal

strongest spiral ridges

thick, corneous operculum is small compared to aperture

INDO-PACIFIC

Range S. India, Sri Lanka	Occurrence 🐚🐚🐚🐚🐚	Size 13cm (5in)

HARPS

A VOLUPTUOUS SHAPE, with exquisite patterns and bright colours, help make harps some of the most attractive of all seashells. About a dozen species occur in shallow, warm tropical water a few in deep water off south Australi Harps lack an operculum and live i sand. The animals are carnivorous.

Superfamily MURICOIDEA	Family Harpidae	Species *Harpa costata* Linnaeus

IMPERIAL HARP

The small, pointed spire of this shell is dwarfed by the inflated body whorl. Upper part of whorls flat; body whorl has a broad ramp. Large aperture; smooth outer lip and columella. Body whorl covered with 30–40 closely-spaced vertical ribs, each pointed at the shoulder and ascending penultimate whorl. Creamy white, with broken spiral bands of brown and pinkish brown; aperture yellowish white; large, reddish brown blotch at centre of columella.
• **REMARK** A rare and highly prized shell, proportional to size and condition.
• **HABITAT** Sand offshore.

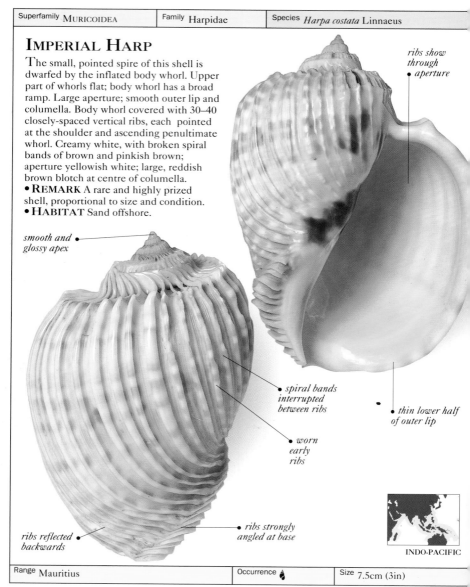

ribs show through aperture

smooth and glossy apex

spiral bands interrupted between ribs

worn early ribs

thin lower half of outer lip

ribs reflected backwards

ribs strongly angled at base

INDO-PACIFIC

Range Mauritius		Occurrence	Size 7.5cm (3in)

Superfamily MURICOIDEA	Family Harpidae	Species *Harpa major* Röding

MAJOR HARP

This thin but sturdy shell has a low spire and a sharp apex. The aperture is large; the outer lip smooth and angled at the top; columella is smooth. About 12 wide or narrow ribs on the body whorl, each one pointed at the shoulder. Thin callus spreads over apertural side of the body whorl and extends over the spire. Creamy white, with brown zigzags down sides of the ribs and broad, paler brown spiral bands; chocolate-brown columella and apertural callus.
• **REMARK** The shell's external pattern shows through the aperture.
• **HABITAT** Shallow water on sand.

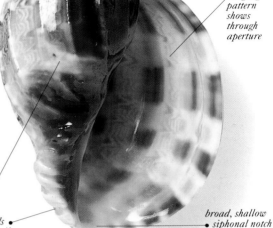

edge thickened at angle

zigzag pattern shows through aperture

broad, shallow siphonal notch

INDO-PACIFIC

constant gap in the brown colouring

curved ends to vertical ribs

Range Tropical Indo-Pacific	Occurrence 🐚🐚🐚🐚	Size 9cm (3½in)

Superfamily MURICOIDEA	Family Harpidae	Species *Harpa doris* Röding

ROSY HARP

A thin, short-spired shell with an elongate body whorl and a pointed apex. Body whorl has a broad ramp below the suture. The columella is smooth; weak teeth project from lower part of outer lip. A dozen low vertical ribs on body whorl: slightly undulating in profile, tops sharply pointed; smooth intervals between ribs. Reddish, blotched brown; spiral bands with whitish crescents.
• **REMARK** The only member of the group from the Atlantic Ocean.
• **HABITAT** Sand offshore.

edge of transparent callus

fine spiral lines on later spire whorls

brown crests on vertical ribs

brown patch by columella

WEST AFRICAN

Range W. Africa	Occurrence 🐚🐚	Size 6cm (2½in)

VOLUTES

T HE VARIED SHAPES and colourful patterns of the volutes make them the darlings of shell collectors everywhere. Most are solid and heavy, but they vary considerably in size and appearance; some species have several named varieties. They occur in warm and temperate seas, and are well rep resented around Australian coasts. A few species have small operculums many have vertical folds or ribs, and a volutes have folds on the columella Most of the animals burrow in san and all of them are carnivorous.

| Superfamily MURICOIDEA | Family Volutidae | Species *Voluta musica* Linnaeus |

MUSIC VOLUTE

A thick shell with a short spire, an inflated body whorl, and a narrow aperture. The apex is smooth and bulbous. The body whorl and later spire whorls have a few massive tubercles at the shoulder; the columella has strong folds. Cream or pinkish, marked with brown spots, and spiral lines; the vertical bars and dots resemble sheet music. A small operculum is present.
• **REMARK** Attempts to extract a tune from the musical notation on this shell have failed!
• **HABITAT** Shallow water.

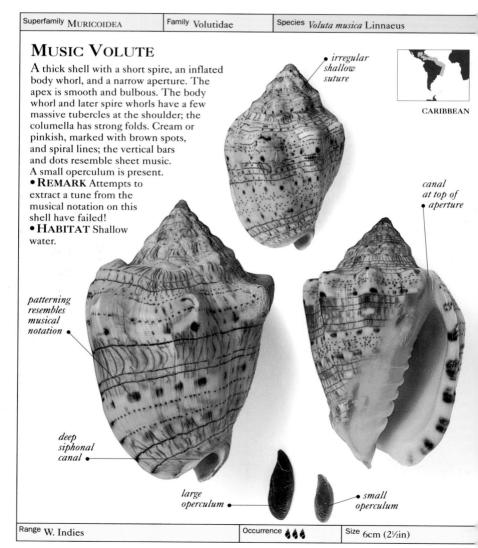

irregular shallow suture

CARIBBEAN

canal at top of aperture

patterning resembles musical notation

deep siphonal canal

large operculum

small operculum

| Range W. Indies | Occurrence 🐚🐚🐚 | Size 6cm (2½in) |

Superfamily MURICOIDEA	Family Volutidae	Species *Voluta ebraea* Linnaeus

HEBREW VOLUTE

The body whorl of this solid, tall, and high-spired shell sometimes appears to have parallel sides, depending on how the outer lip has developed. The outer lip usually slopes towards the siphonal canal. The apex is smooth and rounded; the suture is impressed and wavy. The columella has five strong folds at the bottom and weaker ones above; the long aperture is moderately narrow. Broad, low ridges on all whorls; those on the body whorl are sharply pointed. Creamy yellow, with brown spiral bands and hieroglyphic lines.

• **REMARK** Owes its name to the resemblance of its markings to letters of the Hebrew alphabet.

• **HABITAT** Rocks or sand.

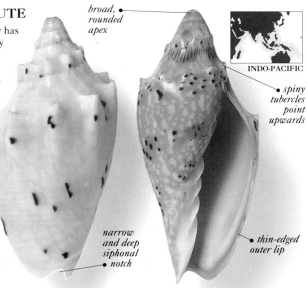

• broad and thin callus

• columellar folds

CARIBBEAN

Range N.E. Brazil	Occurrence ♦♦♦	Size 15cm (6in)

Superfamily MURICOIDEA	Family Volutidae	Species *Cymbiolacca pulchra* Sowerby

BEAUTIFUL VOLUTE

This variable species typically has a short spire, with smooth early whorls and shallow suture, a slender body whorl, and wide aperture. The columella has four strong oblique folds; the lowest descends to the edge of the siphonal canal. The body whorl has pointed tubercles at the shoulder. Reddish or pinkish orange, with small white triangles and three spiral bands with brown spots; columella white; aperture white with pink edge.

• **REMARK** Several forms were once considered to be distinct species.

• **HABITAT** Sand offshore.

broad, rounded apex

INDO-PACIFIC

• spiny tubercles point upwards

• thin-edged outer lip

narrow and deep siphonal notch

Range N.E. Australia	Occurrence ♦♦♦	Size 7.5cm (3in)

Superfamily MURICOIDEA	Family Volutidae	Species *Alcithoe swainsoni* Marwick

SWAINSON'S VOLUTE

A moderately thick shell with a short, narrow spire; elongate body whorl, and long, smooth-lipped aperture. Smooth or with vertical ribs on the early whorls, which become obsolete later. Shell is dark or light brown in colour, with spiral bands of wavy lines.
• **REMARK** Named after William Swainson, who published the first illustration of the shell in 1821.
• **HABITAT** Offshore.

NEOZELANIC

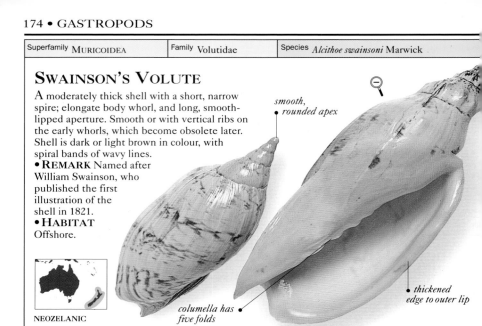

smooth, rounded apex

thickened edge to outer lip

columella has five folds

Range New Zealand	Occurrence 🐚🐚🐚	Size 20cm (8in)

Superfamily MURICOIDEA	Family Volutidae	Species *Fulgoraria hirasei* Sowerby

HIRASE'S VOLUTE

A large, thin, elongate shell with a wide aperture that is more than half the height of the large body whorl. The spire is much shorter than the body whorl, with a shallow suture; the apex is large, smooth, and globular. Each spire whorl has strong vertical folds; these are weaker on the body whorl and become totally obsolete on its lower half. The whole shell has weak spiral lines which help to give it a dull sheen. The columella is lightly glazed and smooth, but sometimes has weak folds. Reddish brown or brown in colour; the aperture is reddish orange with a paler edge to the outer lip.
• **REMARK** The animal is edible and is occasionally sold in fish markets on the Japanese island of Honshu.
• **HABITAT** Moderately deep water.

JAPONIC

smooth, narrow band above suture

callus thickening at top of aperture

edge of outer lip is thin but not sharp

reddish brown zone with pale rim

siphonal notch is broad and shallow

Range Japan	Occurrence 🐚🐚🐚	Size 15cm (6in)

Superfamily MURICOIDEA	Family Volutidae	Species *Lyria delessertiana* Petit

DELESSERT'S LYRIA

Thick, high-spired shell with rounded apex and strong vertical folds. Small canal at top of aperture; folds along columella's entire length. Pink with orange blotches and brown, interrupted spiral lines.
• **REMARK** Named after French shell collector, Baron Benjamin Delessert.
• **HABITAT** Offshore.

operculum

INDO-PACIFIC

• *edge of outer lip greatly thickened*

Range Madagascar, Comoros, Seychelles	Occurrence 🐚🐚	Size 5cm (2in)

Superfamily MURICOIDEA	Family Volutidae	Species *Harpulina lapponica* Linnaeus

BROWN-LINED VOLUTE

A heavy shell with a short spire and inflated body whorl. The apex is bulbous; the succeeding two or three whorls have low vertical ribs; the remaining whorls are smooth. The suture is shallow; the columella has seven or eight folds. Cream, with brown blotches (arranged in three bands on body whorl) and many spiral rows of dashes.
• **HABITAT** Offshore.

INDO-PACIFIC

• *narrow canal at top of aperture*

narrow, deep siphonal notch

• *sharp edge*

Range Sri Lanka, S. India	Occurrence 🐚🐚🐚	Size 9cm (3½in)

Superfamily MURICOIDEA	Family Volutidae	Species *Volutoconus bednalli* Brazier

BEDNALL'S VOLUTE

Instantly recognizable by its bold, distinctive pattern, this is a solid but lightweight, narrow or moderately inflated shell with a high spire. The body whorl is much more than half the shell's total height. Apex broadly rounded, almost dome-like, with a very small spur projecting from the top. The long, narrow aperture ends in a deep and upturned siphonal notch. The columella has four or five folds. The shell is covered in fine vertical lines and usually has broad, low vertical folds on the penultimate whorl and body whorl. Cream, with four spiral, chocolate lines on body whorl, connected by angular lines; aperture pale pink.
• **REMARK** Coveted by collectors since 1878 when it was first made known to science.
• **HABITAT** Muddy sand offshore.

• *chocolate-coloured apex*

• *uppermost fold is the strongest*

• *slightly concave outer lip*

INDO-PACIFIC

Range N. Australia, S.E. Indonesia	Occurrence 🐚	Size 14cm (5 ½in)

Superfamily MURICOIDEA	Family Volutidae	Species *Scaphella junonia* Lamarck

THE JUNONIA

The almost straight-sided body whorl of this shell ends in a broad siphonal notch. Columella has four folds. Pinkish white, with regular spiral rows of brown spots.
• **REMARK** Fine examples of this rare shell continue to be scarce.
• **HABITAT** Sand offshore.

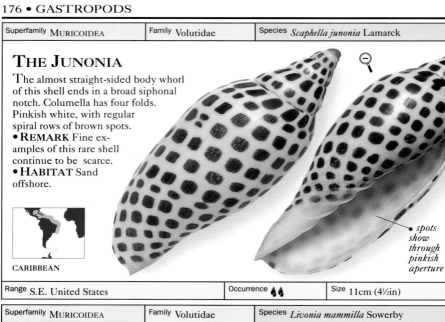

CARIBBEAN

• *spots show through pinkish aperture*

Range S.E. United States	Occurrence 👣👣	Size 11cm (4½in)

Superfamily MURICOIDEA	Family Volutidae	Species *Livonia mammilla* Sowerby

FALSE MELON VOLUTE

This large shell has a capacious body whorl, a short spire of three convex whorls, topped by a bulbous apex, and a very shallow suture. The wide aperture ends in a broad siphonal notch; its reflected outer lip is almost as long as the entire body whorl. The columella has three low, sinuous folds; a thin, transparent glaze covers parietal area. Creamy or yellowish white in colour, with three broad bands of irregular, brown zigzags and triangles; penultimate whorl brown; little ornamentation; columella pinkish orange.
• **REMARK** Occasionally washed up on beaches.
• **HABITAT** Offshore.

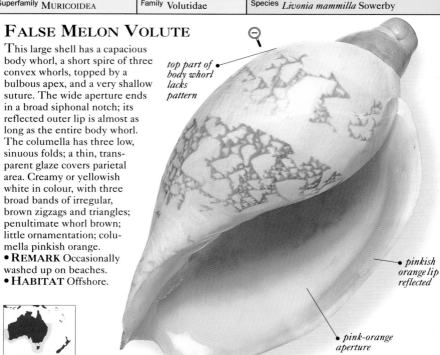

top part of body whorl lacks pattern

• *pinkish orange lip reflected*

• *pink-orange aperture*

AUSTRALIAN

Range S.E. Australia, Tasmania	Occurrence 👣👣	Size 25cm (10in)

Superfamily MURICOIDEA	Family Volutidae	Species *Cymbiolista hunteri* Iredale

HUNTER'S VOLUTE

Lightweight shell with low spire, a large body whorl, and impressed suture. Early spire whorls smooth, later ones ornamented with short, upright spines. Body whorl has about a dozen spines at the shoulder; otherwise lacking ornament. Flared outer lip is almost as long as the body whorl. Four strong, sinuous folds on the almost straight columella. Orange-yellow, with zigzag brown lines and two spiral, darker brown bands.
• **REMARK** First illustration published in 1821 by William Swainson who named it the marbled volute.
• **HABITAT** Offshore.

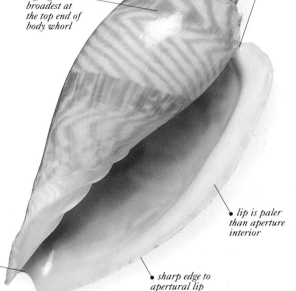

zigzag lines broadest at the top end of body whorl

deep notch

lip is paler than aperture interior

sharp edge to apertural lip

deep siphonal notch

AUSTRALIAN

Range E. Australia	Occurrence 🐚🐚🐚	Size 15cm (6in)

Superfamily MURICOIDEA	Family Volutidae	Species *Cymbium olla* Linnaeus

OLLA VOLUTE

This lightweight but sturdy shell has a short spire largely enveloped by the capacious body whorl. Apex smooth and rounded; suture deeply channelled. The long aperture sometimes projects above the top of the body whorl; outer lip curved, ending in broad, shallow siphonal notch. The convex columella has two sinuous folds. Smooth except for a coarse glaze on the parietal area. Reddish or yellowish brown, with paler aperture; columellar folds whitish.
• **REMARK** The name given by Linnaeus to this species is Latin for "earthenware jar".
• **HABITAT** Offshore.

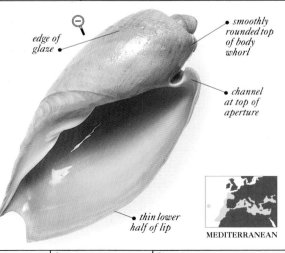

edge of glaze

smoothly rounded top of body whorl

channel at top of aperture

thin lower half of lip

MEDITERRANEAN

Range Mediterranean, N.W. Africa	Occurrence 🐚🐚	Size 11cm (4½in)

MARGIN SHELLS

T HERE IS A CONSIDERABLE size range in this group; most margin shells are below 2cm (¾in) in length, while a few exceed 5cm (2in). All these shells are smooth and glossy, have folds on the columella, and end in a sho[rt] siphonal notch. All species inhab[it] warm and tropical seas; living in san[d] under rocks, or in algae. The anima[ls] mostly prey on other molluscs.

Superfamily MURICOIDEA	Family Marginellidae	Species *Afrivoluta pringlei* Tomlin

PRINGLE'S MARGIN SHELL

This shell has several features, apart from its superior size, which distinguish it from other members of the group. Thin and lightweight, it has a short spire with a large, bluntly rounded apex, and a lightly impressed suture. The long body whorl has a large, opaque callus pad on its apertural side. The aperture is long and narrow. The columella has four, thick, shelf-like folds, each tilted at a different angle. Reddish brown colour, with paler callus pad and edge of outer lip.
• REMARK In 1947, when it was first described, this extraordinary shell was believed to be an unusual kind of volute. Now that its anatomy has been thoroughly examined, however, it is recognized as the second largest margin shell.
• HABITAT Deep water.

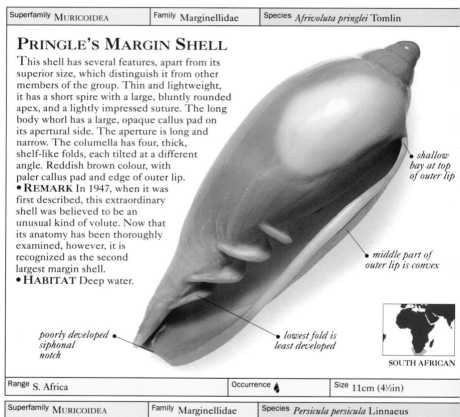

shallow bay at top of outer lip

middle part of outer lip is convex

poorly developed siphonal notch

lowest fold is least developed

SOUTH AFRICAN

Range S. Africa	Occurrence	Size 11cm (4½in)

Superfamily MURICOIDEA	Family Marginellidae	Species *Persicula persicula* Linnaeus

SPOTTED MARGIN SHELL

A thick, ovate shell with sunken spire covered by callus; aperture is as tall as the shell; its thickened outer lip is slightly taller. Up to nine folds on columella. White, yellow, or pale brown, with small brown spots.
• REMARK Both heavily and lightly spotted forms are illustrated.
• HABITAT Offshore.

WEST AFRICAN

lowest fold is longest

Range W. Africa	Occurrence	Size 2cm (¾in)

Superfamily MURICOIDEA	Family Marginellidae	Species *Bullata bullata* Born

BLISTERED MARGIN SHELL

A large, thick shell with sunken spire visible only as a small mound within the rim of the body whorl. The outer lip is just slightly taller than the rest of the body whorl. The aperture is long and narrow; the columella has four strong, oblique folds. The shell is beige in colour, with feint indications of darker spiral bands.

• **REMARK** Fine examples of this shell have always been particularly difficult to obtain.

• **HABITAT** Offshore.

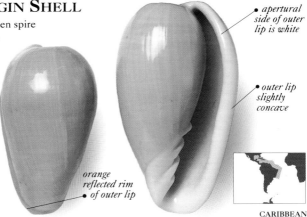

• *apertural side of outer lip is white*

• *outer lip slightly concave*

orange reflected rim • of outer lip

CARIBBEAN

Range Brazil	Occurrence 🐚🐚	Size 6cm (2½in)

Superfamily MURICOIDEA	Family Marginellidae	Species *Marginella glabella* Linnaeus

SMOOTH MARGIN SHELL

This solid, ovate shell has a short spire and a low, rounded apex. The spire whorls are almost imperceptibly rounded; the swollen body whorl has a slightly rounded shoulder. The aperture does not reach as far as the suture; the columella has four strong folds. The thickened outer lip is reflected. Pink, with three spiral bands of pale brown markings and whitish dots.

• **REMARK** This species varies considerably in size and pattern.

• **HABITAT** Offshore.

reddish blotches • below suture

WEST AFRICAN

• *narrow canal*

• *edge of outer lip is paler than aperture*

Range N.W. Africa, Cape Verde Is.	Occurrence 🐚🐚🐚	Size 4cm (1½in)

Superfamily MURICOIDEA	Family Marginellidae	Species *Persicula cingulata* Dillwyn

GIRDLED MARGIN SHELL

An inflated, flat-spired shell with its apex submerged under callus. The outer lip is raised slightly above the body whorl; its inner edge is faintly or distinctly toothed. There are up to seven folds on the columella. Yellowish white, with reddish spiral lines.

• **HABITAT** Sandy mud offshore.

WEST AFRICAN

• *white columella and outer lip*

Range W. Africa	Occurrence 🐚🐚🐚🐚	Size 2cm (¾in)

Superfamily MURICOIDEA	Family Marginellidae	Species *Marginella sebastiani* Marche-Marchad

SEBASTIAN'S MARGIN SHELL

Thick, ovate shell with short spire of four whorls topped by a low, rounded apex. Body whorl swollen, squat, or elongate; suture partially callused. The thick outer lip, which does not reach the top of the body whorl, has strong teeth on its inner side. There are four strong folds on the columella. Cream to orange-brown, with small, pale spots.
• **REMARK** Illustrated examples have larger spots than usual.
• **HABITAT** Mud offshore.

WEST AFRICAN

well-defined canal

lowest fold is the longest

Range W. Africa	Occurrence ♀♀♀	Size 4cm (1½in)

Superfamily MURICOIDEA	Family Marginellidae	Species *Marginella nebulosa* Röding

CLOUDY MARGIN SHELL

A short-spired shell with a low, rounded apex and callused suture. Body whorl is broadest below the shoulder. Aperture large with reflected outer lip; the columella has four strong folds. Off-white or yellow with broken bands of black-edged, grey, or brownish blotches.
• **REMARK** Unlike the examples shown here, those washed up on beaches are nearly always worn, dull, and faded.
• **HABITAT** Sand offshore.

SOUTH AFRICAN

canal almost non-existent

pattern shows through aperture

Range S. Africa	Occurrence ♀♀♀	Size 4cm (1½in)

Superfamily MURICOIDEA	Family Marginellidae	Species *Cryptospira strigata* Dillwyn

STRIPED MARGIN SHELL

A large, thick shell with a depressed spire that is callused over. Usually there is an inflated, ovate body whorl. The thickened and reflected outer lip ends in a broad siphonal notch; the columella has five strong folds. Creamy or greyish, with vertical olive-green streaks and broken spiral stripes; rear of outer lip is orange.
• **REMARK** The illustrated examples show the size range.
• **HABITAT** Shallow water.

apex seen as slight pimple

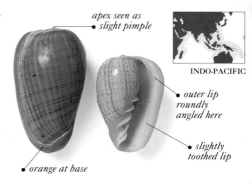

INDO-PACIFIC

outer lip roundly angled here

slightly toothed lip

orange at base

Range S.E. Asia	Occurrence ♀♀	Size 4cm (1½in)

NUTMEGS

MEMBERS OF THIS worldwide group of small shells have vertical ribs, often crossed by spiral ribs which form lattice or cancellate ornament. The columella has strong folds. Most of the species come from deep water in warm and tropical seas. They are vegetable feeders and lack an operculum.

Superfamily CANCELLARIOIDEA	Family Cancellariidae	Species *Cancellaria spirata* Lamarck

SPIRAL NUTMEG

A low-spired shell with rounded whorls separated by a deep suture; the apex is smooth and prominent. The aperture is more than half the height of the well-rounded body whorl; the columella has four folds. Ornamented with vertical and spiral riblets. Yellowish brown, with brown blotches.
• **HABITAT** Shallow water.

slight groove at top of lip

AUSTRALIAN

spiral ridges inside aperture

Range S. Australia	Occurrence ♦♦♦	Size 3cm (1¼in)

Superfamily CANCELLARIOIDEA	Family Cancellariidae	Species *Cancellaria piscatoria* Gmelin

FISHERMAN'S NUTMEG

A thick shell with inflated body whorl and wide ramp below suture. Aperture has thin outer lip; columella smooth. Vertical ridges crossed by spiral riblets, producing points. Yellowish brown, with browner blotches.
• **REMARK** Rare for a nutmeg not to have folds on the columella.
• **HABITAT** Sand inshore.

WEST AFRICAN

spine at edge of lip

dark brown inside aperture

Range W. Africa	Occurrence ♦♦♦	Size 2.5cm (1in)

Superfamily CANCELLARIOIDEA	Family Cancellariidae	Species *Trigonostoma pulchra* Sowerby

BEAUTIFUL NUTMEG

This thick, high-spired shell has a broad body whorl and deep suture. The small aperture has strong spiral ridges inside; the columella has three or four small folds. Vertical ribs are crossed by spiral ridges, producing scales or points on the shell. White, with spiral brown bands.
• **REMARK** The ornament and brown bands give this shell its name.
• **HABITAT** Offshore.

smooth, pointed apex

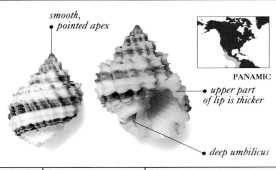

PANAMIC

upper part of lip is thicker

deep umbilicus

Range W. Mexico to Ecuador	Occurrence ♦♦	Size 3cm (1¼in)

| Superfamily CANCELLARIOIDEA | Family Cancellariidae | Species *Cancellaria reticulata* Linnaeus |

COMMON NUTMEG

A thick, moderately high-spired shell with an inflated body whorl and a deep suture. The spire whorls are strongly shouldered. Twisted columella bears two strong folds. Vertical ridges crossed by spiral ribs give a lattice ornament which may appear beaded on spire whorls. Yellowish or cream, with pale or dark brown bands.
• **HABITAT** Shallow water in sand.

TRANSATLANTIC CARIBBEAN

• *subsidiary ridge on larger fold*

• *strong spiral ridges on narrow aperture*

| Range N. Carolina to Brazil | Occurrence 🐚🐚🐚🐚 | Size 4cm (1½in) |

| Superfamily CANCELLARIOIDEA | Family Cancellariidae | Species *Cancellaria nodulifera* Sowerby |

KNOBBED NUTMEG

This inflated, short-spired shell has an incised suture and a deep umbilicus. Straight-sided spire whorls look partly submerged in large body whorl. Three indistinct folds on columella. Vertical ribs on body whorl crossed by spiral ribs; pointed tubercles decorate the shoulder. Apricot coloured.
• **HABITAT** Shallow water.

JAPONIC

• *aperture smooth inside*

• *outer lip thin and jagged*

| Range S. Japan | Occurrence 🐚🐚 | Size 4.5cm (1¾in) |

| Superfamily CANCELLARIOIDEA | Family Cancellariidae | Species *Cancellaria cancellata* Linnaeus |

LATTICE NUTMEG

A high-spired shell with about eight rounded whorls, a deep suture, and a small umbilicus. The aperture is narrowed at top and bottom; the columella has three conspicuous folds, the uppermost fold the strongest. The prominent vertical ridges are crossed by smooth spiral ribs which produce rounded or sharp points at the intersections. Thin varices are occasionally formed. White, with spiral brown bands.
• **HABITAT** Shallow water.

thin varix

WEST AFRICAN

• *grooved outer lip*

• *strong spiral ridges inside aperture*

broken thin outer lip

| Range W. Africa to Algeria | Occurrence 🐚🐚🐚 | Size 4cm (1½in) |

TURRIDS

THIS IS THE LARGEST group of sea-shells, with hundreds of types ccuring in all seas. Most species have tall spire, and a long siphonal canal. All have a long or short slit or notch at the upper end of the outer lip. The operculum is leaf-shaped. The animals prey on marine worms.

Superfamily CONOIDEA	Family Turridae	Species *Lophiotoma indica* Röding

INDIAN TURRID

A many-whorled shell, whose spire is slightly longer than its siphonal canal. Deep, narrow notch towards upper end of outer lip. Straight columella ends in a long, slightly sinuous canal. All whorls sharply keeled. White, with brown streaks.
• **REMARK** One of the larger turrids.
• **HABITAT** Shallow water on sand.

strong spiral ridges below keel

siphonal canal open along its length

INDO-PACIFIC

Range Tropical Indo-Pacific	Occurrence ♦♦♦	Size 7.5cm (3in)

Superfamily CONOIDEA	Family Turridae	Species *Turris babylonia* Linnaeus

BABYLON TURRID

A slender, elegant, many-whorled shell with a pointed apex and spire longer than the body whorl and siphonal canal combined. Outer lip has a deep notch towards its upper end. All whorls have strong spiral ridges. White, with brown spots.
• **HABITAT** Offshore.

rows of largest spots below suture

INDO-PACIFIC

Range Tropical Indo-Pacific	Occurrence ♦♦	Size 7.5cm (3in)

Superfamily CONOIDEA	Family Turridae	Species *Turricula javana* Linnaeus

JAVA TURRID

The spire of this thin shell is less than the combined height of body whorl and siphonal canal. Columella is sinuous; outer lip has a broad notch towards upper end. All whorls keeled and nodulous at their periphery; spiral ribs are weak above keel, progressively stronger below. Buff or darker brown.
• **REMARK** Possibly the commonest large turrid.
• **HABITAT** Mud offshore.

broad, pale rib below suture

smooth nodules

INDO-PACIFIC
JAPONIC

Range Tropical Indo-Pacific	Occurrence ♦♦♦♦	Size 6cm (2½in)

| Superfamily CONOIDEA | Family Turridae | Species *Thatcheria mirabilis* Angas |

JAPANESE WONDER SHELL

This thin shell resembles a winding staircase. The flat upper surface of the whorls ends in a sharp, slightly upturned keel. Body whorl is slightly taller than the spire. When viewed from above, upper part of outer lip is seen to be deeply and broadly grooved. Dull yellow, with white aperture and columella.
• **REMARK** Known only by a unique specimen for more than half a century, this remarkable species is now common in collections.
• **HABITAT** Deep water.

DORSAL VIEW

APERTURAL VIEW

fine spiral lines

lightly glazed straight columella

TOP VIEW

fine growth lines

raised edge to whorl

JAPONIC
INDO-PACIFIC

| Range Japan to Philippines | Occurrence 🌢🌢🌢 | Size 10cm (4in) |

| Superfamily CONOIDEA | Family Turridae | Species *Inquisitor griffithi* Gray |

GRIFFITH'S TURRID

A biconic shell with an acutely pointed apex and a shallow suture. Body whorl is slightly taller than the spire. Outer lip is thickened just before its edge and has a deep notch near its upper end; the columella is straight. All whorls are ornamented with spiral riblets and tubercles at the shoulders. Dark brown, with white tubercles and spiral ribs.
• **REMARK** Named after Edward Griffith who brought out an English edition of a classic work by Cuvier about the animal kingdom.
• **HABITAT** Shallow water.

INDO-PACIFIC

swelling below narrow canal

blunt points at edge of lip

| Range Indo-West Pacific | Occurrence 🌢🌢 | Size 4.5cm (1¾in) |

CONES

NEARLY ALL the species included in this group have a strong family likeness: conical in shape and very substantial. Cone shells are heavy or light, and may be flat-topped or have an extended spire; they may be smooth or have spiral ornament. The great variety of colours and patterns displayed within this group has made cones popular with shell collectors and these features identify most of them readily. Many species of cone have a small, narrow, corneous operculum. The periostracum can be either thin and silky or thick and coarse.

———— • ————

The animals of every single cone are carnivorous, feeding on other molluscs, worms, and small fish. By injecting venom through their teeth, they stun their prey before consuming it. Some species can sting so it is best to take precautions when collecting cones. Most live in the tropics on coral reefs.

Superfamily CONOIDEA	Family Conidae	Species *Conus generalis* Linnaeus

GENERAL CONE

A thick, heavy shell with a short, concave-sided spire ending in a pointed apex; each of the later whorls is channelled. The large body whorl is almost straight-sided and slightly rounded at the shoulder. Variable in colour and pattern, it is usually light or dark brown with three spiral bands of white, each band interrupted by brown streaks and blotches; aperture white.
• **REMARK** During the 18th century, certain cones, including this one, were named as though each was an army or naval officer.
• **HABITAT** Intertidal sand.

APERTURAL VIEW

broad "tongues" of white at shoulder •

DORSAL VIEW

upper spire whorls • often eroded

TOP VIEW

slightly concave body whorl •

purplish • brown at base of aperture

• deep groove at top edge of aperture

• crescent-shaped markings

INDO-PACIFIC

Range Tropical Indo-Pacific	Occurrence 🐚🐚🐚🐚	Size 7cm (2¾in)

Superfamily CONOIDEA	Family Conidae	Species *Conus eburneus* Hwass

IVORY CONE

A solid, heavy shell, broad at the shoulder of the body whorl and almost flat-topped; only the early whorls are raised. Most of shell is smooth except for well-marked spiral grooves towards base. White, sometimes faintly banded with yellow, encircled by bands of dark brown spots.
• **REMARK** Varies greatly in the placing and size of its markings; spots sometimes coalesce to form almost complete spiral bands.
• **HABITAT** Coral and sand.

very low apex

body whorl rounded at shoulder

white aperture patterned at edge of lip

INDO-PACIFIC

Range Tropical Indo-Pacific	Occurrence ♦♦♦♦	Size 6cm (2½in)

Superfamily CONOIDEA	Family Conidae	Species *Conus spectrum* Linnaeus

SPECTRAL CONE

This quite thick shell has a silky sheen; its short spire ends in an acutely pointed apex. Shoulder of convex body whorl is angulated or rounded. Faint spiral striae on body whorl are seen towards the base. White ground shows through brown colour as cloudy blotches.
• **REMARK** Nebulous white markings may have seemed ghost-like to Linnaeus when he named this shell in 1758.
• **HABITAT** Sand offshore.

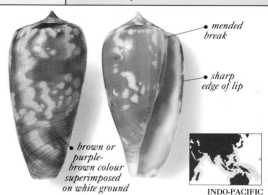

mended break

sharp edge of lip

brown or purple-brown colour superimposed on white ground

INDO-PACIFIC

Range W. Pacific	Occurrence ♦♦♦	Size 6cm (2½in)

Superfamily CONOIDEA	Family Conidae	Species *Conus praecellens* A. Adams

ADMIRABLE CONE

A lightweight, biconic shell with a tall spire of many whorls and a sharply pointed apex. The body whorl is keeled at the shoulder, its upper half convex, its lower half slightly concave; it is encircled by shallow grooves. Cream, with dark brown streaks and squarish spots.
• **REMARK** Specialists dispute the species name, but agree it is like no other cone.
• **HABITAT** Deep water.

slightly concave sides to spire

INDO-PACIFIC

Range W. Pacific	Occurrence ♦♦	Size 4cm (1½in)

Superfamily CONOIDEA	Family Conidae	Species *Conus gloriamaris* Chemnitz

GLORY OF THE SEA

This is a glossy, heavy, fairly tall-spired shell with a body whorl more than twice the spire's height. Spire whorls are slightly concave; body whorl is straight-sided or slightly concave; the suture is a mere line. The long aperture widens slightly towards the base. Early whorls have fine nodules; later whorls are almost smooth. Whitish, bluish white, or cream, with three broad, often ill-defined spiral bands, and crowded, overlapping, pale or darker brown tent-like markings.
• **REMARK** Virtually unobtainable pre-1960s, this elegant species was the most coveted of all seashells. Now readily available from the Philippines, it is still expensive when large and perfect.
• **HABITAT** Deep water.

brown spiral band on each spire whorl

INDO-PACIFIC

tent-like markings are white within

long, narrow columella

Range W. Pacific	Occurrence 🐚🐚	Size 11cm (4½in)

Superfamily CONOIDEA	Family Conidae	Species *Conus textile* Linnaeus

TEXTILE CONE

A light or heavy species, whose short spire has straight or gently concave sides. The body whorl has gently or strongly convex sides, with a rounded or slightly angulated shoulder. Low spiral ridges towards the base; rest of shell is smooth. White, with large and small, overlapping, tent-like markings and three interrupted brown or yellowish spiral bands.
• **REMARK** One of the most venomous of the cone shells.
• **HABITAT** Sand under rocks.

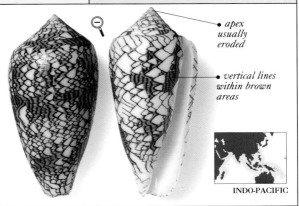

apex usually eroded

vertical lines within brown areas

INDO-PACIFIC

Range Tropical Indo-Pacific	Occurrence 🐚🐚🐚🐚	Size 9cm (3½in)

Superfamily CONOIDEA	Family Conidae	Species *Conus geographus* Linnaeus

GEOGRAPHY CONE

This thin, lightweight, low-
spired shell has an inflated body
whorl which is broadest halfway
down. Base of the body whorl is
encircled by a few low ridges;
undulating ridge on the angle
at the shoulder. Cream or bluish
white in colour, encircled by
two or three broad, pale, or dark
brown bands; brown-edged tent
markings all over.
• **REMARK** This species can
consume fish as large as itself.
• **HABITAT** Coral reefs.

INDO-PACIFIC

strong vertical
growth ridges

columella
abruptly cut
off at its base

Range Tropical Indo-Pacific	Occurrence 🐚🐚🐚	Size 9cm (3½in)

Superfamily CONOIDEA	Family Conidae	Species *Conus imperialis* Linnaeus

IMPERIAL CONE

A thick, heavy, low-spired or
nearly flat-topped shell. Its
body whorl is straight-sided
or very slightly concave;
later spire whorls and the
shoulder of the body whorl
have rounded and blunt
tubercles; the body whorl may
also have spiral rows of small
pits. Creamy white, with pale
brown spiral bands and spiral
rows of dots and dashes.
• **REMARK** Some well-marked
varieties have been optimistically
described as distinct species.
• **HABITAT** Coral reefs in
shallow water.

INDO-PACIFIC

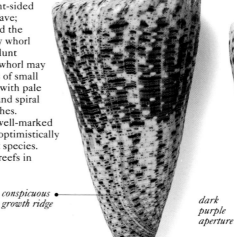

early whorls
eroded

conspicuous
growth ridge

dark
purple
aperture

Range Tropical Indo-Pacific	Occurrence 🐚🐚🐚🐚	Size 7.5cm (3in)

Superfamily CONOIDEA	Family Conidae	Species *Conus pulicarius* Hwass

FLEA-BITE CONE

This heavy, thick shell has a
low spire and a short, fat body
whorl which narrows sharply
at the base. Wide shoulder of
body whorl is roundly angled
and has prominent rounded
tubercles. White, sometimes
tinged pale orange, with black
or reddish brown elongated dots.
• **REMARK** Named late in the
18th century when fleas were
more active on humans.
• **HABITAT** Shallow water.

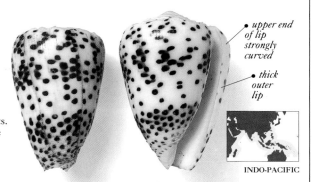

*upper end
of lip
strongly
curved*

*thick
outer
lip*

INDO-PACIFIC

Range Indo-Pacific	Occurrence	Size 6cm (2½in)

Superfamily CONOIDEA	Family Conidae	Species *Conus coccineus* Gmelin

SCARLET CONE

A moderately thin, lightweight shell
with a low spire and a body whorl
which is barrel-shaped below the
shoulder, narrowing sharply towards
base. Spire whorls have undulating
surface; body whorl angled at the
shoulder and covered with low spiral
ridges. Bright red or coffee-coloured,
with a whitish central spiral band variegated with brown spots and blotches.
• **REMARK** Varies greatly in colour and
may lack the spiral ridges.
• **HABITAT** Shallow water.

*undulating
shoulder to
body whorl*

*upper half
of outer lip
straight-edged*

INDO-PACIFIC

Range Tropical Pacific	Occurrence	Size 4cm (1½in)

Superfamily CONOIDEA	Family Conidae	Species *Conus ammiralis* Linnaeus

ADMIRAL CONE

A thick, heavy, glossy shell with
a low, concave-sided, pointed
spire and a straight-sided body
whorl. Shoulder of body whorl
is roundly angled; columella is
short. White, with broad, brown
spiral bands with white patches
and narrow, yellow or pale brown
spiral bands of small marks.
• **REMARK** May have nodules on
shoulder and spiral rows of granules.
• **HABITAT** Sand or coral.

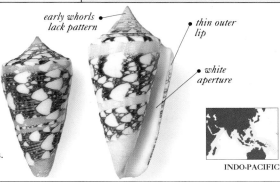

*early whorls
lack pattern*

*thin outer
lip*

*white
aperture*

INDO-PACIFIC

Range Tropical Indo-Pacific	Occurrence	Size 6cm (2½in)

| Superfamily CONOIDEA | Family Conidae | Species *Conus zonatus* Hwass |

ZONED CONE

This thick, heavy, glossy shell has a low spire whose early whorls are eroded and which usually form a dome; later whorls and shoulder of body whorl have low, rounded tubercles. The body whorl is broad-shouldered and spirally ridged at the base; the aperture is about the same width throughout. Bluish grey, with irregular bands of white blotches and encircled by thin, reddish lines.
• **REMARK** May be lighter or darker in colour and spire may be stepped.
• **HABITAT** Shallow reefs.

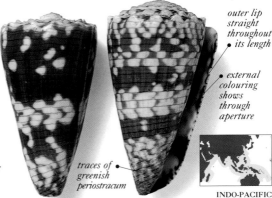

outer lip straight throughout its length

external colouring shows through aperture

traces of greenish periostracum

INDO-PACIFIC

| Range Indian Ocean | Occurrence 🐚🐚 | Size 7cm (2¾in) |

| Superfamily CONOIDEA | Family Conidae | Species *Conus cedonulli* Linnaeus |

MATCHLESS CONE

A thick shell with a short and slightly stepped spire. A broad-shouldered body whorl is covered with fine spiral ridges, strongest at the base. Aperture about the same width throughout. White, largely covered with yellow, orange, or brown, leaving a pattern of spiral bands and lines with dark-edged white blotches and spots.
• **REMARK** Shell was known to most 18th century collectors only from pictures in books.
• **HABITAT** Submerged rock.

early whorls eroded

spots connected like strings of beads

mended break

CARIBBEAN

| Range W. Indies | Occurrence 🐚🐚 | Size 5cm (2in) |

| Superfamily CONOIDEA | Family Conidae | Species *Conus ebraeus* Linnaeus |

HEBREW CONE

A squat, heavy shell with a low, heavily eroded spire and a convex-sided body whorl with a rounded, undulating shoulder and conspicuous spiral ridges above it. Whitish, with three broad spiral bands of large, squarish, black blotches.
• **REMARK** Ground colour often pink, and markings sometimes fuse together.
• **HABITAT** Shallow water.

mended break

INDO-PACIFIC

| Range Tropical Indo-Pacific | Occurrence 🐚🐚🐚🐚🐚 | Size 4cm (1½in) |

Superfamily CONOIDEA	Family Conidae	Species *Conus dorreensis* Peron

PONTIFICAL CONE

A thick but lightweight shell with a stepped spire and a convex-sided body whorl. Later, spire whorls and the shoulder of the body whorl have rounded tubercles. Spiral rows of pits cover all of the body whorl. The shell is white; periostracum yellowish brown, with black spiral band near base and on shoulder.
• **REMARK** Periostracum has only colour.
• **HABITAT** Shallow water.

• *black band often worn away*

AUSTRALIAN

Range W. Australia	Occurrence ♦♦♦♦	Size 3cm (1¼in)

Superfamily CONOIDEA	Family Conidae	Species *Conus arenatus* Hwass

SAND-DUSTED CONE

A thick, heavy shell with a low spire; the slightly convex or straight-sided body whorl is widest just below the well-rounded shoulder. Top of body whorl and spire whorls have prominent rounded tubercles. Suture is deep; columella is short and straight. White or cream, covered with small, oval, brown and black spots.
• **REMARK** Although its name is apt, the dots' size vary greatly.
• **HABITAT** Intertidal.

• *tubercles not spotted*

aperture a uniform width throughout its length

INDO-PACIFIC

Range Tropical Indo-Pacific	Occurrence ♦♦♦♦	Size 5cm (2in)

Superfamily CONOIDEA	Family Conidae	Species *Conus purpurascens* Sowerby

PURPLE CONE

A solid shell with a low spire, sometimes slightly stepped whorls, and a pointed or bluntly rounded apex. Body whorl has angled or rounded shoulders, convex sides, and a narrow base. Usually purplish or bluish, covered with spiral rows of brown dashes and white dots; large brown or greyish areas only thinly covered with these markings.
• **REMARK** Shell occasionally encircled by thin brown lines.
• **HABITAT** Shallow water.

• *mended break*

• *opaque bluish white inside aperture*

low spiral ridges at base

PANAMIC

Range Gulf of California to Peru	Occurrence ♦♦♦	Size 5cm (2in)

Superfamily CONOIDEA	Family Conidae	Species *Conus pulcher* Lightfoot

BUTTERFLY CONE

This is a heavy and sometimes extremely large, low-spired shell. It has a round-shouldered body whorl which may well be either straight-sided or slightly convex.

slightly concave spire whorls

apex always eroded on old shells

flame-like markings at shoulder

The spire whorls on this shell lack any form of spiral orna-ment; they tend to be slightly concave on top. The apex on old shells is always eroded. The body whorl can have up to 12 low, spiral ridges towards the base, but these become obsolete on older examples. The shell is coloured white or cream, with orange-brown spots and dashes distributed all over in a mixture of broad and narrow, spiral bands.
• **REMARK** This is is the world's largest cone shell; specimens exceeding the 20cm (8in) example shown here have been found on occasions, but they are usually less than half that length.
• **HABITAT** Shallow water.

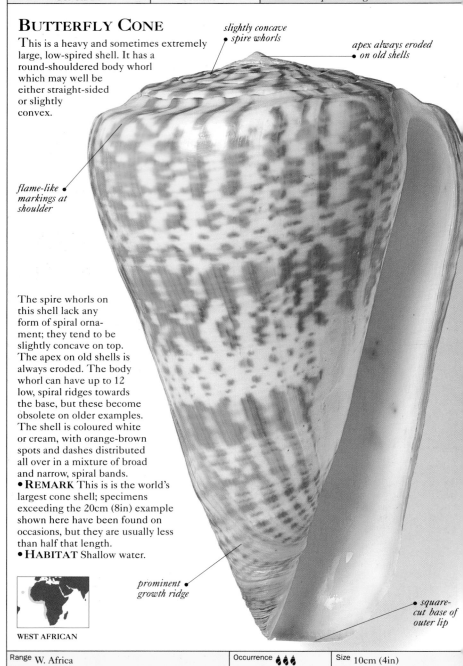

prominent growth ridge

square-cut base of outer lip

WEST AFRICAN

Range W. Africa	Occurrence ▲▲▲	Size 10cm (4in)

Superfamily CONOIDEA	Family Conidae	Species *Conus circumcisus* Born

CIRCUMCISION CONE

A low-spired shell; slightly convex
body whorl; suture indistinct. Sharp
apex; tops of whorls slightly concave.
Low spiral ridges cover body whorl.
White, pink, or tinged violet; spiral
brown bands and occasional black
or purple spots and dashes.
• **REMARK** Brightly coloured and
spotted examples are very rare.
• **HABITAT** Shallow and
deep water.

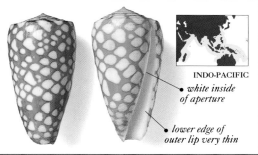

INDO-PACIFIC

*straight edge
to outer lip*

*aperture widens
gradually from
top to bottom*

Range W. Pacific	Occurrence 🌢🌢	Size 6cm (2½in)

Superfamily CONOIDEA	Family Conidae	Species *Conus nobilis* Linnaeus

NOBLE CONE

A solid, low-spired shell with a pointed
apex and a straight-sided or gently convex
body whorl. The tops of the spire whorls
are slightly concave; shoulder of the body
whorl is sharply angled. Pale brown to
dark red, with large, white, closely spaced
patches which are sometimes dark-edged.
• **REMARK** There are several named
varieties of this attractive cone.
• **HABITAT** Shallow and deep water.

INDO-PACIFIC

*white inside
of aperture*

*lower edge of
outer lip very thin*

Range Tropical Indo-Pacific	Occurrence 🌢🌢	Size 5cm (2in)

Superfamily CONOIDEA	Family Conidae	Species *Conus tessulatus* Born

TESSELLATE CONE

On this thick, glossy shell, early
whorls and blunt apex are raised;
spiral ridges on tops of whorls.
Sides of body whorl are straight or
slightly concave; shoulder broad
and rounded or gently angled.
White with orange or red rectangles.
• **REMARK** Old, heavy examples
often have white, not violet, base.
• **HABITAT** Shallow water.

INDO-PACIFIC

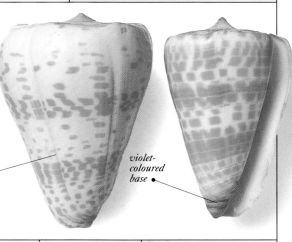

*vertical groove
shows where shell
stopped growing
for a time*

*violet-
coloured
base*

Range Tropical Indo-Pacific	Occurrence 🌢🌢🌢🌢	Size 5cm (2in)

Superfamily CONOIDEA	Family Conidae	Species *Conus genuanus* Linnaeus

GARTER CONE

A glossy shell with low spire.
The body whorl is smooth
except for some indistinct spiral
ridges towards the base. Grey,
tinged with pink or blue
encircled by broad, spiral,
greenish brown bands; the body
whorl is covered with spiral rows
of large and small black and
white dashes and dots.
• **REMARK** The attractive
colours of this species soon fade.
• **HABITAT** Shallow water.

WEST AFRICAN

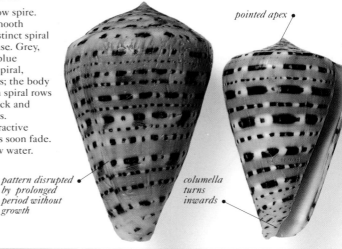

pointed apex

*pattern disrupted
by prolonged
period without
growth*

*columella
turns
inwards*

Range W. Africa	Occurrence 🐚🐚	Size 5cm (2in)

Superfamily CONOIDEA	Family Conidae	Species *Conus amadis* Gmelin

AMADIS CONE

A thin, glossy shell with
a strongly keeled
shoulder and a short
spire. Early whorls are
prominently elevated,
later ones are con-
cave and sometimes
stepped. Outer lip is
curved. White, heavily
or lightly overlaid with
pale or dark brown and
variegated with angular
white blotches; aperture
and columella white.
• **REMARK** One form
has broad dark bands and
extended spire.
• **HABITAT** Offshore.

INDO-PACIFIC

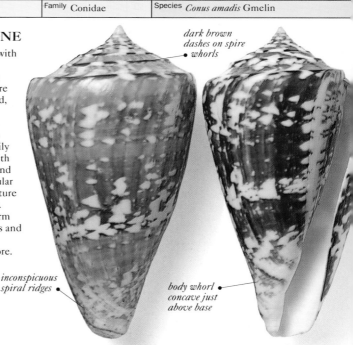

*dark brown
dashes on spire
whorls*

*inconspicuous
spiral ridges*

*body whorl
concave just
above base*

Range Indo-West Pacific	Occurrence 🐚🐚🐚	Size 7.5cm (3in)

AUGER SHELLS

MOST OF THE MANY hundreds of different species of augers to be found have long, slender, glossy shells; some can be thick and heavy, while others are more light and remarkably attenuated. The aperture is small, and usually rectangular, and it ends in a short, wide siphonal canal; the outer lip is thin and sharp-edged, and the columella is spirally twisted. There is always a small, corneous operculum yet there is no periostracum.

•

All species are from warm or temperate waters and most live in the intertidal zone, where they burrow; some hide under rocks and lumps of coral. The animals feed on various marine worms.

Superfamily CONOIDEA	Family Terebridae	Species *Terebra maculata* Linnaeus

MARLINSPIKE

A heavy, glossy shell with broad body whorl; elongate aperture. Later whorls slightly convex. Early whorls have weak vertical ridges; later whorls smooth. Cream, with interrupted spiral bands of brown markings.
• **REMARK** This shell has been used as a boring tool.
• **HABITAT** Shallow water.

no dark markings just above suture •

• markings of lower row smaller than those of upper

• well defined but shallow suture

INDO-PACIFIC

Range Tropical Indo-Pacific	Occurrence 🐚🐚🐚🐚	Size 14cm (5½in)

Superfamily CONOIDEA	Family Terebridae	Species *Terebra subulata* Linnaeus

SUBULATE AUGER

Although this shell is strongly built, early whorls are often missing. Whorls are straight-sided; aperture is rectangular. Spire whorls may have spiral grooves. The shell has strong vertical growth lines. Cream, with large, rectangular brown blotches.
• **REMARK** Name is tautologous, as "subulate" means "auger-shaped".
• **HABITAT** Offshore.

markings may be much smaller than seen here •

early whorls • lack markings

• top of each whorl well rounded

body whorl • has three rows of blotches

• two rows of blotches per spire whorl

INDO-PACIFIC

Range Tropical Indo-Pacific	Occurrence 🐚🐚🐚	Size 13cm (5in)

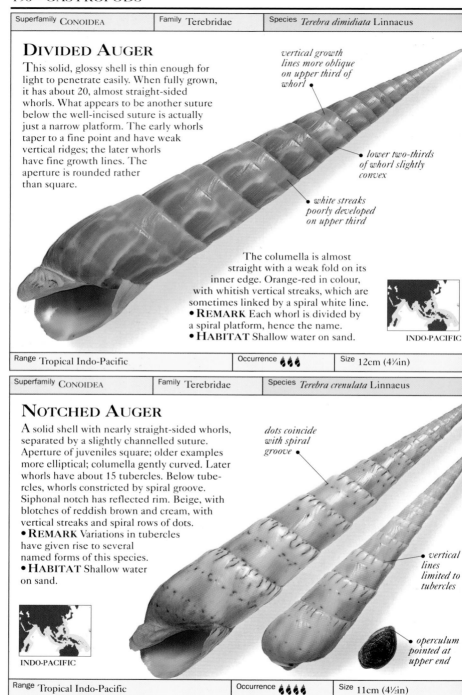

| Superfamily CONOIDEA | Family Terebridae | Species *Terebra dimidiata* Linnaeus |

DIVIDED AUGER

This solid, glossy shell is thin enough for light to penetrate easily. When fully grown, it has about 20, almost straight-sided whorls. What appears to be another suture below the well-incised suture is actually just a narrow platform. The early whorls taper to a fine point and have weak vertical ridges; the later whorls have fine growth lines. The aperture is rounded rather than square.

vertical growth lines more oblique on upper third of whorl

lower two-thirds of whorl slightly convex

white streaks poorly developed on upper third

The columella is almost straight with a weak fold on its inner edge. Orange-red in colour, with whitish vertical streaks, which are sometimes linked by a spiral white line.
• **REMARK** Each whorl is divided by a spiral platform, hence the name.
• **HABITAT** Shallow water on sand.

INDO-PACIFIC

| Range Tropical Indo-Pacific | Occurrence ♦♦♦ | Size 12cm (4¾in) |

| Superfamily CONOIDEA | Family Terebridae | Species *Terebra crenulata* Linnaeus |

NOTCHED AUGER

A solid shell with nearly straight-sided whorls, separated by a slightly channelled suture. Aperture of juveniles square; older examples more elliptical; columella gently curved. Later whorls have about 15 tubercles. Below tubercles, whorls constricted by spiral groove. Siphonal notch has reflected rim. Beige, with blotches of reddish brown and cream, with vertical streaks and spiral rows of dots.
• **REMARK** Variations in tubercles have given rise to several named forms of this species.
• **HABITAT** Shallow water on sand.

dots coincide with spiral groove

vertical lines limited to tubercles

operculum pointed at upper end

INDO-PACIFIC

| Range Tropical Indo-Pacific | Occurrence ♦♦♦♦ | Size 11cm (4½in) |

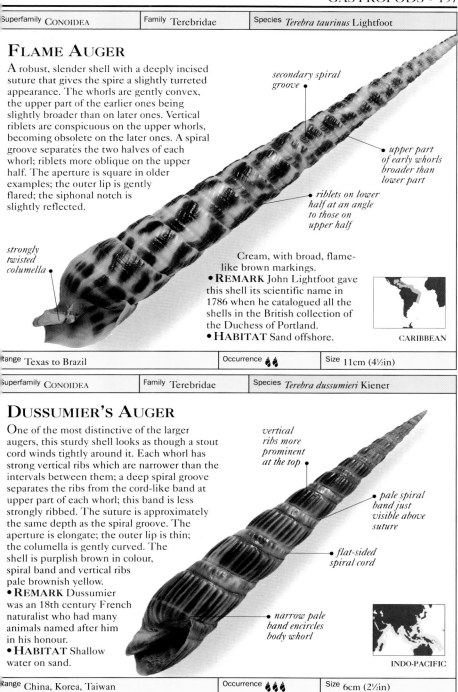

Superfamily CONOIDEA	Family Terebridae	Species *Terebra taurinus* Lightfoot

FLAME AUGER

A robust, slender shell with a deeply incised suture that gives the spire a slightly turreted appearance. The whorls are gently convex, the upper part of the earlier ones being slightly broader than on later ones. Vertical riblets are conspicuous on the upper whorls, becoming obsolete on the later ones. A spiral groove separates the two halves of each whorl; riblets more oblique on the upper half. The aperture is square in older examples; the outer lip is gently flared; the siphonal notch is slightly reflected.

secondary spiral groove

upper part of early whorls broader than lower part

riblets on lower half at an angle to those on upper half

strongly twisted columella

Cream, with broad, flame-like brown markings.
• **REMARK** John Lightfoot gave this shell its scientific name in 1786 when he catalogued all the shells in the British collection of the Duchess of Portland.
• **HABITAT** Sand offshore.

CARIBBEAN

Range Texas to Brazil	Occurrence 👣👣	Size 11cm (4½in)

Superfamily CONOIDEA	Family Terebridae	Species *Terebra dussumieri* Kiener

DUSSUMIER'S AUGER

One of the most distinctive of the larger augers, this sturdy shell looks as though a stout cord winds tightly around it. Each whorl has strong vertical ribs which are narrower than the intervals between them; a deep spiral groove separates the ribs from the cord-like band at upper part of each whorl; this band is less strongly ribbed. The suture is approximately the same depth as the spiral groove. The aperture is elongate; the outer lip is thin; the columella is gently curved. The shell is purplish brown in colour, spiral band and vertical ribs pale brownish yellow.
• **REMARK** Dussumier was an 18th century French naturalist who had many animals named after him in his honour.
• **HABITAT** Shallow water on sand.

vertical ribs more prominent at the top

pale spiral band just visible above suture

flat-sided spiral cord

narrow pale band encircles body whorl

INDO-PACIFIC

Range China, Korea, Taiwan	Occurrence 👣👣👣	Size 6cm (2½in)

Superfamily CONOIDEA	Family Terebridae	Species *Terebra commaculata* Gmelin

MANY-SPOTTED AUGER

An extremely tall, solid shell of at least 25 whorls, ending in a sharp, usually complete apex. The spire coils so gradually that the whorls seem to have almost parallel sides. Below suture are two spiral bands ornamented with rounded tubercles, the uppermost band being the larger; from about halfway down the spire of a mature example, the tubercles become progressively less distinct. White, with broad, flame-like strips.

• **REMARK** Distinguished from most of the other augers by the length, breadth, and continuity of its brown markings.

• **HABITAT** Shallow water on sand.

early whorls have slightly concave sides

groove between rows of tubercles

tubercles become less distinct from here down

lattice ornament on all whorls

INDO-PACIFIC

Range Indo-West Pacific	Occurrence	Size 7.5cm (3in)

Superfamily CONOIDEA	Family Terebridae	Species *Terebra babylonia* Lamarck

BABYLON AUGER

A glossy, solid shell with an acutely pointed spire. The slightly convex whorls are encircled by a band of rectangular nodules below the suture; the whorls appear stepped because the band projects slightly. A spiral groove separates the band from the rest of the whorl which has wavy vertical grooves crossed by two more spiral grooves; the base of the body whorl has lesser spiral grooves. The appearance of the lower half of the body whorl is evidence that the surface ornament of the rest of shell doubles its thickness. Reddish brown, overlaid with opaque white ornament which becomes pure white on the upper whorls.

• **REMARK** The name implies a resemblance to a type of tapestry associated with the ancient city of Babylon.

• **HABITAT** Shallow water.

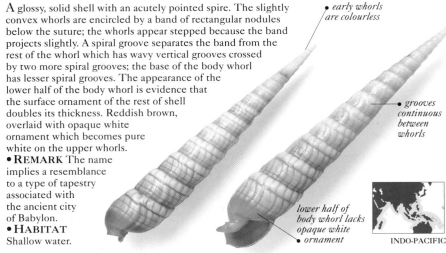

early whorls are colourless

grooves continuous between whorls

lower half of body whorl lacks opaque white ornament

INDO-PACIFIC

Range Tropical Indo-Pacific	Occurrence	Size 7.5cm (3in)

Superfamily CONOIDEA	Family Terebridae	Species *Terebra areolata* Link

FLY-SPOTTED AUGER

A tall, glossy, almost straight-sided shell of about 20 whorls. The earlier whorls have vertical ridges, which tend to become obsolete on later whorls. A deep groove encircling all whorls divides each of them in the ratio of one-third to two-thirds. The colour is cream or pale yellowish brown with spiral rows of brown blotches.
• **REMARK** The scientific name comes from a Latin word meaning "little open spaces" and refers to the brown blotches.
• **HABITAT** Shallow water on sand.

vertical ridges begin to die out

blotches just above the suture larger than the others

upper half of outer lip angled

INDO-PACIFIC

Range Tropical Indo-Pacific	Occurrence ♦♦♦	Size 12cm (4¾in)

Superfamily CONOIDEA	Family Terebridae	Species *Hastula lanceata* Linnaeus

LANCE AUGER

A moderately thick, sturdy, and glossy shell, whose common name accurately describes the appearance presented by its narrow spire and sharply pointed apex. The smoothly rounded vertical ridges developed on the early whorls rapidly diminish in strength and become indistinct or obsolete on the last few whorls. The suture, though shallow, is very distinct. The slightly stepped appearance of the early whorls is replaced by the almost straight sides of the later ones. Upper half of columella is concave, lower half recurved. It is white, with thin, vertical brown streaks which are interrupted on the body whorl.
• **REMARK** Of all the many auger shells, this is one of the least variable and is unlikely to be mistaken for any other species.
• **HABITAT** Shallow water on sand.

vertical streaks begin just below suture

apex often missing

equidistant vertical streaks

small and narrow aperture

INDO-PACIFIC

Range Tropical Indo-Pacific	Occurrence ♦♦♦♦	Size 5cm (2in)

PYRAMS

THIS IS A WORLDWIDE GROUP of high-spired shells with a smooth or ribbed surface. There may be folds on the columella; a thin, corneous operculum is usually present. Som larger shells are colourful but others ar white or translucent. The animals ar parasitic upon other invertebrates.

Superfamily PYRAMIDELLOIDEA	Family Pyramidellidae	Species *Pyramidella dolabrata* Linnaeus

HATCHET PYRAM

One of the larger and more attractive pyrams, the smooth, shiny shell has a tall and almost straight-sided spire of roughly ten whorls. The apex, of less than two whorls, is turned on its side – quite a normal condition among pyrams – but it is often missing from adult specimens. There is a narrow and deep umbilicus. The outer lip is thin and sharp and there are three strong folds on the columella. Older specimens develop a columellar lip. Creamy white or greyish white, with three, spiral dark or light brown bands on each spire whorl and four on the body whorl.
• **REMARK** There may be one less colour band per whorl.
• **HABITAT** Sand offshore.

apex missing from adult shell

INDO-PACIFIC

top of lip slightly thickened

bands show through aperture

deep groove above folds

Range Circumtropical	Occurrence ♦♦♦♦	Size 3cm (1¼in)

BUBBLE SHELLS

INCLUDED IN this particular group are species which, although they share certain anatomical features, do in fact belong to different families. Most have thin bubble-like shells; som have an operculum. Many feed o algae, others on invertebrates. Som burrow in muddy sand in warm seas.

Superfamily PHILINOIDEA	Family Bullinidae	Species *Bullina lineata* Gray

LINED BUBBLE

A thin, fragile, globular, or egg-shaped shell with whorls separated by a deep suture and covered by regularly spaced, flat-topped spiral riblets. Whitish in colour, with two spiral, red lines crossed by thinner, disjointed, wavy red lines.
• **HABITAT** Shallow water.

INDO-PACIFIC
JAPONIC

white columella

Range Tropical Indo-Pacific, S. Japan	Occurrence ♦♦♦♦	Size 2.5cm (1in)

Superfamily PHILINOIDEA	Family Acteonidae	Species *Pupa solidula* Linnaeus

SOLID PUPA

Shaped like an elongated tear-drop, the outer lip of this solid shell is almost straight edged. There is a double fold on the lower half of the columella, and a single one on the upper half. Rounded ribs encircle the shell. White in colour, with square black, red, or fawn spots on the ribs; the aperture and columella are both white.
• **REMARK** Red-spotted shells are the most commonly found variety.

rib may lack
• *spots*

INDO-PACIFIC

• *groove on top of fold*

Range Tropical Indo-Pacific	Occurrence 🐚🐚🐚	Size 2.5cm (1in)

Superfamily PHILINOIDEA	Family Acteonidae	Species *Pupa sulcata* Gmelin

FURROWED PUPA

A thick, short-spired shell with a well-marked suture and a large, gently rounded body whorl. A massive, twisted fold at the lower end of the columella is separated by a groove from a lesser fold just above. Broad, flat-topped ribs encircle the body whorl. The shell is white in colour, with smudged blackish or brownish spots on the ribs.
• **HABITAT** Shallow water on sand.

INDO-PACIFIC

• *porcelain-white aperture*

ribs closer
• *at base*

Range Tropical Indo-Pacific	Occurrence 🐚🐚	Size 2.5cm (1in)

Superfamily PHILINOIDEA	Family Acteonidae	Species *Acteon eloiseae* Abbott

THE ELOISE

A globose shell, the whorls of its short spire seem partly telescoped into each other because a deep, channelled suture separates them. The apex is low and the spire whorls are gently rounded. Low, flattened ribs encircle all whorls; these are crossed by fine growth striae. There is a strong, twisted fold towards base of the columella. The most remarkable feature of this shell is its striking colour pattern: displayed against a white ground are large, orange-pink blotches, each blotch with a dark, reddish-brown edge; three rows of blotches encircle the body whorl.
• **REMARK** This lovely shell, first classified in 1973, is named after one of its original discoverers, Eloise Bosch.
• **HABITAT** Muddy sand at low tide.

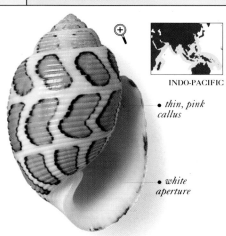

INDO-PACIFIC

• *thin, pink callus*

• *white aperture*

Range Masirah Island (Oman)	Occurrence 🐚🐚	Size 3cm (1¼in)

Superfamily PHILINOIDEA	Family Hamineidae	Species *Atys naucum* Linnaeus

WHITE PACIFIC ATYS

Thin and globose, this shell really does have a bubble-like appearance. The spire is deeply submerged within the body whorl; there is a small umbilicus. Glossy and superficially smooth. The entire body whorl is encircled by grooves, shallow and widely spaced in the middle portion, but becoming deeper and more crowded towards the top and bottom. Faint growth lines cross the spiral grooves. White, with orange-brown periostracum.
• **REMARK** Illustrated specimen has a well-developed, slightly reflected lip.
• **HABITAT** Washed up on beaches.

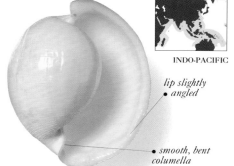

INDO-PACIFIC

lip slightly • *angled*

smooth, bent • *columella*

Range Tropical Indo-Pacific	Occurrence 🐚🐚🐚	Size 4cm (1½in)

Superfamily PHILINOIDEA	Family Hydatinidae	Species *Micromelo undata* Bruguière

MINIATURE MELO

Thin and globose, with a spire enveloped by the large body whorl, the shell has a broadly rounded top which is just slightly taller than the aperture. Creamy white, encircled by three spiral, red lines with paler red, vertical lines between them.
• **REMARK** With its bluish, pink-spotted foot and head lobes protruding from the shell, the animal is a beautiful sight crawling about among feathery green algae.
• **HABITAT** Low tide on algae.

apex sunk into • *later whorls*

⊕

CARIBBEAN

equidistant • *spiral lines*

crescent-shaped vertical lines •

Range S.E. Florida to Brazil, Ascension Is.	Occurrence 🐚🐚	Size 1.2cm (½in)

Superfamily PHILINOIDEA	Family Hydatinidae	Species *Hydatina amplustre* Linnaeus

ROYAL PAPER BUBBLE

Thin, smooth, globular shell with a flat, slightly sunken spire. The columella is smooth and straight. The body whorl normally has two spiral, pink zones edged with dark brown bands, and three white zones, one of which is central.
• **REMARK** Examples show brown (not white) central band .
• **HABITAT** Shallow water in sand or mud.

⊕

INDO-PACIFIC

aperture has thin white glaze •

columella cut off at base •

Range Tropical Pacific	Occurrence 🐚🐚🐚	Size 2.5cm (1in)

Superfamily PHILINOIDEA	Family Hydatinidae	Species *Hydatina albocincta* van der Hoeven

LINED PAPER BUBBLE

There is so little calcium carbonate in the composition of this paper-thin shell that it is flexible when touched. Smooth and glossy, it has a sunken spire and an aperture which is taller than it is wide. The columella is strongly curved and there is a thin, transparent, parietal callus. Encircling the body whorl are five white bands and four broader brown bands; each brown band is variegated with thin, vertical, paler streaks. A thin, pale amber periostracum covers the shell.
• **HABITAT** Offshore.

uneven edges to bands

INDO-PACIFIC

perio-stracum flaking at edge

Range Tropical Indo-Pacific	Occurrence 🐚🐚	Size 5cm (2in)

Superfamily PHILINOIDEA	Family Hydatinidae	Species *Hydatina physis* Linnaeus

GREEN PAPER BUBBLE

A thin, fragile shell with a very large aperture which flares towards the lower end. Its shiny surface has irregular growth lines and may show mended breaks. The spire is sunken and the suture is deeply channelled. A narrow umbilicus is almost concealed by the reflected edge of the smooth, straight columella. Creamy yellow colour, with crowded, wavy, spiral lines which vary in width; the aperture is white.
• **REMARK** Fresh examples have an orange-brown or greenish periostracum.
• **HABITAT** Shallow water on silty sand.

INDO-PACIFIC

upper end of aperture slightly constricted

lip edge slightly thickened

Range Circumtropical	Occurrence 🐚🐚🐚	Size 3cm (1¼in)

Superfamily PHILINOIDEA	Family Bullidae	Species *Bulla ampulla* Linnaeus

FLASK BUBBLE

A thin, opaque shell. The sunken apex looks like a narrow and deep umbilicus. The outer lip rises above the rest of the shell; it is narrowed above, and broadly expanded below. Opaque parietal callus is continuous with the straight columella. Grey or brownish, with purple blotches or streaks and white spots; rare examples with two spiral bands. Aperture white, with external colour showing through.
• **REMARK** Buried in sand all day, the animal emerges to feed on seaweeds at night.
• **HABITAT** Intertidal on sand.

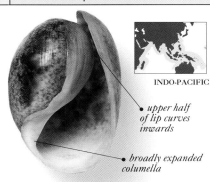

INDO-PACIFIC

upper half of lip curves inwards

broadly expanded columella

Range Indo-Pacific, S. Africa	Occurrence 🐚🐚🐚🐚🐚	Size 5cm (2in)

SEA BUTTERFLIES

THE FRAGILE AND GLASSY SHELLS of pteropods may often be found washed up on beaches, although these small molluscs spend their lives in the upper layers of the world's oceans. Called sea butterflies because of their wing-like extensions, they are among the most abundant of marine animals.

Superfamily THECOSOMATA	Family Cavoliniidae	Species *Cavolinia uncinata* Rang

HOOKED CAVOLINE

A small and fragile shell which resembles a curious insect (a similar species was classified as such by Linnaeus in 1758). Shiny and plump, its aperture is narrow and is partly covered by a ridged shield whose rear end extends into three sharp points. The shell is amber coloured.
• **REMARK** Prefers warmer waters.
• **HABITAT** Open sea.

narrow aperture

ridged hood

WORLD

Range Worldwide	Occurrence 🐚🐚🐚🐚🐚	Size 1.2cm (½in)

Superfamily THECOSOMATA	Family Cavoliniidae	Species *Cavolinia tridentata* Niebuhr

THREE-TOOTHED CAVOLINE

Shiny, transparent, and smooth, the shell has a swollen upper side (shown upside down in top illustration). The longer, more flattened, underside has a rim-like extension. A long slit separates each side. There is a long, straight, central spur. Amber coloured.
• **REMARK** Like others in its family, this species lacks an operculum.
• **HABITAT** Open sea.

WORLD

ridge ends in blunt point

Range Worldwide	Occurrence 🐚🐚🐚🐚🐚	Size 2cm (¾in)

Superfamily THECOSOMATA	Family Cavoliniidae	Species *Diacria trispinosa* Blainville

THREE-SPINED DIACRIA

This tiny shell is shiny, transparent, and slightly convex. Each lip of the aperture is thickened, the upper one being straight sided and upturned. There are two sharp spines each side of the aperture, as well as a long funnel-like spine at the base. Colourless with brown edges.
• **HABITAT** Open sea.

brown edges

WORLD

reflected upper lip

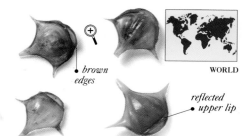

Range Worldwide	Occurrence 🐚🐚🐚	Size 1.2cm (½in)

TUSK SHELLS

TUSK SHELLS

THE TAPERING, tubular shell that is typical of this class has very few conspicuous ornamental features other than its longitudinal ribs and concentric lines. The hole at the rear end may be bordered by a notch or slit, or it may contain a short pipe. Tusk shells live buried in sand offshore.

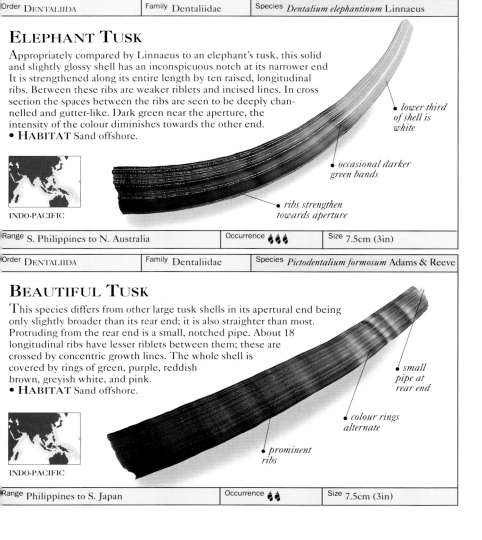

Order DENTALIIDA	Family Dentaliidae	Species *Dentalium elephantinum* Linnaeus

ELEPHANT TUSK

Appropriately compared by Linnaeus to an elephant's tusk, this solid and slightly glossy shell has an inconspicuous notch at its narrower end It is strengthened along its entire length by ten raised, longitudinal ribs. Between these ribs are weaker riblets and incised lines. In cross section the spaces between the ribs are seen to be deeply channelled and gutter-like. Dark green near the aperture, the intensity of the colour diminishes towards the other end.
• **HABITAT** Sand offshore.

lower third of shell is white

occasional darker green bands

ribs strengthen towards aperture

INDO-PACIFIC

Range S. Philippines to N. Australia	Occurrence 🐚🐚🐚	Size 7.5cm (3in)

Order DENTALIIDA	Family Dentaliidae	Species *Pictodentalium formosum* Adams & Reeve

BEAUTIFUL TUSK

This species differs from other large tusk shells in its apertural end being only slightly broader than its rear end; it is also straighter than most. Protruding from the rear end is a small, notched pipe. About 18 longitudinal ribs have lesser riblets between them; these are crossed by concentric growth lines. The whole shell is covered by rings of green, purple, reddish brown, greyish white, and pink.
• **HABITAT** Sand offshore.

small pipe at rear end

colour rings alternate

prominent ribs

INDO-PACIFIC

Range Philippines to S. Japan	Occurrence 🐚🐚	Size 7.5cm (3in)

Order DENTALIIDA	Family Dentaliidae	Species *Fissidentalium vernedei* Sowerby

VERNEDE'S TUSK

Compared with its considerable length, this gently curved tusk shell enlarges very little from end to end. The rear end has an internal pipe bearing a notch, and the edge of the aperture is very thin. In cross section the shell is round because the surface ornament is poorly developed. Fine, longitudinal riblets, with narrow grooves between them, are crossed by occasional growth rings. Mended breaks are usually present towards the aperture of older specimens. White ground colour is variegated with occasional, broad or narrow rings of yellow or pale brown.
• **REMARK** The world's largest tusk shell, named after a Victorian shell collector.
• **HABITAT** Sand offshore.

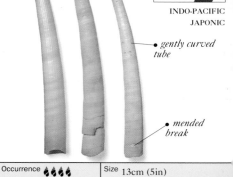

INDO-PACIFIC
JAPONIC

• *gently curved tube*

• *mended break*

Range Philippines to Japan	Occurrence ♦♦♦♦	Size 13cm (5in)

Order DENTALIIDA	Family Dentaliidae	Species *Antalis longitrorsum* Reeve

ELONGATE TUSK

This thin, shiny shell is long and slender; it is gracefully curved and has a rough edge to the aperture. The narrower rear end has a very small notch. Juvenile specimens are almost needle-sharp at the rear end. Some tusk shells may be as long and as slender, but none is more gracefully curved. Except for very fine, longitudinal lines at the rear end, and occasional growth rings, it is almost smooth. The shell's uniformly white colour often has a somewhat yellowish or greenish tinge.
• **REMARK** Specimens which have a pinkish or apricot colour are occasionally found.
• **HABITAT** Sand offshore.

• *greenish tinge*

INDO-PACIFIC

• *juveniles have sharply pointed rear end*

Range Tropical Indo-Pacific	Occurrence ♦♦	Size 9.5cm (3¾in)

Order DENTALIIDA	Family Dentaliidae	Species *Antalis dentalis* Linnaeus

EUROPEAN TUSK

A rough-edged shell, its apertural end is wider than its rear. Gently curved at first, it bends more sharply towards the rear, sometimes being slightly angled in the middle. Strong longitudinal ribs are weakest just above aperture. May be white, pale brown, or pink.
• **REMARK** Although this is not a robust shell, it seldom displays evidence of mended breaks.
• **HABITAT** Sand offshore.

MEDITERRANEAN

• *jagged edge*

Range Mediterranean and Adriatic	Occurrence ♦♦♦♦	Size 3cm (1¼in)

CHITONS

CHITONS

THE HALLMARK of these molluscs is their overlapping, eight-piece shell; the pieces (also known as valves) are movable, and are held in place by a muscular girdle which may be smooth or variously ornamented. Chitons, also known as coat-of-mail shells, live on or under rocks and stones in most seas.

Order NEOLORICATA	Family Chitonidae	Species *Chiton tuberculatus* Linnaeus

WEST INDIAN CHITON

Like most chitons, this shell is longer than it is broad, and the valves are prominently arched. The central strip of valves is smooth with crowded, wavy, vertical riblets covering triangular areas each side; the triangular areas next to the girdle each have about six beaded, transverse riblets. End valve has crowded, radiating, beaded riblets. The girdle is almost equally wide all around, covered with small, smooth scales. Greyish green or brownish in colour, with pale green on scales and beads.
• **REMARK** The girdle ornamentation resembles shark-skin.
• **HABITAT** Rocky shores.

SIDE VIEW UNDER VIEW TOP VIEW

CARIBBEAN

dark bands on girdle *valves overlap* *front end*

Range S.E. Florida and W. Indies	Occurrence ♦♦♦♦	Size 6cm (2½in)

Order NEOLORICATA	Family Chitonidae	Species *Chiton marmoratus* Gmelin

MARBLED CHITON

An elongate, almost parallel-sided chiton, its valves are smooth and rather flattened. The narrow girdle is covered with flat, lozenge-shaped scales. Colour and pattern varies considerably; may be olive-green, brown, or greyish with paler blotches and streaks; girdle has alternating bands of green and greyish scales.
• **REMARK** The shell is distinguished by the completely smooth surface of the valves.
• **HABITAT** Rocky shores.

rear end

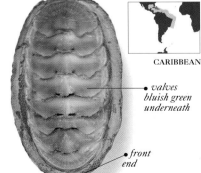

CARIBBEAN

valves bluish green underneath

front end

Range S.E. Florida and W. Indies	Occurrence ♦♦♦♦♦	Size 6cm (2½in)

| Order NEOLORICATA | Family Chitonidae | Species *Chiton striatus* Barnes |

MAGNIFICENT CHITON

A large, well-arched chiton surrounded by a broad girdle. The central portion of each valve has crowded, straight riblets which are usually worn smooth at the highest point. The triangular side areas of each valve have coarse, transverse ribs. Head and tail valves have coarse radiating ribs. Polished, square-sided granules cover the girdle. Blackish-brown colour with a dark green girdle.
• **HABITAT** Intertidal rocks.

slight gloss on valves

PERUVIAN

front end

| Range Chile | Occurrence 🐾🐾🐾 | Size 9cm (3½in) |

| Order NEOLORICATA | Family Ischnochitonidae | Species *Ischnochiton comptus* Gould |

DECKED CHITON

An elongate chiton with broad valves, its narrow girdle is densely covered with tiny scales. Valves are smooth and may be red, blackish, white or yellow, or combinations of these colours; the girdle is greenish.
• **REMARK** One of several related species with scales covering the girdle.
• **HABITAT** Shallow water under stones.

narrow girdle

JAPONIC

contrasting colours

| Range Japan | Occurrence 🐾🐾🐾🐾 | Size 2.5cm (1in) |

| Order NEOLORICATA | Family Ischnochitonidae | Species *Ischnochiton contractus* Reeve |

LATTICE CHITON

The two middle valves of this chiton are broader than others. Tail valve about as broad as it is long. Median valves have ribs and pimples. Girdle is scaly. Varies greatly in colour and pattern. Valves often streaked centrally.
• **REMARK** Varieties of this shell have on occasion been described as species.
• **HABITAT** Intertidal stones and shells.

pimples on outer part of valves

AUSTRALIAN

ridges on inner part of valves

| Range S. Australia | Occurrence 🐾🐾🐾🐾🐾 | Size 4cm (1½in) |

| Order NEOLORICATA | Family Chitonidae | Species *Tonicia chilensis* Frembly |

ELEGANT CHITON

A thin, broad, smooth girdle surrounds this chiton. The median valve behind the head valve is larger than the others. Reddish brown, streaked and blotched with yellow, especially on head and tail, and on central valves.
• **REMARK** When dry, the girdle has a tendency to wrinkle up at the sides.
• **HABITAT** Shallow water on rocks.

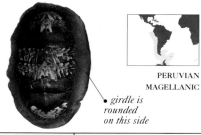

PERUVIAN
MAGELLANIC

girdle is rounded on this side

| Range Peru to Chile | Occurrence ♦♦♦♦ | Size 5cm (2in) |

| Order NEOLORICATA | Family Ischnochitonidae | Species *Chaetopleura papilio* Spengler |

BUTTERFLY CHITON

A fairly large chiton surrounded by a broad girdle covered with stiff bristles when fresh. The valves are gently arched, slightly ridged down the mid-line, and highly polished. Dark brown, with a mottled and flecked yellowish brown area at the centre of each valve. The bases of the valves are whitish, and their sides may have bluish white stains. The girdle is dark brown and the undersides of the valves are yellowish white.
• **REMARK** Valves look like polished mahogany.
• **HABITAT** Under rocks at low tide.

back end

smooth valves

SOUTH AFRICAN

front end

pale-edged valves

| Range S. Africa | Occurrence ♦♦♦ | Size 6cm (2½in) |

| Order NEOLORICATA | Family Chitonidae | Species *Acanthopleura granulata* Gmelin |

FUZZY CHITON

A strongly humped chiton surrounded by a thick girdle which is thickly covered with coarse spines. The valves, if unworn, are granulated. Valves are brown when unworn, but usually appear greyish brown with darker brown crests and sides. The girdle is whitish with blackish bands.
• **REMARK** Valves usually heavily eroded.
• **HABITAT** Intertidal rocks.

CARIBBEAN

front end

| Range S. Florida, W. Indies | Occurrence ♦♦♦♦♦ | Size 6cm (2½in) |

BIVALVES

AWNING CLAMS

T HIS GROUP OF fragile, elongate shells are covered by a polished periostracum. The hinge lacks teeth; the long ligament may be external or internal. The thin periostracum is reddish brown in colour, often with pale radiating bands. A widely distributed primitive group, it has few species.

Superfamily SOLEMYOIDEA	Family Solemyidae	Species *Solemya togata* Poli

TOGA AWNING CLAM

A fragile, cigar-shaped bivalve which gapes at each end; its polished periostracum extends well beyond the valve edges, especially at the front. The umbones are so poorly developed that the hinge line appears to be almost straight. In front of the rear muscle scar there is a poorly developed radial rib. The shell is colourless, and the periostracum is dark brown in colour with paler rays.
• **HABITAT** Mud and sand. *valve edge*

MEDITERRANEAN

WEST AFRICAN
SOUTH AFRICAN

Range Mediterranean to S. Africa	Occurrence 🐚🐚	Size 5cm (2in)

NUT SHELLS

T HESE SMALL, triangular shells have prominent umbones; the front end projects more than the rear end. In each valve, the conspicuously arched hinge has a series of sharp teeth arranged in two rows, one each side of the umbo. Species live in mud or sand offshore, and occur worldwide.

Superfamily NUCULOIDEA	Family Nuculidae	Species *Nuculata sulcata* Bronn

FURROWED NUT SHELL

A solid, dull, triangular shell with small, pointed umbones. Fine concentric ribs are crossed by indistinct radial lines. Each valve has a row of pointed teeth on either side of the umbo. The lower edges of the valves are serrated. The shell is yellowish green in colour; pearly inside.
• **HABITAT** Mud and sand offshore.

BOREAL
MEDITERRANEAN

front end

Range North Sea to Angola	Occurrence 🐚🐚🐚	Size 2cm (¾in)

ARKS

T HE SHELLS IN THIS LARGE group are elongate and strongly ribbed; the hinge has a series of teeth along its length. There is a wide ligamental area.

The shells are usually fixed to solid objects by filaments (byssus) which protrude through a gap in the valves. There are many species worldwide.

Superfamily ARCOIDEA	Family Arcidae	Species *Arca noae* Linnaeus

NOAH'S ARK

A very elongate shell with umbones situated towards the rear end. Many tiny teeth on hinge; two muscle impressions on each valve are of equal size. Coarse radial ribs. Whitish, with zigzag brown streaks.
• **REMARK** Valves gape below umbones.
• **HABITAT** Rocks offshore.

shell thinnest below umbo

broad ligamental area

MEDITERRANEAN

Range Mediterranean and E. Atlantic	Occurrence 🐚🐚🐚🐚	Size 7cm (2¾in)

Superfamily ARCOIDEA	Family Arcidae	Species *Anadara uropygimelana* Bory

BURNT-END ARK

An inflated, thick shell, which is almost rectangular in its outline; it has broad umbones set close together. Strong radial ribs smooth and flattened. Inside edges of valves deeply grooved. White with brown periostracum; inside yellowish.
• **HABITAT** Intertidal rocks and crevices.

close-set small teeth

INDO-PACIFIC

Range Tropical Indo-Pacific	Occurrence 🐚🐚🐚🐚🐚	Size 6cm (2½in)

Superfamily ARCOIDEA	Family Arcidae	Species *Anadara granosa* Linnaeus

GRANULAR ARK

A thick, heavy shell with broad umbones centrally above the hinge. Serial teeth are shortest beneath the umbones. Strong radial ribs have regularly spaced, thick scales down their length. The shell is white in colour, with a thick, brown periostracum.
• **REMARK** Recognizable by the scales on the ribs.
• **HABITAT** Muddy sand inshore.

broadly serrated edge

INDO-PACIFIC

Range S.W. Pacific	Occurrence 🐚🐚🐚🐚🐚	Size 6cm (2½in)

Superfamily ARCOIDEA	Family Arcidae	Species *Barbatia amygdalumtostum* Röding

BURNT-ALMOND ARK

The shell's edges are parallel and the two ends rounded. Teeth are much larger at ends of hinge. Concentric and radial ridges become stronger with successive shell growth. Dark purplish brown, with brown, fibrous periostracum; muscle scars purplish brown.
• **REMARK** The periostracum is easily scraped away.
• **HABITAT** Under rocks and coral.

INDO-PACIFIC

whitish inside

Range Tropical Indo-Pacific	Occurrence 🐚🐚🐚🐚🐚	Size 4cm (1½in)

Superfamily ARCOIDEA	Family Arcidae	Species *Barbatia foliata* Forsskåhl

LEAFY ARK

A compressed shell with a wide gape between lower edges of valves. Ligament as long as hinge. Strong radial ribs; weak or strong concentric ribs are sometimes ornamented. White under dark brown, bristly periostracum.
• **HABITAT** Under rocks inshore.

INDO-PACIFIC

deeply grooved ligamental area

Range Indo-Pacific and S. Africa	Occurrence 🐚🐚🐚🐚🐚	Size 6cm (2½in)

Superfamily ARCOIDEA	Family Arcidae	Species *Trisidos tortuosa* Linnaeus

PROPELLOR ARK

The valves are strongly twisted, producing a fold at an acute angle to the hinge line (seen as a gully internally). The long hinge is almost straight, but the lower edge of each valve is curved. The shell has thin, radiating ribs and coarse, concentric growth ridges. Yellowish white in colour; brown periostracum.
• **REMARK** The hinge teeth are poorly developed.
• **HABITAT** Shallow water.

INDO-PACIFIC

curved lower edge

Range Tropical Pacific	Occurrence 🐚🐚🐚	Size 7.5cm (3in)

BITTERSWEET CLAMS

T HE EXISTENCE of serial teeth indicate that these thick shells are related to the arks. Totalling about 150 species worldwide, the shells have an oval or circular outline, prominent umbones, an external ligament, and are ribbed or almost smooth. The animals burrow in sand or gravel offshore.

Superfamily LIMOPSOIDEA	Family Glycymerididae	Species *Glycymeris glycymeris* Linnaeus

EUROPEAN BITTERSWEET

This is a solid, thick shell with an almost circular outline. The ligament occupies a broad, triangular area below the centrally placed umbones. White, with dark and pale brown markings in bands and zigzags.
• **REMARK** Shell has a dark brown periostracum.
• **HABITAT** Mud and sand offshore.

serrated edge

BOREAL
MEDITERRANEAN

Range North Sea to Mediterranean	Occurrence 🐚🐚🐚🐚	Size 6cm (2½in)

Superfamily LIMOPSOIDEA	Family Glycymerididae	Species *Glycymeris reevei* Mayer

REEVE'S BITTERSWEET

This inflated shell is angled at the front, and slopes each side of the umbones. The radial ribs are broad. Brown, with yellowish grooves between the ribs, and white smears at the front end.
• **REMARK** The shell is distinguished by its quadrangular outline.
• **HABITAT** Shallow water in sand.

dark brown muscle scar

INDO-PACIFIC

Range S.W. Pacific	Occurrence 🐚🐚🐚	Size 5cm (2in)

Superfamily LIMOPSOIDEA	Family Glycymerididae	Species *Glycymeris formosa* Reeve

BEAUTIFUL BITTERSWEET

This thick, compressed shell has a nearly circular outline. The hinge line is gently curved. Lower inside edge of each valve is closely serrated. Pale yellow, with dark brown radial dashes; the inside white and brown.
• **REMARK** Umbones are small and pointed.
• **HABITAT** Sand offshore.

broad hinge

WEST AFRICAN

Range W. Africa	Occurrence 🐚🐚🐚	Size 4cm (1½in)

SEA MUSSELS

T HESE ARE THE MOST abundant of all bivalves, found on rocky and stony shores worldwide. The valves are thin, lack prominent teeth on the short hinge, and are joined by a long ligament in the front half. The animals affix themselves to solid objects by a bunch of filaments (byssus).

Superfamily MYTILOIDEA	Family Mytilidae	Species *Mytilus edulis* Linnaeus

COMMON BLUE MUSSEL

A thin but solid shell; it is approximately triangular in outline, with umbones at the front. The ligamental area is straight and reaches about halfway to the highest point of the shell. The inside of the valves may be partially or completely covered by a pearly layer. Brown or blue in colour, the shell often has darker radial bands; the inside of the shell is white.
• **REMARK** This mussel is eaten in great quantities worldwide.
• **HABITAT** Intertidal rocks and stony shores.

small teeth at front end

WORLD

Range Most seas	Occurrence ♦♦♦♦♦	Size 7.5cm (3in)

Superfamily MYTILOIDEA	Family Mytilidae	Species *Choromytilus chorus* Molina

CHORUS MUSSEL

P robably the largest of all mussels when fully grown, this is one of several species with no muscle scar at the front internally. The largest specimens are thick and opaque; they have prominent growth ridges and slightly curved umbones. The ligament is long, occupying almost half the length of the shell, the space it occupies being bordered by a thin, sharp ridge. Towards the rear end of each valve is a very large muscle scar. Fresh specimens are covered by a thick, greenish periostracum, beneath which the shell is bluish in colour; the inside is a blue colour, overlaid with pearly white.
• **REMARK** The shell takes a high polish and is used to make into decorative ornaments.
• **HABITAT** Rocks in shallow water.

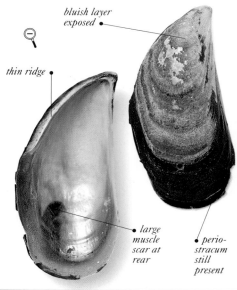

bluish layer exposed

thin ridge

large muscle scar at rear

periostracum still present

PERUVIAN
MAGELLANIC

Range Peru to Tierra del Fuego	Occurrence ♦♦♦♦	Size 10cm (4in)

PEN SHELLS

T HESE SHELLS are mostly thin and compressed, medium to large, broadly or narrowly paddle shaped, and often with fluted or tubular scales. The umbones are at the front end, and the ligament is as long as the straight, toothless hinge. Widely distributed in warm and temperate seas.

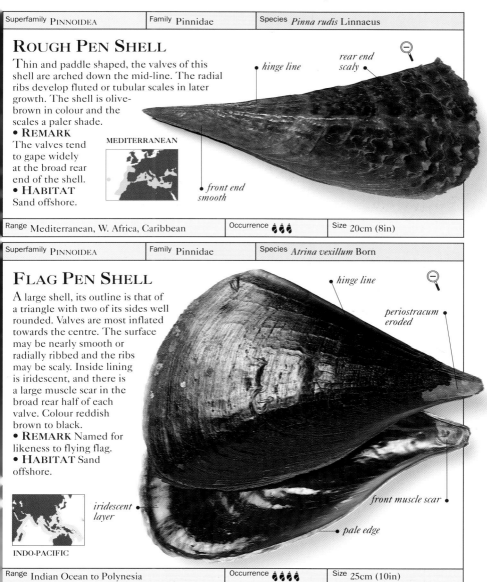

Superfamily PINNOIDEA	Family Pinnidae	Species *Pinna rudis* Linnaeus

ROUGH PEN SHELL

Thin and paddle shaped, the valves of this shell are arched down the mid-line. The radial ribs develop fluted or tubular scales in later growth. The shell is olive-brown in colour and the scales a paler shade.
• **REMARK** The valves tend to gape widely at the broad rear end of the shell.
• **HABITAT** Sand offshore.

hinge line

rear end scaly

MEDITERRANEAN

front end smooth

Range Mediterranean, W. Africa, Caribbean	Occurrence	Size 20cm (8in)

Superfamily PINNOIDEA	Family Pinnidae	Species *Atrina vexillum* Born

FLAG PEN SHELL

A large shell, its outline is that of a triangle with two of its sides well rounded. Valves are most inflated towards the centre. The surface may be nearly smooth or radially ribbed and the ribs may be scaly. Inside lining is iridescent, and there is a large muscle scar in the broad rear half of each valve. Colour reddish brown to black.
• **REMARK** Named for likeness to flying flag.
• **HABITAT** Sand offshore.

hinge line

periostracum eroded

iridescent layer

front muscle scar

pale edge

INDO-PACIFIC

Range Indian Ocean to Polynesia	Occurrence	Size 25cm (10in)

WING OYSTERS

MANY OF THESE bivalves have wing-like extensions at the front and rear; they are attached by their byssus threads to solid objects. Others, including pearl mussels, are wingless, rounder, and often live among sea fans. Hinge teeth are feeble or absent; the inside of the valves is pearly.

Superfamily PTERIOIDEA	Family Pteriidae	Species *Pteria tortirostris* Dunker

TWISTED WING OYSTER

Like others in its genus, this thin-shelled species has the right valve smaller than the left. The hinge line has small wing-like extensions at each end, the rear extension being the longer and broader. There are two indistinct teeth in the right valve below the umbo, and one in the left. A long, thin ridge lies below the hinge, behind the umbo, in each valve. Towards the centre of the valves is a large muscle impression. The shell is dark to pale brown in colour, sometimes with wavy concentric bands or radial lines; inside pearly.
• **REMARK** The wing-like extensions help the mollusc to orientate itself.
• **HABITAT** Sea fans offshore.

small tooth

INDO-PACIFIC

gap for byssus

front muscle scar

right valve

Range Indo-Pacific	Occurrence 🐚🐚	Size 7.5cm (3in)

Superfamily PTERIOIDEA	Family Pteriidae	Species *Pinctada radiata* Leach

RAYED PEARL OYSTER

The several species of pearl oyster vary so much throughout their range that they are difficult to identify. This species is oval or saucer shaped and its right valve is slightly smaller than its left. The concentric ridges on its surface have overlapping scales towards the edges. At each end of the long hinge is a small tooth and there is a large muscle impression in the centre of each valve. Pale brown or greyish, heavily rayed with reddish brown; the inside surface is pearly.
• **REMARK** Larger examples are found in deeper water.
• **HABITAT** Rocks in shallow water.

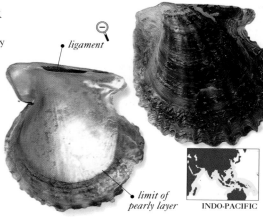

ligament

limit of pearly layer

INDO-PACIFIC

Range Tropical Indo-Pacific	Occurrence 🐚🐚🐚🐚🐚	Size 7.5cm (3in)

TREE OYSTERS

CLOSE RELATIVES of the wing oysters, these bivalves are given the name tree oysters because many attach themselves to the aerial roots of mangroves. The ligament lies in a series of grooves or pits along the hinge of the shell. Each valve has a single large muscle impression.

Superfamily PTERIOIDEA	Family Isognomonidae	Species *Crenatula picta* Deshayes

PAINTED TREE OYSTER

This, very flattened shell, almost rectangular in outline, with small pointed umbones near the front end. Along the hinge is a series of small pits for the reception of the ligament. Yellowish with wavy, brown, radiating bands; pearly just below the hinge.
• **HABITAT** Among sponges.

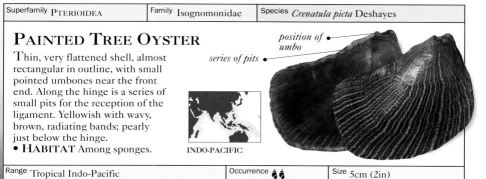

position of umbo

series of pits

INDO-PACIFIC

Range Tropical Indo-Pacific	Occurrence 🐚🐚	Size 5cm (2in)

HAMMER OYSTERS

THIS SMALL GROUP gets its name from the somewhat hammer-headed appearance of one or two species. The elongated valves have undulating edges. There are no hinge teeth. Below the short ligament is a large muscle scar. The shells anchor themselves in sand or sandy mud.

Superfamily PTERIOIDEA	Family Malleidae	Species *Malleus albus* Lamarck

WHITE HAMMER

The elongated, narrow shell has undulating sides. Wings give it the form of a T-square. At the top of each valve, next to the short ligament, is the small, pointed umbo. Inside, just below the ligament, is a large muscle scar. The shell is dirty white in colour, and the muscle scar is black.
• **REMARK** This hammer-shaped shell has occasionally been mistaken for an encrusted hammer.
• **HABITAT** Sand in shallow water.

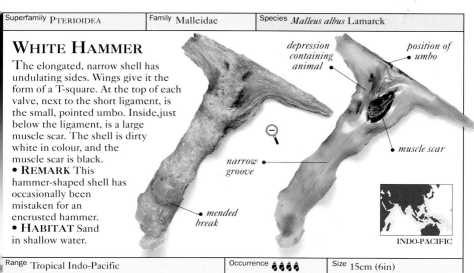

depression containing animal

position of umbo

muscle scar

narrow groove

mended break

INDO-PACIFIC

Range Tropical Indo-Pacific	Occurrence 🐚🐚🐚	Size 15cm (6in)

SCALLOPS

A MONG THE BEST KNOWN of all the bivalves, scallops have fan-shaped shells, with unequally sized "ears" on either side of the umbones.

———— • ————

The internal ligament occupies a triangular pit below the umbones. The hinge is toothless when adult. There is a single, large muscle scar at the centre of each valve (the site of the muscle is eaten as a delicacy). Young scallops usually attach themselves to hard objects with their byssus. There are many species found worldwide.

Superfamily PECTINOIDEA	Family Pectinidae	Species *Pecten maximus* Linnaeus

GREAT SCALLOP

Adopted as a commercial symbol, widely used as an ashtray, and immortalized in Botticelli's painting "The Birth of Venus", this is probably the best known of all seashells. Almost circular in outline, the convex right (lower) valve slightly overlaps the flat left (upper) valve. The ears are very prominent and almost equal in length. About 15–17 broad radial ribs on each valve are crossed by fine concentric lines. The edges of the valves are broadly serrated. The shell can vary in colour from white to yellowish to brown, and sometimes with darker brown concentric bands and zigzags; the inside is white.
• **REMARK** Scallops settle on the sea-bed, flat valve uppermost.
• **HABITAT** Sand or gravel offshore.

ribs of left valve flat-topped

ribs of right valve rounded

right valve strongly curved

BOREAL
MEDITERRANEAN

Range Norway to Mediterranean	Occurrence 🐚🐚🐚🐚	Size 13cm (5in)

Superfamily PECTINOIDEA	Family Pectinidae	Species *Chlamys islandica* Müller

ICELAND SCALLOP

Narrowly fan-shaped shell with one
ear twice as long as the other, and
both valves slightly and equally
convex. About 50 closely spaced,
coarse ribs, each of which divides
into two near the edges of
the valves; the valves are
correspondingly grooved
inside. Creamy yellow
in colour, and usually
concentrically banded;
the ears may be lighter.
• REMARK Colours are
similar but darker inside.
• HABITAT Shallow and
deep water.

finely serrated edge

BOREAL   CIRCUMPOLAR

Range Arctic seas to N.W. and N.E. United States	Occurrence	Size 9cm (3½in)

Superfamily PECTINOIDEA	Family Pectinidae	Species *Chlamys australis* Sowerby

AUSTRAL SCALLOP

The sides of each valve slope down steeply from the
umbo and then broaden rapidly to become fully fan
shaped. One ear is much longer and more scaly than the
other. There are about 20 rounded radial ribs on each
valve with rounded grooves between them. Each
rib has small pointed scales along its length, the
scales being more conspicuous on the shorter
ribs. This shell ccurs in several colours,
including orange, purple, and yellow.
• HABITAT Offshore.

COLORATION
*The colours of
this shell are
bright and
unmixed.
Different
shades of one
colour can
occur together.*

*scales more
noticeable
on short ribs*

AUSTRALIA

*strongly
scalloped edge*

Range S. and W. Australia	Occurrence	Size 7.5cm (3in)

Superfamily PECTINOIDEA	Family Pectinidae	Species *Aequipecten opercularis* Linnaeus

QUEEN SCALLOP

The left valve is more convex than the
right; the sides slope gradually from the
umbones. Ears slightly unequal in size.
About 20 rounded and finely corrugated
radial ribs. Colours include pink, red,
brown, yellow, and purple.
• **REMARK** One of the more
striking colour forms is illustrated.
• **HABITAT** Gravel and sandy
mud offshore.

*ear
shorter on
rear side*

**BOREAL
MEDITERRANEAN**

front edge •

left valve •

Range Norway to Mediterranean	Occurrence 🐚🐚🐚🐚	Size 7.5cm (3in)

Superfamily PECTINOIDEA	Family Propeamussidae	Species *Amusium pleuronectes* Linnaeus

ASIAN MOON SCALLOP

The saucer-shaped valves of this delicate,
smooth shell are very compressed and have
almost equal ears. About 30-35 radial ribs on
the inside of each valve. Right valve is white,
the left dull pink with purplish radial lines and
reddish-brown concentric lines.
• **REMARK** One of several similar species.
• **HABITAT**
Offshore.

*dark
brown ears*

*ears have
rounded
• sides*

*sharp
edge* •

*dark pink
left valve*

*• white-coloured
right valve*

INDO-PACIFIC

Range India, S.W. Pacific	Occurrence 🐚🐚🐚🐚	Size 9cm (3½in)

Superfamily PECTINOIDEA	Family Pectinidae	Species *Cryptopecten pallium* Linnaeus

ROYAL CLOAK SCALLOP

A thick shell with two equally convex valves but slightly un-equal ears. It is ornamented with about 13–14 broad, well raised and evenly spaced radial ribs with two or three riblets on each; ribs and riblets bear tiny scales. Ribs have corresponding grooves on the inside of each valve. White, blotched and spotted with reddish purple; the umbonal area of the shell is often white; inside white except for the edges which duplicate the exterior colour.
• **HABITAT** Coral reefs.

• *ears have scaly ribs*

INDO-PACIFIC

overlapping • scales on ribs

left valve •

Range Tropical Indo-Pacific	Occurrence 🐚🐚🐚🐚	Size 6cm (2½in)

Superfamily PECTINOIDEA	Family Pectinidae	Species *Lyropectnen nodosus* Linnaeus

LION'S PAW

This thick, heavy shell is about as broad as it is high, and has one ear twice as long as the other. Each valve has from seven to nine large, broad ribs which incorporate large, hollow nodules. Strong radial riblets cover the shell and are crossed by thin, concentric ridges. Colours include dark or bright red, orange and yellow.
• **REMARK** The nodules are poorly developed on the shell shown.
• **HABITAT** Offshore.

CARIBBEAN

purplish • brown inside

Range S.E. U.S.A. to Brazil	Occurrence 🐚🐚🐚	Size 10cm (4in)

THORNY OYSTERS

T HESE COLOURFUL bivalves cement themselves, at an early stage, by the right (lower) valve to hard objects - for life. Spines camouflage and protect them. Two strong teeth in each valve fit into corresponding pits; the deep-seated ligament lies between poorly developed "ears". Tropical distribution.

Superfamily PECTINOIDEA	Family Spondylidae	Species *Spondylus princeps* Broderip

PACIFIC THORNY OYSTER

A heavy shell with thick, often blunt-ended spines which are broad, slightly curved and, at later stages of growth, crowded together. Between rows of longer spines are shorter, more pointed spines and radial ribs. Colour usually red or pink with spines over white; inside white with edges of valves the same colour as the outside.
• **REMARK** A collectors' favourite.
• **HABITAT** Hard objects.

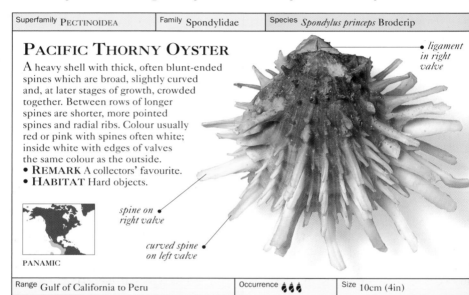

ligament in right valve

spine on right valve

curved spine on left valve

PANAMIC

Range Gulf of California to Peru	Occurrence ♦♦♦	Size 10cm (4in)

Superfamily PECTINOIDEA	Family Spondylidae	Species *Spondylus linguaefelis* Sowerby

CAT'S-TONGUE OYSTER

The oval outline of this shell is difficult to discern in adult examples because it is obscured by sharp-pointed spines at edges of valves. There is usually an area around umbones relatively free of spines. Orange-brown, yellowish, or pale purple; the umbonal area is often rosy; inside white.
• **REMARK** Spines may be longer on shells from protected habitats.
• **HABITAT** Corals.

no long spines below umbo

spines longest at edge

spines on ribs

INDO-PACIFIC

Range S. Pacific	Occurrence ♦♦	Size 7.5cm (3in)

JINGLE SHELLS

T HE CHARACTERISTIC FEATURE of these fragile, shapeless bivalves is the large hole in the lower (right) valve; through this the animal extrudes a plug for cementing itself to hard objects. The internal ligament lies in a crescent-shaped pit. When knocked together the pearly valves "jingle".

Superfamily ANOMIOIDEA	Family Anomiidae	Species *Anomia ephippium* Linnaeus

EUROPEAN JINGLE SHELL

Thin, glistening, and irregular in outline, this bivalve moulds itself to the object it adheres to. Its left valve has three small muscle impressions, its right valve a single large one.
• **REMARK** Left valve overlaps right.
• **HABITAT** Shallow water.

remains of ligament

BOREAL
MEDITERRANEAN

elongate byssal hole

Range N.W. Europe, Mediterranean, W. Africa	Occurrence 🐚🐚🐚🐚🐚	Size 4cm (1½in)

TRUE OYSTERS

T HESE ECONOMICALLY important bivalves are shapeless and hard to identify. They cement themselves to rocks and other shells by the left (lower) valve. The ligament is internal and the hinge is toothless. Several species have jagged edges. Most are edible and some are cultivated.

Superfamily OSTREOIDEA	Family Ostreidae	Species *Lopha cristagalli* Linnaeus

COCK'S-COMB OYSTER

Each valve of this solid, thick shell is sharply ridged, forming a series of four to six vaulted arches at the edges; the arches of both valves interlock. Ridges have spiny projections which are more prominent towards the umbonal area. Surface is covered with pustules. Dark purple; inside brownish purple.
• **REMARK** May be more corrugated and often covered with scaly ridges.
• **HABITAT** Clumps offshore.

spine near umbo

lines of small pustules

large pustules on inside edges

smooth internal floor

INDO-PACIFIC

Range Tropical Indo-Pacific	Occurrence 🐚🐚🐚	Size 9cm (3½in)

FILE CLAMS

T HESE LOPSIDED BIVALVES have short ears and a central ligament pit. They are so-called because some species have sharp scales along the radial ribs. The hinge is toothless and there is one muscle scar in each valve. They swim by clapping their valves together. Many species worldwide.

Superfamily LIMOIDEA	Family Limidae	Species *Lima vulgaris* Link

PACIFIC FILE SHELL

The valves of this paddle-shaped shell are equally convex and the hinge line slopes down sharply either side of the triangular ligament pit. Radiating from the broadly rounded umbo are about 20 closely spaced, rounded ribs, each bearing along its length a row of sharp, fluted scales. The inner edges of the valves are broadly serrated; they gape slightly at the rear. Yellowish white; inside white.
• **REMARK** Shell bleaches to pure white.
• **HABITAT** Shallow water.

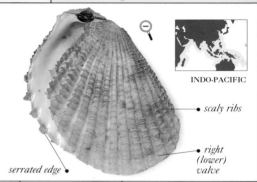

INDO-PACIFIC

• *scaly ribs*

• *right (lower) valve*

serrated edge •

Range Tropical Indo-Pacific	Occurrence 🦪🦪🦪🦪	Size 6cm (2½in)

BROOCH CLAMS

T HE FEW STILL EXISTING SPECIES of brooch clam are relics of an ancient group of "living fossils", now restricted to the offshore waters of Australia. The triangular shells, pearly inside, have three hinge teeth in one valve, and two in the other. Various kinds of ornament have been made from them.

Superfamily TRIGONIOIDEA	Family Trigoniidae	Species *Neotrigonia margaritacea* Lamarck

AUSTRALIAN BROOCH-CLAM

A solid, triangular shell with granulated ribs. Inside pearly, including large hinge teeth. Pinkish white; inside gold tinged.
• **REMARK** The shell has a brown periostracum when fresh.
• **HABITAT** Mud offshore.

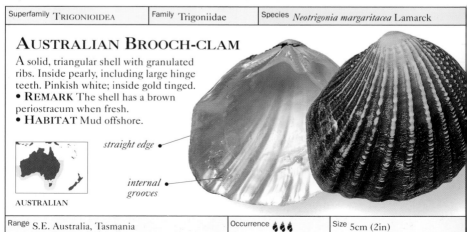

straight edge •

internal grooves •

AUSTRALIAN

Range S.E. Australia, Tasmania	Occurrence 🦪🦪🦪	Size 5cm (2in)

LUCINE CLAMS

T HESE MOSTLY DISCOIDAL shells have a very small lunule and a long ligament, which may be internal or external. The large, narrow, front muscle scar and the absence of a pallial sinus distinguish lucine from the otherwise similar Venus clams. Mainly warm-water species, they burrow in sand or mud.

Superfamily LUCINOIDEA	Family Lucinidae	Species *Codakia punctata* Linnaeus

PITTED LUCINE

The discus-shaped valves of this thick-shelled species have pointed umbones, a very small lunule, and a long internal ligament. Irregular radial grooves are crossed by strong growth lines. Two cardinal teeth in each valve; there is no pallial sinus. Creamy, tinged with violet; inside yellow within the pallial line, orange-red beyond.
• **HABITAT** Shallow water in sand.

INDO-PACIFIC

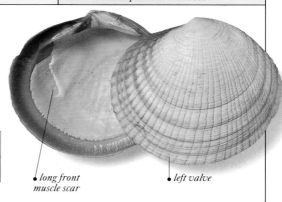
long front muscle scar   *left valve*

Range Tropical Indo-Pacific	Occurrence ♦♦♦♦	Size 7.5cm (3in)

Superfamily LUCINOIDEA	Family Lucinidae	Species *Lucina pectinata* Gmelin

THICK LUCINE

The thick, compressed valves have a rounded ridge from the umbo to the rear edge. Wide-spaced, concentric, sharp ridges; long, narrow front muscle scar. Raised lunule gives valves a sinuous, front-edge profile. Yellowish.
• **HABITAT** Shallow water.

front muscle scar

CARIBBEAN
TRANSATLANTIC

Range N. Carolina to Brazil	Occurrence ♦♦♦♦	Size 5cm (2in)

Superfamily LUCINOIDEA	Family Lucinidae	Species *Divaricella huttoniana* Vanatta

HUTTON'S LUCINE

One of several similar species in its genus, this inflated bivalve has an almost circular outline. Narrow grooves form characteristic, closely spaced, broad chevrons across the valves. The front muscle scar is long and narrow; the ligament is long. All white.
• **HABITAT** Sand or mud offshore.

ligament

NEOZELANIC

right valve

Range New Zealand	Occurrence ♦♦♦♦	Size 4cm (1½in)

ASTARTE CLAMS

THESE THICK-SHELLED, brownish bivalves are mostly triangular in outline and are either smooth or concentrically ribbed. All have a thick periostracum when fresh. The two muscle scars in each valve are joined by the pallial line; there is no pallial sinus. Most live in very cold water.

Superfamily ASTARTOIDEA	Family Astartidae	Species *Astarte castanea* Say

CHESTNUT ASTARTE

The compressed valves have a rounded-triangular outline. Umbones are prominently raised, almost hooked. Smooth, except for low, concentric ridges. The broad hinge has three teeth in each valve, and there is a small ligament. Serrated inside edges. Pale brown.
• **REMARK** The periostracum rubs off.
• **HABITAT** Mud, sand, and gravel offshore.

ligament

right (lower) valve

BOREAL, U.S. ONLY

Range Nova Scotia to New Jersey	Occurrence ♠♠♠♠	Size 2.5cm (1in)

CRASSATELLAS

THESE TRIANGULAR SHAPED shells are heavy, compressed, and have a thick, brown periostracum. Several may have concentric ribs. The internal ligament lies in a triangular pit; there are three cardinal teeth in the right valve, two in the left. Crassatellas are common off southern Australian coasts.

Superfamily CRASSATELLOIDEA	Family Crassatellidae	Species *Eucrassatella decipiens* Reeve

DECEPTIVE CRASSATELLA

This thick, heavy shell has pointed umbones from which the hinge line slopes steeply down each side. Triangular internal ligament; rear lateral teeth longer than front ones. Brown, with occasional reddish rays; inside, creamy below, apricot above.
• **REMARK** Muscle scars always chestnut brown.
• **HABITAT** Offshore.

ligament

right valve

AUSTRALIAN

Range S.W. and S. Australia	Occurrence ♠♠	Size 7.5cm (3in)

CARDITA CLAMS

T HESE SOLID, BOAT-SHAPED shells have strong radial ribs which may themselves be concentrically ribbed. The well developed hinge is towards the front end; the ligament is external. Each valve has two muscle scars; there is no pallial sinus. Inside edges of valves are serrated. Widespread in warm seas.

Superfamily CARDITOIDEA	Family Carditidae	Species *Megacardita incrassata* Sowerby

THICKENED CARDITA

A thick, heavy shell whose boat-shaped valves have about 16 broad, rounded ribs. Minute lunule; long ligament. White, with concentric brown bands, sometimes pink; inside white.
• **REMARK** Illustrated example is the commonly occurring pink variety.
• **HABITAT** Under intertidal rocks.

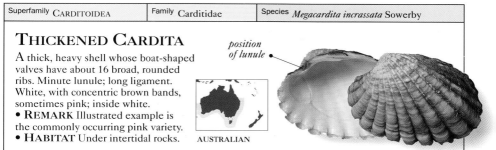

position of lunule

AUSTRALIAN

Range Australia (except southern coast)	Occurrence ♦♦♦	Size 4cm (1½in)

JEWEL BOXES

T HESE THICK AND HEAVY shells resemble colourful oysters with curved umbones. All species cement themselves firmly to solid objects. The surface bears scales or spines, but these features are usually obscured by encrustations. With few exceptions, jewel boxes live in tropical waters.

Superfamily CHAMOIDEA	Family Chamidae	Species *Chama lazarus* Linnaeus

LAZARUS JEWEL BOX

One of the larger jewel boxes, it is cemented to solid objects by its shallow left valve; convex right valve is articulated to it by a broad hinge. Right valve has leafy, overlapping plates arranged concentrically from umbo to lower edge. White; two or three reddish-violet rays; inside white.
• **REMARK** Young shells brighter.
• **HABITAT** Shallow water on rocks.

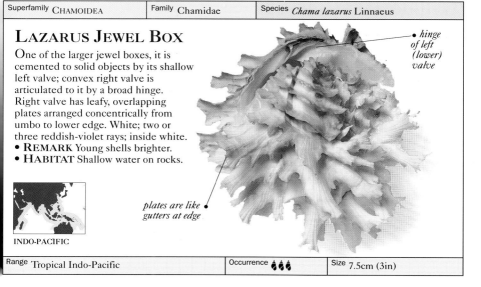

hinge of left (lower) valve

plates are like gutters at edge

INDO-PACIFIC

Range Tropical Indo-Pacific	Occurrence ♦♦♦	Size 7.5cm (3in)

COCKLES

SPECIES IN THIS WIDESPREAD group include several which are well known as food items. They have equal valves, with radial ribs which may well bear spines, and the inside edges are serrated. There are two equal-sized muscle scars but no pallial sinus. The external ligament is situated behind the umbones; there are two cardinal teeth in each valve. Most species burrow in sand or mud; some occur in astronomical numbers over a small area.

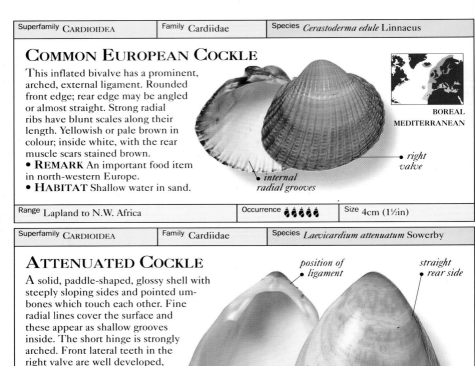

Superfamily CARDIOIDEA	Family Cardiidae	Species *Cerastoderma edule* Linnaeus

COMMON EUROPEAN COCKLE

This inflated bivalve has a prominent, arched, external ligament. Rounded front edge; rear edge may be angled or almost straight. Strong radial ribs have blunt scales along their length. Yellowish or pale brown in colour; inside white, with the rear muscle scars stained brown.
• **REMARK** An important food item in north-western Europe.
• **HABITAT** Shallow water in sand.

BOREAL
MEDITERRANEAN

• *right valve*

• *internal radial grooves*

Range Lapland to N.W. Africa	Occurrence 🐚🐚🐚🐚🐚	Size 4cm (1½in)

Superfamily CARDIOIDEA	Family Cardiidae	Species *Laevicardium attenuatum* Sowerby

ATTENUATED COCKLE

A solid, paddle-shaped, glossy shell with steeply sloping sides and pointed umbones which touch each other. Fine radial lines cover the surface and these appear as shallow grooves inside. The short hinge is strongly arched. Front lateral teeth in the right valve are well developed, the innermost one being the larger. Inside edges are serrated. Yellow, with orange-red mottlings and concentric bands.
• **REMARK** Pink umbones.
• **HABITAT** Shallow water.

position of ligament

straight rear side

yellow inside edge

finely serrated edge

INDO-PACIFIC

Range Tropical Indo-Pacific	Occurrence 🐚🐚	Size 5cm (2in)

Superfamily CARDIOIDEA	Family Cardiidae	Species *Fragum unedo* Linnaeus

STRAWBERRY COCKLE

A quadrangular, thick shell, with prominent umbones and a short external ligament. About 25–30 radial ribs are ornamented with low scales. The inside edges of the valves are serrated; serrations on rear edges are produced into points. White or yellow, with lilac scales; inside white.
• **HABITAT** Shallow water.

two front lateral teeth •

INDO-PACIFIC

Range Tropical Indo-Pacific	Occurrence 🐚🐚🐚🐚	Size 4cm (1½in)

Superfamily CARDIOIDEA	Family Cardiidae	Species *Lyrocardium lyratum* Sowerby

LYRE COCKLE

A rather thin shell with rounded, touching umbones; its valves are almost circular in outline. The hinge is thin and gently curved. Front half of each valve has about 16 widely spaced, oblique ridges, the hallmark of the genus. Reddish purple; inside pink and yellow.
• **HABITAT** Offshore.

right valve •

**INDO-PACIFIC
JAPONIC**

Range Japan to N. Australia	Occurrence 🐚🐚🐚	Size 4cm (1½in)

Superfamily CARDIOIDEA	Family Cardiidae	Species *Acanthocardia echinata* Linnaeus

EUROPEAN PRICKLY COCKLE

This very inflated shell has broad umbones which rise well above the hinge line. Surface has many radial ribs bearing sharp spines which are linked at their bases. Spines sparsely distributed around umbones, but they become progressively more numerous, more crowded, and longer towards the rear and below; longest at the rear. At the front, the spines tend to be replaced by wart-like, smooth nodules. The inner edges are serrated. Yellow or pale brown, sometimes mottled.
• **HABITAT** Sand offshore.

few spines on umbonal area •

longest spines •

right valve •

thickened scales at • front

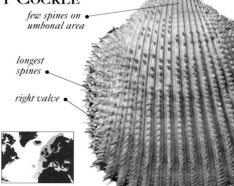

**BOREAL
MEDITERRANEAN**

Range Norway to Mediterranean	Occurrence 🐚🐚🐚🐚	Size 6cm (2¼in)

Superfamily CARDIOIDEA	Family Cardiidae	Species *Plagiocardium pseudolima* Lamarck

GIANT COCKLE

One of the largest and certainly the heaviest, of all cockles. The valves are very thick and inflated; the in-rolled umbones almost touch. Seen from the front or rear ends, the joined valves are heart shaped. Broad, flat ribs are separated by narrow, V-shaped grooves; in later growth the ribs have blunt spines. Orange-brown turning purplish; inside white, flushed pink.
• **REMARK** Marked growth stages.
• **HABITAT** Sand offshore.

right valve •

INDO-PACIFIC

occasional • blunt spines

rear • muscle scar

interlocking • serrations

Range E. Africa to Indonesia	Occurrence 🐚🐚🐚	Size 15cm (6in)

Superfamily CARDIOIDEA	Family Cardiidae	Species *Corculum cardissa* Linnaeus

TRUE HEART COCKLE

The delicate, translucent valves of this exquisite cockle together form a heart-shaped outline. Sharply keeled edges turn slightly forwards and may be jagged. Front half of valves is radially ribbed. Yellow, violet, white, pink, sometimes pink-spotted.
• **REMARK** The right umbo overlaps the left.
• **HABITAT** Sand, shallow water.

overlapping umbones •

ligament visible externally •

flattened • radial ribs

INDO-PACIFIC

jagged edge •

Range Philippines and W. Pacific	Occurrence 🐚🐚🐚	Size 5cm (2in)

GIANT CLAMS

T HESE THICK, HEAVY SHELLS have strong radial ribs, with or without fluted scales. The scalloped edges of the valves interlock. The byssus is ex- truded through a gape between the valves; there are two adjacent muscle scars. A dozen species occur in the tropical Indo-Pacific, around coral reefs.

Superfamily TRIDACNOIDEA	Family Tridacnidae	Species *Tridacna squamosa* Lamarck

FLUTED GIANT CLAM

This very thick shell has cupped, fan-shaped valves. For its size, it is the heaviest species in the group, but it never reaches the dimensions or the weight of the quintessential Giant Clam (*Tridacna gigas* Linnaeus). It has a wide gape behind the umbones through which the byssus protrudes. Four to twelve well-rounded, raised, radial ribs expand rapidly in width from the umbo to the edge of each valve. The ribs are ornamented with fluted scales which enlarge progressively to the edge. The valve edges correspond to the contours of the ribs and intervening channels. White, often tinged with orange and yellow; inside white.

• **REMARK** The projecting scales are the identifying hallmark for this species of giant clam.
• **HABITAT** Coral reefs.

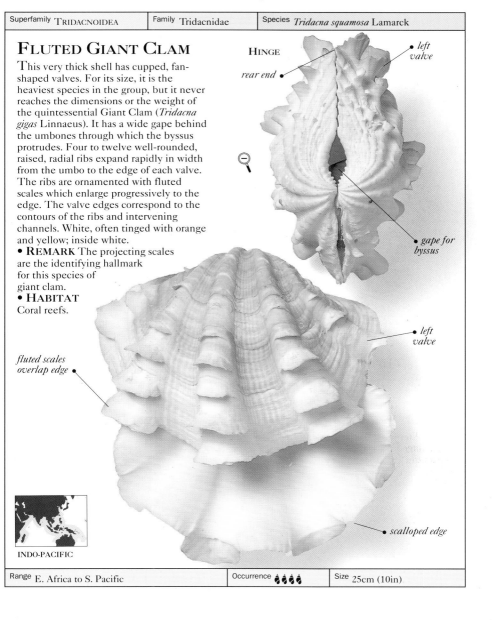

HINGE

rear end •

• left valve

• gape for byssus

• left valve

fluted scales overlap edge •

• scalloped edge

INDO-PACIFIC

Range E. Africa to S. Pacific	Occurrence 🐚🐚🐚	Size 25cm (10in)

TROUGH SHELLS

S HELLS IN THIS WORLDWIDE group are boat shaped or triangular, with central umbones. They have a deep pallial sinus, and two muscle scars in each valve. The main distinguishing feature of this group is a chondrophore, a trough-like pit to hold the internal ligament. The animals burrow in sand.

Superfamily MACTROIDEA	Family Mactridae	Species *Mactra corallina* Linnaeus

RAYED TROUGH SHELL

A thin, glossy shell, triangular in outline, with a slightly angular front end. Below umbones is the broad, triangular chondrophore. Pallial sinus is broad and deep. Whitish, tinged with purple; white or purple inside.
• **REMARK** The valves may sometimes have pale rays.
• **HABITAT** Clean sand offshore.

chondrophore in left valve

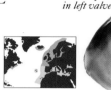

BOREAL
MEDITERRANEAN

Range Norway to Senegal, Mediterranean	Occurrence ♦♦♦♦	Size 5cm (2in)

Superfamily MACTROIDEA	Family Mactridae	Species *Mactrellona exoleta* Gray

MATURE TROUGH SHELL

Large, thin, and translucent, each valve has fine concentric lines and a keel from the umbo to the rear end. Deep chondrophore; lateral teeth short. Yellowish white inside and out.
• **HABITAT** Sand offshore.

chondrophore

short lateral tooth

PANAMIC

Range Gulf of California to Peru	Occurrence ♦♦♦	Size 10cm (4in)

Superfamily MACTROIDEA	Family Mactridae	Species *Spisula solida* Linnaeus

SOLID TROUGH SHELL

This solid shell has equally convex valves, a thick hinge, and low, rounded umbones. Fine concentric lines and grooves cover shell. Right valve has three separate cardinal teeth, two front lateral teeth, and two rear. White inside and out.
• **REMARK** Always has distinct growth stages.
• **HABITAT** Sand offshore.

right valve • *cardinal teeth*

BOREAL
MEDITERRANEAN

Range Norway to Mediterranean	Occurrence ♦♦♦♦	Size 4cm (1½in)

RAZOR SHELLS

K NOWN AS "JACK-KNIFE CLAMS" in the U.S.A., "stickbait" in South Africa, and "finger oysters" in Australia, razor shells are sharp edged and smooth. The hinge, with its external ligament, inconspicuous cardinal teeth, and thin lateral teeth, is at the front end. The animals burrow into sand.

Superfamily SOLENOIDEA	Family Cultellidae	Species *Ensis siliqua* Linnaeus

GIANT RAZOR SHELL

The long, narrow valves are O-shaped in cross-section and, when the animal is removed, the cardinal teeth are clearly visible through the front end. Whitish, with violet-brown streaks and blotches divided by a diagonal line running the length of the shell. Olive-green periostracum overlaps edges.
• **REMARK** Muscle scars provide important identification features.
• **HABITAT** Fine sand in shallow water.

ligament

position of cardinal tooth

right valve

obliquely cut rear end

BOREAL
MEDITERRANEAN

Range Norway to Mediterranean	Occurrence 🌢🌢🌢🌢	Size 15cm (6in)

Superfamily SOLENOIDEA	Family Cultellidae	Species *Siliqua radiata* Linnaeus

SUNSET SILIQUA

The very thin, polished, boat-shaped valves gape at the front end but meet together at the rear. A broad, flat ridge extends obliquely from below the umbo in each valve to the opposite edge. The shell is purple, with four white rays.
• **REMARK** The foremost ray corresponds to the internal ridge.
• **HABITAT** Mud in shallow water.

position of internal rib

ligament

INDO-PACIFIC

Range Indian Ocean	Occurrence 🌢🌢🌢🌢	Size 7.5cm (3in)

TELLINS

BRIGHTLY COLOURED and elegant in their outline, many species of tellin have laterally compressed valves, rounded in front and angular behind. The external ligament is in the rear half of the hinge. The pallial sinus is large and deep. Many species are found in warm and temperate waters.

Superfamily TELLINOIDEA	Family Tellinidae	Species *Tellina virgata* Linnaeus

STRIPED TELLIN

A compressed, triangularly oblong shell, rounded in front and angular behind, it has a slight ridge from the umbo to the rear edge. Fine radial ribs cover the surface of the shell. White rays on pink.
• **HABITAT** Shallow water in sand.

ridge on rear slope •

INDO-PACIFIC

Range Tropical Indo-Pacific	Occurrence ♦♦♦♦	Size 6cm (2¼in)

Superfamily TELLINOIDEA	Family Tellinidae	Species *Tellina madagascariensis* Gmelin

WEST AFRICAN TELLIN

This thin, compressed shell has almost central umbones, a straight lower edge, and bluntly pointed rear end. Fine concentric lines produce a silky sheen. There is a deep pallial sinus. Pink outside; reddish pink inside.
• **HABITAT** Shallow water.

large front muscle scar •

WEST AFRICAN

Range West Africa	Occurrence ♦♦♦♦	Size 7.5cm (3in)

Superfamily TELLINOIDEA	Family Tellinidae	Species *Tellina radiata* Linnaeus

SUNRISE TELLIN

This elongate, highly polished shell is rather inflated. Rear end has a slight embayment below; front end rounded. Large pallial sinus almost touches the front muscle scar. Creamy white, with pink, yellow, or pale-red rays.
• **REMARK** Variable in colour, the umbones are usually red.
• **HABITAT** Shallow water in coral sand.

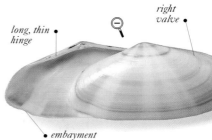

right valve •

long, thin hinge •

CARIBBEAN
TRANSATLANTIC

• *embayment*

Range S.E. U.S.A. to N.E. S.America	Occurrence ♦♦♦♦	Size 7.5cm (3in)

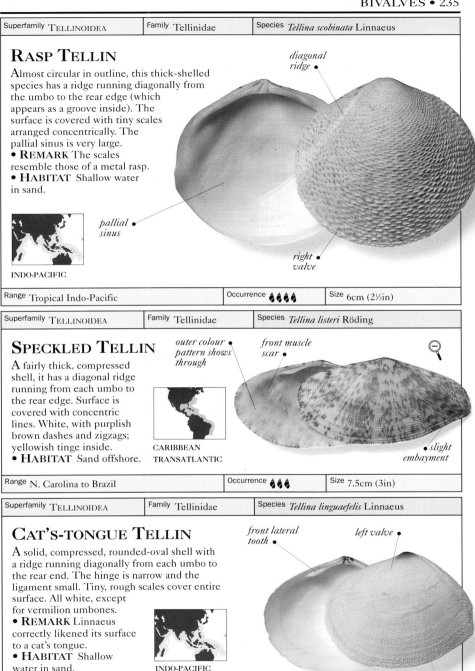

| Superfamily TELLINOIDEA | Family Tellinidae | Species *Tellina scobinata* Linnaeus |

RASP TELLIN

Almost circular in outline, this thick-shelled
species has a ridge running diagonally from
the umbo to the rear edge (which
appears as a groove inside). The
surface is covered with tiny scales
arranged concentrically. The
pallial sinus is very large.
• REMARK The scales
resemble those of a metal rasp.
• HABITAT Shallow water
in sand.

*diagonal
ridge*

*pallial
sinus*

*right
valve*

INDO-PACIFIC

| Range Tropical Indo-Pacific | Occurrence ♦♦♦♦ | Size 6cm (2½in) |

| Superfamily TELLINOIDEA | Family Tellinidae | Species *Tellina listeri* Röding |

SPECKLED TELLIN

A fairly thick, compressed
shell, it has a diagonal ridge
running from each umbo to
the rear edge. Surface is
covered with concentric
lines. White, with purplish
brown dashes and zigzags;
yellowish tinge inside.
• HABITAT Sand offshore.

*outer colour
pattern shows
through*

*front muscle
scar*

CARIBBEAN
TRANSATLANTIC

*slight
embayment*

| Range N. Carolina to Brazil | Occurrence ♦♦♦ | Size 7.5cm (3in) |

| Superfamily TELLINOIDEA | Family Tellinidae | Species *Tellina linguaefelis* Linnaeus |

CAT'S-TONGUE TELLIN

A solid, compressed, rounded-oval shell with
a ridge running diagonally from each umbo to
the rear end. The hinge is narrow and the
ligament small. Tiny, rough scales cover entire
surface. All white, except
for vermilion umbones.
• REMARK Linnaeus
correctly likened its surface
to a cat's tongue.
• HABITAT Shallow
water in sand.

*front lateral
tooth*

left valve

INDO-PACIFIC

| Range S.W. Pacific | Occurrence ♦♦ | Size 4.5cm (1¾in) |

Superfamily TELLINOIDEA	Family Tellinidae	Species *Phylloda foliacea* Linnaeus

LEAFY TELLIN

Lightweight, very compressed, translucent shell, broadly triangular in outline with low, central umbones. Front edges of the valves gape slightly and there is a ridge running diagonally from the umbo to the rear edge in each valve. Smooth except for fine corrugations on the area between the ridge and the hinge. Yellowish orange, with whitish concentric lines. There is a thin, brown periostracum.
• **HABITAT** Sand offshore.

position of ligament

diagonal ridge at rear

INDO-PACIFIC

right valve

Range Tropical Indo-Pacific	Occurrence	Size 7.5cm (3in)

Superfamily TELLINOIDEA	Family Tellinidae	Species *Tellidora burneti* Broderip & Sowerby

BURNET'S TELLIN

An odd-looking shell, it has a flat left valve and a slightly inflated right valve. Each valve has sides sloping sharply down-wards from the pointed umbo which bear a jagged crest. The lower edge is gracefully curved. Irregular, thin, concentric lines cover both valves and there are well-marked concentric growth ridges. All white in colour, sometimes tinged with blue.
• **HABITAT** Shallow water.

PANAMIC

growth ridge

right valve

Range Gulf of California to Ecuador	Occurrence	Size 4cm (1½in)

Superfamily TELLINOIDEA	Family Tellinidae	Species *Tellina laevigata* Linnaeus

SMOOTH TELLIN

This sturdy, rounded-oval, slightly compressed shell has a rounded ridge running diagonally from the umbo to the rear edge in each valve. The surface is glossy and superficially smooth but there are fine radial and concentric lines all over. All white, or rayed and banded with orange; inside may be white or yellow.
• **HABITAT** Shallow water in sand.

two cardinal teeth

TRANSATLANTIC CARIBBEAN

right valve

sharp edge

Range S.E. U.S.A. to Caribbean	Occurrence	Size 7.5cm (3in)

DONAX CLAMS

S HELLS IN THIS WORLDWIDE group are either triangular or wedge shaped and have the umbones nearer the rear end. The external ligament is short and there are two cardinal teeth in each valve. The pallial sinus is deep. The animals burrow in sand. A few are colorful; some are edible.

Superfamily TELLINOIDEA	Family Donacidae	Species *Hecuba scortum* Linnaeus

LEATHER DONAX

A triangular shell with in-rolled umbones, its rear end is drawn out and pointed. A sharp ridge runs from umbo to the rear end, and concentric ridges cover the surface. Pale brown; inside violet.
• **REMARK** Dark brown periostracum.
• **HABITAT** Shallow water in mud.

single cardinal tooth

left valve

INDO-PACIFIC

ridges project at edge

Range Indian Ocean	Occurrence 🐚🐚🐚🐚	Size 5cm (2in)

Superfamily TELLINOIDEA	Family Donacidae	Species *Donax cuneatus* Linnaeus

CRADLE DONAX

Like most donax clams this species is triangular, compressed, has the front end more rounded than the rear, and has a short, external ligament. The pallial sinus is exceptionally large. Grayish white, with brownish or purple rays.
• **HABITAT** Sandy beaches.

INDO-PACIFIC

growth ridge

left valve

Range Indo-Pacific	Occurrence 🐚🐚🐚	Size 4cm (1½in)

Superfamily TELLINOIDEA	Family Donacidae	Species *Donax trunculus* Linnaeus

TRUNCATE DONAX

A moderately inflated, triangular-elongate shell with rounded umbones, much longer in front of the ligament than behind. Fine radial lines on surface. Inside edges closely serrated. Colors include orange, brown, yellow, violet, and white, often rayed; inside usually violet.
• **HABITAT** Shallow water in sand.

cardinal teeth in left valve

MEDITERRANEAN

white inside edge

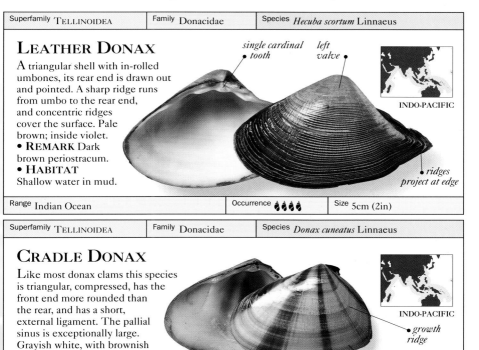

Range S.W. Europe to Mediterranean	Occurrence 🐚🐚🐚🐚	Size 3cm (1¼in)

SANGUIN CLAMS

T HE BOAT-SHAPED shells of this mud-dwelling group have almost central umbones, and the valves may be unequal. The external ligament is set on a thin plate (nymph) projecting upwards from the hinge. There is usually a large pallial sinus. Shells are mostly smooth and violet or pink.

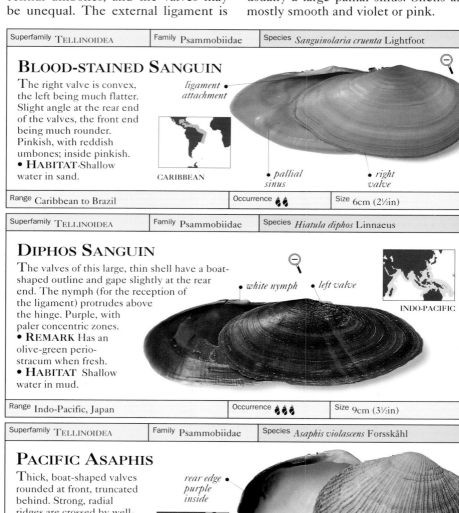

Superfamily TELLINOIDEA	Family Psammobiidae	Species *Sanguinolaria cruenta* Lightfoot

BLOOD-STAINED SANGUIN

The right valve is convex, the left being much flatter. Slight angle at the rear end of the valves, the front end being much rounder. Pinkish, with reddish umbones; inside pinkish.
• HABITAT Shallow water in sand.

ligament attachment

CARIBBEAN

pallial sinus

right valve

Range Caribbean to Brazil	Occurrence 🐚🐚	Size 6cm (2½in)

Superfamily TELLINOIDEA	Family Psammobiidae	Species *Hiatula diphos* Linnaeus

DIPHOS SANGUIN

The valves of this large, thin shell have a boat-shaped outline and gape slightly at the rear end. The nymph (for the reception of the ligament) protrudes above the hinge. Purple, with paler concentric zones.
• REMARK Has an olive-green periostracum when fresh.
• HABITAT Shallow water in mud.

white nymph

left valve

INDO-PACIFIC

Range Indo-Pacific, Japan	Occurrence 🐚🐚🐚	Size 9cm (3½in)

Superfamily TELLINOIDEA	Family Psammobiidae	Species *Asaphis violascens* Forsskåhl

PACIFIC ASAPHIS

Thick, boat-shaped valves rounded at front, truncated behind. Strong, radial ridges are crossed by well-marked, concentric growth lines. Yellowish white, tinged with purple.
• HABITAT Shallow water.

rear edge purple inside

INDO-PACIFIC

Range Tropical Indo-Pacific	Occurrence 🐚🐚🐚🐚	Size 6cm (2½in)

SEMELE CLAMS

THESE OFTEN COLOURFUL shells have slightly gaping valves and central umbones. The internal ligament is in a deeply excavated groove.

There are two cardinal teeth in each valve and the pallial sinus is deep and broad. Inhabitants of estuaries and bays, they burrow in sand.

Superfamily TELLINOIDEA	Family Semelidae	Species *Semele purpurascens* Gmelin

PURPLISH SEMELE

This bivalve has a narrow hinge with two prominent cardinal teeth in each valve. Fine concentric ribs cover surface. Cream or grey, with purple or orange blotches: large purple patch inside.
• **HABITAT** Shallow water in sand.

CARIBBEAN

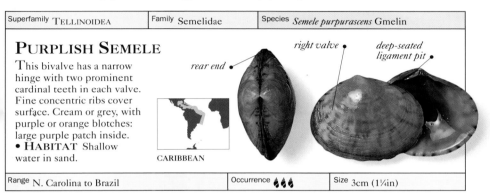

rear end •

right valve •

deep-seated ligament pit •

Range N. Carolina to Brazil	Occurrence 🐚🐚🐚	Size 3cm (1¼in)

TRAPEZIUM CLAMS

THE FEW SPECIES in this group of bivalves have boat-shaped or trapezoidal shells which are solid, sometimes coarsely ribbed, and have an external ligament situated behind the umbones. Below the ligament the

hinge plate is narrowed. The cardinal teeth on each side are short but often very thick. The pallial sinus is usually poorly developed. Shells are mainly white but some are also purple inside. They occur mostly around coral reefs.

Superfamily ARCTICOIDEA	Family Trapeziidae	Species *Trapezium oblongum* Linnaeus

OBLONG TRAPEZIUM

A solid, often thick and heavy shell, its valves are broader than they are tall, and have a trapezoidal outline, with umbones at front. Short but well-developed lateral teeth. Behind the umbones is the short ligament. The surface may be smooth or have coarse radial ribs and prominent concentric growth ridges. White or greyish.
• **HABITAT** Shallow water near coral reefs.

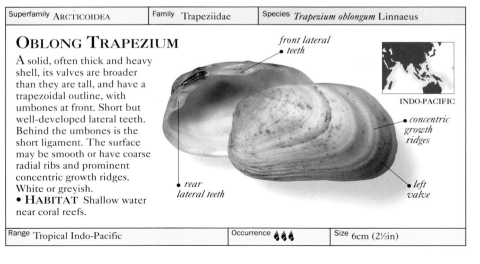

front lateral teeth •

INDO-PACIFIC

• *concentric growth ridges*

• *rear lateral teeth*

• *left valve*

Range Tropical Indo-Pacific	Occurrence 🐚🐚🐚	Size 6cm (2½in)

VENUS CLAMS

O NE OF THE MOST colourful of the bivalve groups. Shells may vary in shape from circular to triangular, and are smooth or ribbed. Escutcheon and lunule are well developed and there is often a pallial sinus. Most burrow in sand and may occur in estuaries. From warm and temperate waters worldwide.

Superfamily VENEROIDEA	Family Veneridae	Species *Circe scripta* Linnaeus

SCRIPT VENUS

A solid, very compressed shell, it has a poorly developed ridge from umbo to rear edge. Strong, concentric ribs cover the shell. There are three large cardinal teeth. Yellowish, with brown rays, bands, and zigzags; inside white.
• **REMARK** Colour pattern varies considerably on different specimens.
• **HABITAT** Shallow water in sand.

ligament in left valve •

INDO-PACIFIC

Range Tropical Indo-Pacific	Occurrence ♦♦♦	Size 4cm (1½in)

Superfamily VENEROIDEA	Family Veneridae	Species *Gafrarium divaricatum* Gmelin

FORKED VENUS

A thick, compressed, roundly triang-ular shell with broad umbones and a sunken ligament. Front half of each valve has weak, nodulose ribs which meet similar ribs to form chevrons. Finely serrated inside lower edges. Creamy white, with reddish-brown streaks, lines, and tent-like markings.
• **HABITAT** Shallow water in sand.

muscle scar in right valve •

INDO-PACIFIC

Range Tropical Indo-Pacific	Occurrence ♦♦♦♦	Size 4cm (1½in)

Superfamily VENEROIDEA	Family Veneridae	Species *Pitar dione* Linnaeus

ROYAL COMB VENUS

The top edge of this shell slopes in a gentle curve from the umbones to the rear edge. There is a ridge running below bearing long spines; these are placed at the end of a series of concentric ridges. The shell is pinkish violet in colour; inside is white.
• **REMARK** This is one of only two spiny species of Venus clam.
• **HABITAT** Offshore sand.

ligament in right valve •

rear end lacks ridges •

CARIBBEAN

Range West Indies	Occurrence ♦♦♦	Size 4cm (1½in)

Superfamily VENEROIDEA	Family Veneridae	Species *Callista erycina* Linnaeus

RED CALLISTA

A large, robust, inflated, boat-shaped shell with prominent umbones pointing forwards, and a long external hinge. The front end is more rounded than the rear. Regularly spaced, broad, and flattened ribs have narrow grooves between them. Muscle scars are clearly outlined and the ligament is long. Coloured cream, pale brown, and orange-red with reddish-brown rays; inside yellowish white with orange-red edges.

• **HABITAT** Sand at low tide.

INDO-PACIFIC

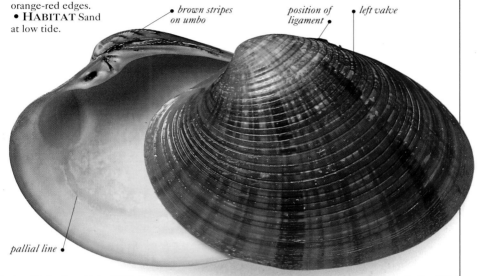

brown stripes on umbo

position of ligament

left valve

pallial line

Range Indo-West Pacific	Occurrence ♦♦♦♦	Size 7.5cm (3in)

Superfamily VENEROIDEA	Family Veneridae	Species *Dosinia anus* Philippi

OLD-WOMAN DOSINIA

One of a few dozen species with almost circular, compressed shells and subdued colouring, which differ in subtle ways. Has small, pointed umbones directed forwards; the lunule is heart shaped and sunken. Coarse, concentric ribs cover the shell and become almost scale-like where the hinge line slopes down behind the umbones. The hinge is broad and massive, the cardinal teeth well developed. Beige in colour with concentric, reddish-brown zones; inside white.

• **HABITAT** Sandy beaches.

growth rings

NEOZELANIC

scale-like ribs

left valve

Range New Zealand	Occurrence ♦♦♦♦	Size 7cm (2¾in)

Superfamily VENEROIDEA	Family Veneridae	Species *Chamelea gallina* Linnaeus

CHICKEN VENUS

This thick, boat-shaped shell has a pointed rear end and is rounded in front. The lunule is short and heart shaped with fine radial ridges. Regular concentric ridges cover the shell and the grooves between them have fine concentric lines. Yellowish white, with reddish-brown rays.
• **HABITAT** Sand offshore.

pallial line in the right valve

BOREAL
MEDITERRANEAN

growth ridge

Range N.W. Europe to Mediterranean	Occurrence 🐚🐚🐚🐚🐚	Size 4cm (1½in)

Superfamily VENEROIDEA	Family Veneridae	Species *Paphia alapapilionis* Röding

BUTTERFLY-WING VENUS

An elegant, boat-shaped, porcelain-like shell, it has broad, forward-pointing umbones and is rounded at the front and the rear. Broad, flattened ribs cover the shell and are separated by narrow grooves. The thin hinge bears a long ligament and three cardinal teeth. Yellowish orange, spotted and flecked with pale brown; four interrupted, reddish-brown rays.
• **HABITAT** Shallow water in sand.

ligament in right valve

interrupted rays

INDO-PACIFIC

Range Tropical Indo-Pacific	Occurrence 🐚🐚🐚🐚	Size 7.5cm (3in)

Superfamily VENEROIDEA	Family Veneridae	Species *Lioconcha castrensis* Linnaeus

CAMP PITAR-VENUS

This solid shell has prominent, rounded umbones. Fine concentric lines give the shell a silky sheen. Large escutcheon; internal ligament; shallow pallial sinus. Front lateral teeth well developed. White, with tent-like or hieroglyphic markings.
• **HABITAT** Shallow water in sand.

front lateral teeth

INDO-PACIFIC

Range Tropical Indo-Pacific	Occurrence 🐚🐚🐚🐚	Size 4.5cm (1¾in)

Superfamily VENEROIDEA	Family Veneridae	Species *Chione subimbricata* Sowerby

STEPPED VENUS

A triangular shell with broad, flat-topped umbones, it has large, widely spaced, concentric ribs. Lunule and escutcheon not clearly visible; internal ligament short. White, with brown zigzag lines, and two or three darker brown rays.
• **REMARK** Ridges vary considerably in number and strength.
• **HABITAT** Intertidal sand flats.

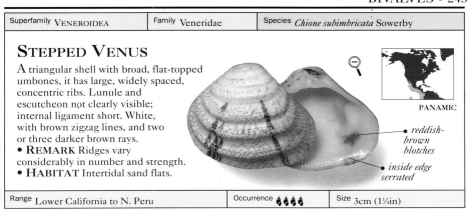

PANAMIC

• reddish-brown blotches

• inside edge serrated

Range Lower California to N. Peru	Occurrence 🦪🦪🦪🦪	Size 3cm (1¼in)

GEODUCKS

T HE SHELLS OF THESE large clams belong to molluscs which burrow deeply into mud intertidally or off-shore. The few species are widely distributed in cold and temperate waters, but only along the coasts of North America are they common and well known. The shells can vary in shape according to habitat, but are more or less rectangular and gape on all sides, except for the hinge.

———— • ————

The large and broad pallial sinus is impressed inside. There is a single, prominent, cardinal tooth in each valve and the ligament is external.

Superfamily HIATELLOIDEA	Family Hiatellidae	Species *Panopea glycymeris* Born

EUROPEAN PANOPEA

This large, obliquely rectangular shell is inflated and gapes on three sides, the hinge being the only point of contact. The umbones are low and broad. Irregular, concentric growth lines cover the shell. There is one small cardinal tooth in each valve, and the pallial sinus is wide but not deep.
• **HABITAT** Mud offshore.

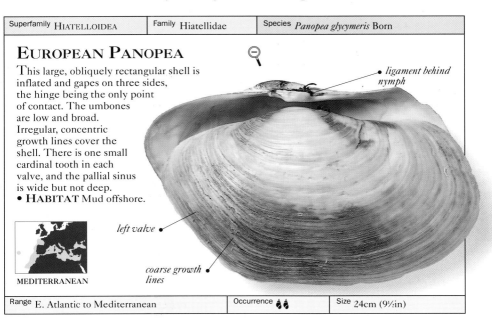

• ligament behind nymph

left valve •

coarse growth lines •

MEDITERRANEAN

Range E. Atlantic to Mediterranean	Occurrence 🦪🦪	Size 24cm (9½in)

HEART CLAMS

ALTHOUGH WELL REPRESENTED in the fossil record, there are few species of these clams living today. Thick shelled and very inflated, they have large, in-rolled umbones and an external ligament. The surface is smooth or ribbed. Some species have a keel from umbo to rear edge.

Superfamily GLOSSOIDEA	Family Glossidae	Species *Glossus humanus* Linnaeus

OX-HEART CLAM

With its great in-rolled umbones and heart-shaped outline, this bulky, heavy shell is unique among living molluscs. Fine, concentric lines cover the shell, except for the umbones. There are three cardinal teeth in each valve and the pallial line is not interrupted by a sinus. Yellowish brown or yellowish white; inside white. A brown periostracum covers most specimens.
• **HABITAT** Sand or mud offshore.

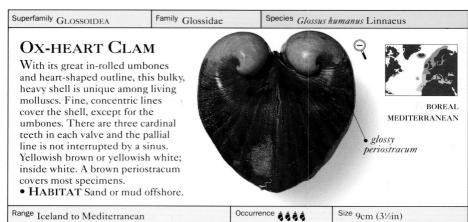

BOREAL
MEDITERRANEAN

glossy periostracum

Range Iceland to Mediterranean	Occurrence 🐚🐚🐚🐚	Size 9cm (3½in)

SOFT-SHELL CLAMS

THE DRAB, CHALKY, rather thin shells in this group belong to cool-water molluscs which burrow in mud. One valve may be smaller than the other, and the ligament may be internal. A projecting chondrophore in the middle of the hinge of the left valve receives the ligament.

Superfamily MYOIDEA	Family Myidae	Species *Mya arenaria* Linnaeus

SOFT-SHELL CLAM

The right valve of this elongate shell may be slightly more convex than the left and the valves gape front and rear. Coarse growth lines cover the shell. The chondrophore in the left valve is large and projects deeply into the right valve. The pallial sinus is long and narrow. Dirty white colour.
• **HABITAT** Intertidal mud flats.

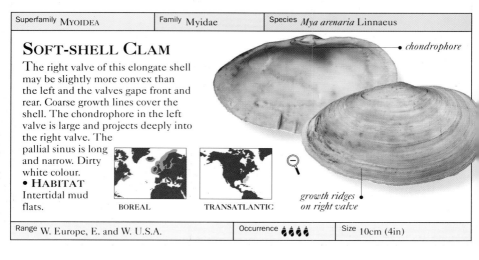

chondrophore

BOREAL   TRANSATLANTIC

growth ridges on right valve

Range W. Europe, E. and W. U.S.A.	Occurrence 🐚🐚🐚🐚	Size 10cm (4in)

PIDDOCKS

T HIN, ELONGATE, and frequently gaping, these shells are adapted for boring into clay, wood, or rock. The valves are often scaly, particularly towards the front. Several additional shell plates give the animal extra protection. There is also a finger-like process (the apophysis) in each valve.

| Superfamily PHOLADOIDEA | Family Pholadidae | Species *Pholas dactylus* Linnaeus |

EUROPEAN PIDDOCK

The long, boat-shaped valves have scaly, concentric ridges. Below each umbo is a long apophysis. Above each umbo the hinge margin is raised and reflected. The pallial sinus is broad and deep.
• **HABITAT** Wood, rock, and sand.

BOREAL
MEDITERRANEAN

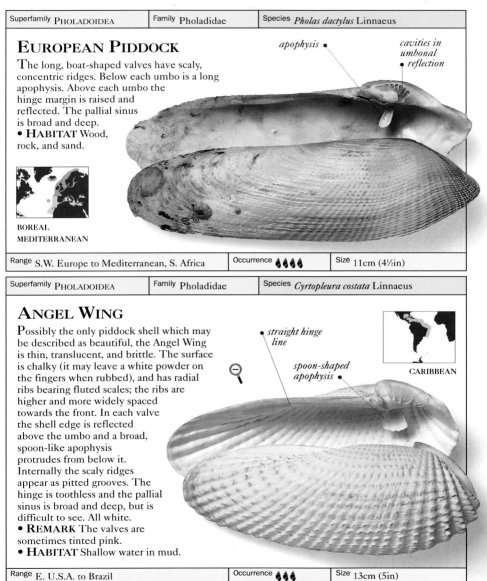

apophysis

cavities in umbonal reflection

| Range S.W. Europe to Mediterranean, S. Africa | Occurrence ♦♦♦♦ | Size 11cm (4½in) |

| Superfamily PHOLADOIDEA | Family Pholadidae | Species *Cyrtopleura costata* Linnaeus |

ANGEL WING

Possibly the only piddock shell which may be described as beautiful, the Angel Wing is thin, translucent, and brittle. The surface is chalky (it may leave a white powder on the fingers when rubbed), and has radial ribs bearing fluted scales; the ribs are higher and more widely spaced towards the front. In each valve the shell edge is reflected above the umbo and a broad, spoon-like apophysis protrudes from below it. Internally the scaly ridges appear as pitted grooves. The hinge is toothless and the pallial sinus is broad and deep, but is difficult to see. All white.
• **REMARK** The valves are sometimes tinted pink.
• **HABITAT** Shallow water in mud.

straight hinge line

spoon-shaped apophysis

CARIBBEAN

| Range E. U.S.A. to Brazil | Occurrence ♦♦♦ | Size 13cm (5in) |

LYONSIA CLAMS

THESE FRAGILE shells belong to molluscs living in mud or inside sponges and sea-squirts. Some species attach sand grains to their shells. Under the thin periostracum, the shell is pearly. The front end tends to be the more convex; the valves gape at the rear end. There are no hinge teeth.

Superfamily PANDOROIDEA	Family Lyonsiidae	Species *Lyonsia californica* Conrad

CALIFORNIAN LYONSIA

Very thin and translucent, the umbones of this shell are near the front end. The internal ligament is set behind a small, shelly plate below the umbo. Whitish.
• **HABITAT** Sandy mud offshore.

CALIFORNIAN

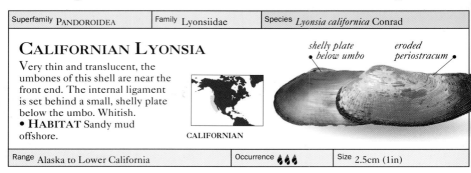

shelly plate
• below umbo

eroded
periostracum •

Range Alaska to Lower California	Occurrence ♦♦♦	Size 2.5cm (1in)

THRACIA CLAMS

THIN, LIGHTWEIGHT, and fragile, the umbo of the smaller left valve may puncture the umbo of the right one. There are no hinge teeth, the ligament is mostly internal, and the pallial sinus is well developed. Most species are from cool waters where they burrow in sand or mud.

Superfamily PANDOROIDEA	Family Thraciidae	Species *Thracia pubescens* Pulteney

DOWNY THRACIA

The left valve of this brittle, boat-shaped shell is rather flat, and its umbo punctures a hole in the umbo of the larger right valve. Except for occasional growth lines, the surface is smooth. The shell is white or cream in colour.
• **HABITAT** Sand and mud offshore.

BOREAL MEDITERRANEAN

WEST AFRICAN

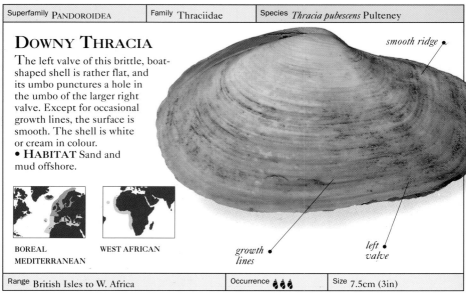

smooth ridge •

growth
lines •

left •
valve

Range British Isles to W. Africa	Occurrence ♦♦♦	Size 7.5cm (3in)

LANTERN CLAMS

AMONG THE MOST delicate of bivalve shells, lantern clams are boat shaped. The hinge is toothless, but there is a projecting chondrophore below the umbo in each valve. The colourless valves are dull on the outside and glossy on the inside. Lantern clams are tropical mud dwellers.

Superfamily PANDOROIDEA	Family Laternulidae	Species *Laternula anatina* Linnaeus

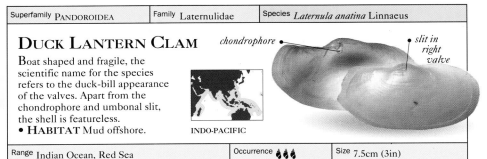

DUCK LANTERN CLAM

Boat shaped and fragile, the scientific name for the species refers to the duck-bill appearance of the valves. Apart from the chondrophore and umbonal slit, the shell is featureless.
• **HABITAT** Mud offshore.

chondrophore

slit in right valve

INDO-PACIFIC

Range Indian Ocean, Red Sea	Occurrence ♦♦♦	Size 7.5cm (3in)

WATERING POT SHELLS

STARTING LIFE as a tiny bivalve, the shell develops into a calcareous tube with the embryonic valves attached to its outer surface. At its base is a perforated, raised disc, fringed with small tubes. The life history of these curious, warm-water molluscs is almost completely unknown.

Superfamily CLAVAGELLOIDEA	Family Clavagellidae	Species *Penicillus strangulatus* Chenu

PHILIPPINE WATERING POT

A close inspection will reveal the presence of embryonic shell valves on the side of the tube representing the mature form of this aberrant bivalve. Sand grains and shell fragments also adhere to the tube. The fringed disc is embedded in the sand while the other end protrudes above it.
• **REMARK** Specimens may form small clumps.
• **HABITAT** Sand offshore.

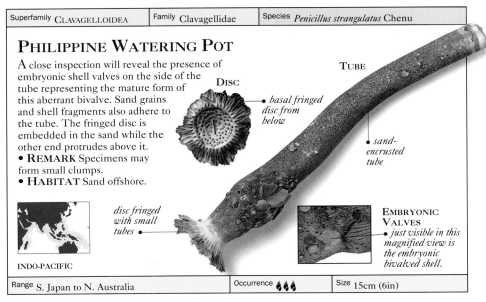

TUBE

DISC

basal fringed disc from below

sand-encrusted tube

disc fringed with small tubes

INDO-PACIFIC

EMBRYONIC VALVES
just visible in this magnified view is the embryonic bivalved shell.

Range S. Japan to N. Australia	Occurrence ♦♦♦	Size 15cm (6in)

CEPHALOPODS

NAUTILUS SHELLS

THE ONLY CEPHALOPODS with true external shells are the nautilus shells. Once they were one of the most dominant invertebrates in the sea; now only a few species survive in the Indo-Pacific region. The lightweight shells have chambers filled with a gas which helps them control their buoyancy.

Subclass NAUTILOIDEA	Family Nautilidae	Species *Nautilus pompilius* Linnaeus

CHAMBERED NAUTILUS

A lightweight, thin-shelled species, it is spirally coiled, but this is only obvious when the shell is sectioned. The shell is also partitioned; the resulting chambers are connected to each other by a hollow tube. It is bilaterally symmetrical, with a large aperture but no umbilicus. White or creamy colour, with zebra-like, reddish stripes radiating from the umbilical region though not extending onto the broadest part of the body whorl.
• **HABITAT** Free swimming.

WORLD

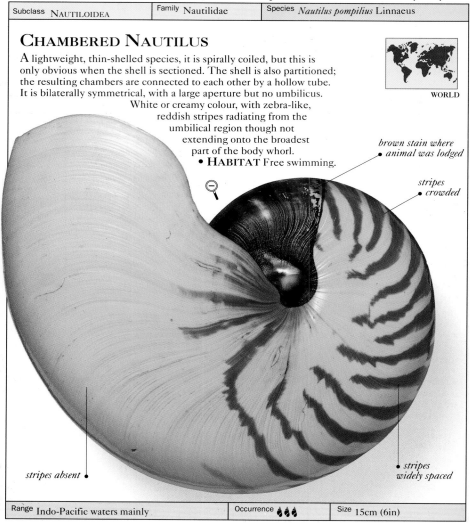

brown stain where
• animal was lodged

stripes
• crowded

stripes absent •

• stripes
widely spaced

Range Indo-Pacific waters mainly	Occurrence 🐾🐾🐾	Size 15cm (6in)

SPIRULA

T HE DIMINUTIVE SPIRULA shares with the nautilus shells the distinctive internal feature of a succession of gas-filled chambers. However, the coiled spirula shell is completely enclosed within the animal, which is unlike any of the nautilus shells. There is only one species.

Subclass NAUTILOIDEA	Family Nautilidae	Species *Spirula spirula* Linnaeus

COMMON SPIRULA

This thin, fragile, loosely coiled shell is partitioned inside, the chamber walls being visible on the outside as shallow grooves. In life the shell is contained within the body of a squid-like animal.
• **REMARK** Circular aperture.
• **HABITAT** Free swimming.

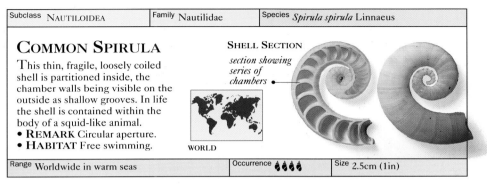

SHELL SECTION
section showing series of chambers •

WORLD

Range Worldwide in warm seas	Occurrence 🐚🐚🐚🐚	Size 2.5cm (1in)

ARGONAUTS

T HE SO-CALLED "SHELLS" of the argonauts are, in fact, nothing more than the calcareous secretions made by the females of octopus-like molluscs which lack true shells. Used to hold eggs, they are discarded once the eggs have hatched out. Argonauts occur worldwide in warm seas.

Subclass ARGONAUTOIDEA	Family Argonautidae	Species *Argonauta hians* Lightfoot

BROWN PAPER-NAUTILUS

One of the smaller argonauts, its thin and fragile "shell" (actually the egg case carried by the female) is inflated, with widely spaced, radiating ribs ending at the periphery in large, sometimes spiny knobs. Brownish, with darker brown knobs.
• **REMARK** The knobs may not be present.
• **HABITAT** Free swimming.

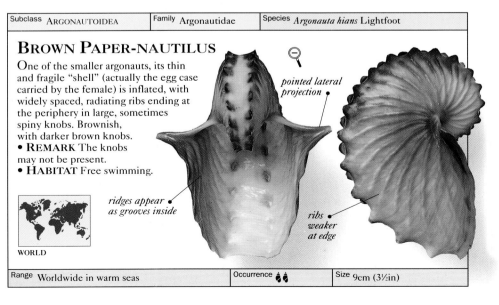

pointed lateral projection •

ridges appear • as grooves inside

ribs • weaker at edge

WORLD

Range Worldwide in warm seas	Occurrence 🐚🐚	Size 9cm (3½in)

GLOSSARY

Technical expressions have been avoided wherever possible but a limited use of them is unavoidable in a book of this nature. The terms listed below, many of them peculiar to molluscs and their shells, are defined in a concise manner. Some definitions have been simplified and generalized in order to avoid obscure language, and they are to be regarded as definitive for this book only. Words that appear in bold type in the definitions are explained elsewhere in the glossary. You may find it helpful to look at the annotated illustrations on pages 18–19 to clarify some of the terms relating to the parts of a shell.

• **APERTURE**
The opening at the front end of gastropod shell and a tusk shell.

• **APEX**
The starting point of shell growth, the "top" of a gastropod spire.

• **APOPHYSIS**
A projecting spur inside a bivalve shell below the **umbo**, the site of a muscle attachment.

• **BASE**
The last-formed part of the shell of a gastropod.

• **BEAK**
The tip of a bivalve shell's **umbo**.

• **BICONIC**
Tapering at both ends, like two cones placed with their broad ends together.

• **BILATERAL SYMMETRY**
When the left side is an exact counterpart of the right.

• **BIVALVE**
A mollusc with a shell formed of two pieces.

• **BODY WHORL**
The last-formed **whorl** of an adult gastropod shell.

• **BYSSUS**
A bunch of silky threads anchoring some bivalves to solid objects.

• **CALCAREOUS**
Made of calcium carbonate, chalky.

• **CALLUS**
A thick or thin layer of shelly substance, usually smooth and glossy, often transparent.

• **CANAL**
A channel at the top or bottom (i.e. rear or front end respectively) of the **aperture** to accommodate the **siphon** of a gastropod.

• **CANCELLATE**
Having a lattice-like ornament, formed when ridges or threads meet at right angles.

• **CARDINAL TOOTH**
A projection on the hinge plate below the umbo.

• **CHITON**
A mollusc with a foot, a head bearing tentacles, and eight shelly plates held together by a **girdle**.

• **CHONDROPHORE**
The spoon-like projection in a bivalve shell below the **umbo**, the attachment for an internal **ligament**.

• **COLUMELLA**
The central pillar of a gastropod shell visible within the **aperture**.

• **CONCENTRIC**
Describes the direction of the raised or depressed **ornament** on a bivalve, parallel to the valve's edge.

• **CONCHOLOGIST**
A student of molluscs and their shells.

• **CORNEOUS**
Made of chitin, a non-calcareous substance.

• **DENTICLE**
A small, usually rounded, tooth.

• **EAR**
An extension of the **hinge** region of a bivalve shell, as in scallops.

• **ESCUTCHEON**
A depression found behind the **umbones** of a bivalve shell, often encompassing an external **ligament**.

• **FAMILY**
A unit containing two or more closely related species belonging to one **genus** or two or more genera, subordinate to a **superfamily**.

• **FLUTED**
Scalloped or arched.

• **FOOT**
The fleshy sole that a gastropod creeps or glides upon, or by which it adheres.

• **GASTROPOD**
Literally "stomach-footed"; a mollusc with a head bearing tentacles and eyes, a foot, and a one-piece shell (sometimes with no shell at all).

• **GENUS** (plural **GENERA**)
A unit containing one or more **species**, subordinate to a **family**.

• **GIRDLE**
The muscular ribbon surrounding and binding together a **chiton's** shelly plates.

• **GLOBOSE**
Tending to be inflated, like a ball.

• **GRANULOSE**
Covered with small raised pimples.

• **GROWTH LINE** or **RIDGE**
A fine or coarse, raised line defining a temporary pause in the growth of the shell.

• **HINGE**
Inner edge of the valve of a bivalve shell, usually joined by a **ligament** to the opposite valve and usually bearing teeth that interlock with teeth in that valve.

• **IMPRESSED**
Indented or sunken.

• **INCISED**
Finely scratched.

• **INCURVED**
Turned inwards.

• **IRIDESCENT**
Reflecting rainbow colours.

• **KEEL**
A more or less sharp edge.

• **LIGAMENT**
The elastic, corneous structure joining the valves of a bivalve.

• **LIP**
The inside or outside edge of the **aperture** of a gastropod shell.

• **LUNULE**
A usually heart-shaped depression in front of the **umbones** of a bivalve shell.

• **MANTLE**
A fleshy lobe which secretes the mollusc's shell and lines the inside of the shell wall.

• **MARGIN**
The shell edge.

• **MOLLUSC**
A soft-bodied, legless, invertebrate

animal which usually secretes a calcareous shell.

• **MOTHER-OF-PEARL**
A shelly layer, or the inner lining of a shell, displaying a pearly (nacreous) surface.

• **MUSCLE SCAR**
The impression inside the valve of a bivalve shell made by an adductor muscle (a muscle holding valves together).

• **NACREOUS**
See **mother-of-pearl**.

• **NODE**
A lumpy protuberance, smaller than a **tubercle**.

• **NODULE**
A knob, smaller than a **node**.

• **NODULOUS**
Covered with **nodules**.

• **NUCLEUS**
The initial growth stage of a molluscan shell or of an **operculum**.

• **NYMPH**
The narrow ledge, on the hinge behind the **umbo**, to which the external ligament is attached.

• **OBSOLETE**
Ceasing to exist, no longer present.

• **OPERCULUM**
The corneous or calcareous structure attached to a gastropod's foot, used to close the shell's **aperture**.

• **ORNAMENT**
Raised or depressed features on the shell surface.

• **OVATE**
Egg shaped.

• **PALLIAL**
Relevant to the **mantle**.

• **PALLIAL LINE**
An impressed line inside the valve of a bivalve shell parallel to the **margin**, which marks the position of the **mantle** edge.

• **PALLIAL SINUS**
A more or less conspicuous indentation of the **pallial line**, showing where the muscles operating the **siphons** were formerly attached.

• **PARIETAL**
Describes that part of the inner lip of a gastropod shell behind the **columella**.

• **PERIOSTRACUM**
The external, often fibrous coating of corneous material covering many shells when fresh.

• **PIPE**
A small tube protruding from the rear end of some tusk shells.

• **PLUG**
The shelly infilling at the rear end of a tusk shell tube.

• **PUSTULE**
A small, rounded protuberance, smaller than a **node**.

• **RADIAL**
Describes the direction of the raised or depressed ornamental feature on a bivalve, running from the **umbo** towards the edge of the valve.

• **RAMP**
A broad, flat-topped ledge below the **suture** of a whorl.

• **RANGE**
The total distribution of a **species**.

• **RECURVED**
Curving upwards or downwards.

• **RIB**
The continuous elevation of the shell surface.

• **RIBLET**
The continuous elevation of the shell surface, subordinate to **rib**.

• **SCALE**
Raised, sharp-edged, ornamental feature, sometimes **fluted**.

• **SERRATED**
A term applied to the edge of a shell when it exhibits a series of grooves or points.

• **SHELF**
A thin plate obscuring the **aperture** of some species of gastropod shells.

• **SHELL TUBE**
The hollow tube, coiled or not, occupied by most gastropods, all tusk shells, and a few bivalves.

• **SHOULDER**
The angulation of a **whorl** at or just below the **suture**.

• **SINUOUS**
Gently waved.

• **SINUS**
See **pallial sinus** and **stromboid notch**.

• **SIPHON**
A retractable fleshy tube of gastropods and bivalves, used for various purposes, including feeding and the expulsion of waste products.

• **SIPHONAL CANAL** or **NOTCH**
The tube or gutter at the front (lower) end of the **aperture**, to hold the front **siphon** of a gastropod.

• **SLIT**
A shallow or deep cut in the shell **margin** of some gastropods and in the **umbones** of some bivalves.

• **SPECIES**
A group of beings sharing virtually identical characteristics not shared by any other group; it is subordinate to and contained within a **genus**.

• **SPINE**
A blunt or sharp projection.

• **SPIRAL**
On gastropod shells and tusk shells, going in a transverse direction (i.e. at right angles to the vertical).

• **SPIRE**
The coiled part of a gastropod shell apart from the **body whorl.**

• **STRIA**
(plural **STRIAE**)
A scratch-like furrow on the surface of the shell.

• **STROMBOID NOTCH**
An embayment, or **sinus**, on the lower edge of the outer lip in the shell of strombs; the animal's right eye protrudes from under it.

• **SUPERFAMILY**
An agglomeration of related **families**.

• **SUTURE**
The line on gastropod shells where the **whorls** connect.

• **TOOTH / TEETH**
Pointed or blunt structure(s) inside the outer or inner **lip** of gastropod shells, and on the **hinges** of bivalve shells.

• **TUBERCLE**
A large rounded protuberance.

• **UMBILICUS**
The opening at the base of a gastropod shell around which the **body whorl** is coiled; it is also present at the centre of the spire whorls.

• **UMBO**
(plural **UMBONES**)
The earliest-formed part of a bivalve shell's valve.

• **VALVE**
One piece of a bivalve shell or of a **chiton**.

• **VARIX**
(plural **VARICES**)
Thickening at former lip edge of a gastropod shell.

• **VERTICAL**
Going in the direction of the **apex** to the base of gastropod shells; in the direction of front to rear of **chiton** valves.

• **WHORL**
One complete turn of the tube of a gastropod shell about its imaginary axis.

INDEX

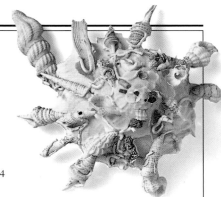

ACKNOWLEDGMENTS

THIS BOOK COULD not have been completed without the help, material and otherwise, of several persons and institutions. The author and publisher are greatly indebted to the following people for their kindness in making available for photography most of the shells illustrated: David Heppell and the National Museum of Scotland, Edinburgh; Alex Arthur of Dorling Kindersley, London; Alan Seccombe of London; Geoff Cox of North Warnborough, Hampshire; Tom and Celia Pain of London; Donald T. Bosch of Muscat, Oman; Noel Gregory of Farnham Common, Bucks; Kenneth Wye of The Eaton Shell Shop, Covent Garden, London.

The author is also extremely grateful to the following individuals: David Heppell, for providing information about shells and other subjects, usually at very short notice; Kathie Way, of the Zoology Department, The Natural History Museum of London, for checking the text, correcting some of his identifications, and making encouraging comments; Una Dance, for using her camera and her wifely patience to good effect on his behalf; and Robert Dance, for ensuring that the publisher received a timely succession of disks and printouts from his father for whom the computer is, and will remain, an unfathomable mystery.

Dorling Kindersley would like to thank: Debra Skinner for her shell illustrations on pages 18-19; Caroline Church for the endpaper illustrations; Salvo Tomasselli for the illustration of the world map on pages 12-13 and all the miniature maps throughout the book; the Royal Masonic Hospital for the X-ray on page 17; Peter Howlett of Lemon Graphics for placing all the leader lines on the shell photographs; Steve Dew for his original map artworks.

We are also indebted to Irene Lyford and David Preston for their invaluable editorial help; Joanna Pocock for her design expertise; and Michael Allaby for compiling the Index.

PICTURE CREDITS
All photographs are by Matthew Ward except for: Robert E. Lipe 7, 14, 15 *(middle left)*, 16; Una Dance 15 *(top left and right)* and author photograph on jacket; J. Hoggesteger (Bifotos) 15 *(middle right)*; S. Peter Dance 15 *(bottom left)*; Shelagh Smith *(bottom right)*; Dave King 17; James Carmichael 16.